Investigating Identity Theft

Investigating Identity Theft

A Guide for Businesses, Law Enforcement, and Victims

Judith M. Collins

John Wiley & Sons, Inc.

For general information on our other products and services, or technical support, please contact our Customer Care Department within the United States at 800-762-2974, outside the United States at 317-572-3993 or fax 317-572-4002.

Wiley also publishes its books in a variety of electronic formats. Some content that appears in print may not be available in electronic books.

For more information about Wiley products, visit our Web site at *http://www.wiley.com*.

Library of Congress Cataloging-in-Publication Data:

Collins, Judith M.
  Investigating identity theft: a guide for businesses, law enforcement, and victims / Judith M. Collins.
      p. cm.
    Includes index.
    ISBN-13: 978-0-471-75724-5 (cloth)
    ISBN-10: 0-471-75724-1 (cloth)
    1. Identity theft—United States. I. Title.

HV6679.C64 2006
363.25'963222

                                                                    2005031926

Printed in the United States of America

10   9   8   7   6   5   4   3   2   1

To all of the police officers who completed
the CyberCrime Investigator Certification (CCI) courses at the MSU
Crime and Research Lab, in appreciation for all you taught me.

CONTENTS

A MESSAGE TO
INVESTIGATORS

This "how-to" book is written for investigators new to the Internet—police officers, corporate fraud investigators, criminal justice teachers, and even victims who wish to investigate their own identity thefts. In *Investigating Identity Theft*, the role of the investigator is to use the Internet to gather, retain, and organize information pertaining to a crime. In no case should an investigator "tip off" perpetrators by placing telephone calls to individuals or businesses or by placing themselves or others in harm's way by confronting possible suspects. It is imperative that *all identity theft investigations be conducted in collaboration with a sworn police officer who has the authority and the professional training to make decisions about the course of events an investigation takes.* In effect, a victim-investigator assumes the role of a "police research assistant" whose tasks are to assist the officer in locating and obtaining chains of evidentiary information that can lead to the apprehension and conviction of the perpetrator.

ACKNOWLEDGMENTS

This book could not have been written without the help of my colleagues at the Michigan State Identity Theft Crime and Research Lab, particularly Sandra Hoffman, who, since 1999, has been my partner in identity theft investigations. Together, we traversed the Internet while investigating hundreds of cases and teaching as many classes to law enforcement officers and corporate and private investigators. The material for this book is derived from those online experiences in, sometimes remote, places in cyberspace, from class lecture notes, and from practical experience.

I will always remain deeply indebted to Timothy Burgard, my editor at John Wiley & Sons, Inc., who gave me the opportunity to publish another recent book, *Preventing Identity Thefts in Your Business: How to Protect Your Business, Customers, and Employees,* and who, subsequently, recognized the potential importance of the present book for combating identity theft. Throughout, Tim provided valuable and timely comments, even when I was less timely with meeting some deadlines.

I thank also others at John Wiley & Sons, including especially Kerstin Nasdeo, Senior Production Editor, and Helen Cho, Editorial Assistant, but also the many others responsible for the preparing, polishing, printing, and publishing of *Investigating Identity Theft.* Thank you, everyone.

FOREWORD

In early 2005, the FBI announced the scrapping of it's new $170 million information sharing technology that was intended to help fight terrorism.[1] The system had been under development for two years but failed to work. Instead, beginning in early 2006 with full deployment expected in 2009, the FBI will develop a new system, named "Sentinel." This new system will be used for information sharing and intelligence gathering and will have Internet search capabilities.

Since 1999, investigators at the Michigan State University Identity Theft Crime and Research Lab have successfully tracked criminals using the Internet as a search tool, and, in February 2003, we trained agents at the FBI Academy, Quantico, VA, on how to use the Internet to track terrorists. Using hands-on exercises and actual cases we had stumbled upon while conducting other online investigations, we demonstrated

[1] Mueller, Robert S., III. Statement made before the United States Senate, Committee on the Judiciary, July 27, 2005.

how one Web site, *www.infocomcorp.com*,[2] had links to a terrorist group in the Middle East.[3] Not only FBI agents, but others as well, can similarly learn how to uncover potentially valuable information online.

In *Investigating Identity Theft* even novice investigators can become professionals at online investigations. No multi-million-dollar technology is required. Armed with a basic laptop computer and an Internet connection, readers will learn to track criminal cases by following the book's detailed instructions and hands-on exercises, most of which are based on actual cases.

Investigating Identity Theft is written for a broad audience—law enforcement officers, corporate fraud investigators, private investigators, and even victims who wish to investigate their own identity thefts. The book is written for investigators new to computers and the Internet, but also for those investigators who, although they have advanced knowledge of computers, have not yet used the Internet as an investigative tool. *Investigating Identity Theft* is not about technology—it is about how to *use* technology for crime investigations, specifically those crimes committed using stolen identities.

---

[2] The *www.infocomcorp.com* Web site no longer exists, however, many of the pages of this Web site have been archived and a few remain intact, online. You may view the site by going to *www.archive.org*: enter the term *http://www.infocomcorp.com* into the search field. Here you will find a page advertising the infocomcorp Web hosting business. To locate the address and technical contact person for infocomcorp, go to *www.samspade.org*: enter the term infocomcorp into the "DO STUFF" field. Click on "DO STUFF." Note that, although the Web site no longer is online, the domain name was last updated September 14, 2005, and the subscription was paid for through March 28, 2006.

[3] Infocom Corporation and its owners were convicted in July 2004 of illegally aiding Hamas terrorists.

Investigating Identity Theft

CHAPTER 1

"REAL WORLD" CASES: SOLVED AND UNSOLVED

The following four identity theft cases are examples of investigations conducted at the Identity Theft Crime and Research Lab at Michigan State University. To protect their anonymities, the names of individuals and their addresses have been changed; any resemblance to actual names or addresses is coincidental. These cases reveal some of the processes involved in identity theft investigations and also provide an insight into the ease with which some cases can be resolved while others may never be. This book is based on practical experiences learned from investigating these and hundreds of other identity frauds. The overriding goal is to provide business fraud investigators and victims themselves with tools for investigating identity theft cases. Law enforcement investigators, particularly those new to conducting investigations on the Internet, may also find this book useful. Beginning with Julie Ann Blakely, the cases dealt with some of the common types of identity thefts and describe steps that were taken to resolve them.

1

THE JULIE ANN BLAKELY CASE: INCARCERATION FRAUD

The call from the victim came into the Identity Theft Crime Lab on Thursday, December 16, 2004, at 9:30 A.M. Julie Ann Blakely had applied for a job at Belmont Hospital and was denied employment because of her criminal record in Detroit, Michigan. Julie claims to have never been involved in any criminal activity. The police will not help her. Would we?

Our first step was to determine whether Julie was actually a victim or was masking as one, which happens with increasing frequency as perpetrators find new ways to avoid detection of frauds they commit. To verify Julie's authenticity as a victim, we first went to the Detroit courthouse to search for any court records on "Julie Ann Blakely" and discovered that she, purportedly, had appeared in traffic court on six different occasions.

The second step was to conduct an Internet search of the records of offenders from the State of Michigan Corrections Department, using that state's public domain search system and the keyword "Blakely." The search revealed the name, date of birth, racial identification, gender, hair, and eye color, height, and weight, arrest, and incarceration records of a perpetrator with the last name of "Blakely," a list of aliases that included the names "Julie Blakely," "Julie Blake," and "Charlene Smith," and a photo of this offender who had recently been incarcerated. The photo was not a picture of the Julie Ann Blakely who had come to our crime lab for help.

The third step, therefore, was to arrange a meeting with Julie and the police officer whose name was on the court records as having apprehended her for a traffic violation. In the meeting, the officer described the incident in which, on September 10, 1999, a driver he had stopped for a traffic violation gave her name as "Charlene Ann Smith." A search of the police database, however, showed that no such person existed. The driver, therefore, after being issued citations for using improper plates, interfering with a police officer, having false ID, possessing drug paraphernalia, and having no operator's license and no valid proof of insurance was processed and booked under the name of Jane Doe. She served 10 days in the jail at the Detroit Police Department.

Of particular note, however, was that while in jail, "Jane Doe" required medical treatment for a diabetic condition; she was admitted to a local hospital, where she admitted her name was not "Charlene Ann Smith" but, rather, was "Julie Ann Blakely"—the name imprinted on a medical card she had in her possession at the time of arrest.

Because of her incarceration, Charlene Ann Smith alias Julie Ann Blakely had been fingerprinted. We now had the following evidence to clear the real Julie Ann Blakely from crimes she did not commit: (1) DNA evidence (the fingerprints), (2) the photo of the since imprisoned Charlene Ann Smith who used the alias Julie Ann Blakely, and (3) the police officer's recognition that the person he arrested matched the photo we had obtained of the now imprisoned Charlene Ann Smith and that Julie Ann Blakely did not fit the description on the arrest report. The case, however, despite this evidence, could not yet be closed—Julie's criminal records would first have to be cleared.

Because of the charges, Julie now had a criminal history, which may be difficult to erase owing to the bureaucracy of government agencies. We, therefore, carefully documented every detail about the case to provide evidence that would clear the driving suspension recorded with the Secretary of State and the Bureau of Driver & Vehicle Records, the outstanding liabilities for debts incurred as part of the court hearings and processing, and the criminal records maintained in the databases of the Michigan State Department of Corrections and the Detroit Police Department.

We sent the documents of evidence, through U.S. certified mail so as to confirm their deliveries, to the personal attention of the directors of each government agency. We also sent copies of all the documents to each of the judges who had fined or sentenced "Julie Ann Blakely" on different occasions as well as to the Chief Judge of that district's court. The cover letters requested the judiciary to ensure that all records of court hearings and violations would be reversed and purged from the criminal databases.

Finally, we sent copies of all the documents to the Department of Human Resources, Belmont Hospital. Julie Ann Blakely, a 21-year-old single mother, was hired for the job for which she had applied at Belmont Hospital, she regained her driving privileges, and was, eventually, resolved from crimes she had never committed. Julie did not incur any great financial losses; the emotional costs, however, were immense and remain to this day.

Several lessons can be learned from this investigation: first, police departments may lack the resources to investigate or spend much time on some identity theft cases; second, some cases are easily resolved with simple strategies and detailed documentation; third, criminals impersonate others not only to commit crimes but also when they are apprehended (and most eventually are); fourth, the Internet is an important tool for identity theft investigations—in this case, it provided the key evidence; fifth, to circumvent bureaucracies, correspondence should be sent to the government officials personally; and sixth, documents should be sent using methods that will confirm receipt. This case illustrates that the process is not difficult; the investigation required only a plan of action that almost anyone could perform. The next case, also using the Internet as a tool could not, unfortunately, be solved.

THE RAY C. LAPIER CASE: SHIPMENTS TO ROMANIA

Unless there is clear evidence for organized crime, in which case federal law enforcement agencies will become involved, identity theft cases involving foreign countries are difficult to investigate and nearly impossible to solve. The best one can do is to help prevent further abuse of the victim whose identity was stolen and also of the merchant where merchandise or services were fraudulently purchased. Victims, nonetheless, sometimes wish to pursue the perpetrator, despite the odds against any apprehension. This is one such case.

On October 10, 2002, Ray C. Lapier received a telephone call from the fraud department at his Visa Credit Card Company. Had he authorized the use of his Visa Signature Rewards card for a shipment of merchandise to Romania?

Perhaps not coincidentally, two weeks earlier, Mr. Lapier had taken his family on a weeklong cruise with the "ACME" Cruise Lines, where many employees are Romanian. Before contacting our crime lab, Mr. Lapier had already filed a complaint with the local police department. The police officer referred the case to us for investigation—the MSU Crime Lab collaborates with local and also federal law enforcement agencies on identity theft cases (when we collect sufficient evidence for a subpoena, search warrant, or arrest, the case is returned to the police officer for further action). In this case, Mr. Lapier wanted to know who his impersonator was, a concern common to most victims of identity theft.

In fact, with few exceptions, the majority of victims express a pressing need to know who their impersonators were. Many victims suspect their coworkers. Others may not point to a specific person but may claim to know the location where the identity theft had happened, often citing the workplace as the source of the theft. Regardless of who stole the identity or where it was stolen from and even when losses are negligible, most victims want to know the identity of their abusers.

Unfortunately, while stolen identities can be secured from further criminal use, at least temporarily, the offenders are difficult to track because, in most cases, the direct thief is a member of a larger, more or less organized, identity theft network in which crimes are "layered" so that only the front criminals are caught. These are the members of the network's cell who are responsible for opening postal boxes, renting apartments, or locating vacant houses for the deliveries of fraudulently ordered merchandise.

Once delivered to these locations by UPS, FedEx, or U.S. Mail, members of a second cell retrieve and transfer the merchandise to members of yet a third cell, who market the merchandise on the street. It is because of this network structure in which many perpetrators are intentionally involved in different aspects of the identity frauds that the leaders of the cells usually remain unknown—to both the police and also to the cell's members at lower levels of the network. (Identity theft networks are further discussed in Chapter 2.) A given perpetrator, therefore, may be only the front person and not the organizer of the network.

Mr. Lapier was persistent. Prior to visiting the MSU Crime Lab, he had already taken the first step: the placing of "fraud alerts" on his credit files at each of the four credit reporting agencies—Experian, Equifax, TransUnion, and Innovis. (Innovis is a data broker—a seller of personal identifying information; so are the other three credit agencies. Innovis, as do the other three agencies, maintains and provides businesses with credit reports, but the U.S. Federal Trade Commission identifies only the first three as credit reporting agencies.) Merchants who wish to verify the name and creditworthiness of a prospective customer will contact one of these agencies, which maintain financial files on all or most U.S. citizens. The fraud alert on a financial record warns the merchant of the possibility of an impersonator.

The next step to be taken in this case was ours, and that was to obtain information from the fraud investigator at the credit card company. In the past, fraud investigators rarely gave any information to the victim and many still do not, despite the Fair and Accurate Credit Transactions Act (FACTA) that requires them to do so (see Chapter 5). At the time of this investigation, however, FACTA had not yet been enacted. In Mr. Lapier's case, we sought the following information: (1) the authenticity of the credit card charge, (2) the amount of the charge, (3) the type of merchandise that was fraudulently purchased, (4) the method of purchase, that is, physical store versus business Web site, (5) the name given by the purchaser, and (6) the address given for the delivery of the merchandise. This information is important for the following reasons.

Even when we have a copy of the credit card statement showing the amount of charge, it is necessary to verify the authenticity of a claim of identity theft.

Second, the Federal Bureau of Investigation should be notified of fraudulent transactions when the amounts are in the $50,000 range or more.

Third, the type of merchandise purchased provides clues, such as the gender of the offender and the extent to which the crime is organized. For example, discount store purchases of ladies' and children's clothing, cookware, and household items suggest a crime of a different nature as compared to purchases of expensive cameras, video, computer, and other technological equipment that are known to be sold in the black market, often to obtain cash to support a drug habit or to fund some other criminal activity.

Fourth, the method used to make the purchase can reveal the offender's identity. If the merchandise was purchased in a physical store versus an online Web site, video cameras positioned inside or outside may have captured the transaction or the license plate number and description of the getaway car. If the purchase was made online, Internet addresses can be traced (Chapters 9 and 10).

Finally, the address given on an application for the delivery of merchandise is where surveillance will be conducted to identify the front person whose task is to retrieve the fraudulently ordered merchandise. The delivery point is the end of the trail, the place where most identity theft investigations begin. This is because the crime scene—the place where the identity was stolen—is rarely known and so is the person who stole the identity that facilitated the identity fraud—the fraudulent purchase of merchandise.

The Visa company investigator was cooperative and so was the fraud investigator for L.L.Bean, the company where the credit card order was placed—for a pair of $105 men's shoes. (The police would not investigate this $105 crime; many police still do not recognize that this type of small offense may be a test of the system and tied into a larger network operation.) Clearly, the sole purpose of the pursuit by Mr. Lapier, as with most victims, was to find and bring to justice his impersonator.

We learned the following: an Anghel Castnel, or someone using that name, placed an Internet order on the Web site of the L.L.Bean Company for a pair of men's shoes costing $105 to be delivered to a person with the same name at Peniei-AL-7-BL-PA-11, 6000-L-BACAU, Romania. Further, the Internet e-mail address that was used to place the order, using a credit card number issued to Ray C. Lapier, was CNEL_8@Yahoo.com.

With this information, we planned a specific approach, or strategy. The first step was to conduct Internet searches (the Internet is a valuable tool and a major focus of this book) to verify the name and address listed on the purchase form. The first search for the name "Anghel Costel" using smartpages.com (*www.smartpagers.com*) proved unsuccessful. The next search, using the Yahoo's People Search directory, was for the e-mail address that was used to place the order. We also searched the Yahoo Member Directory (*www.members.yahoo.com*). The Yahoo Member Directory search uncovered no information, but the Yahoo.com e-mail search revealed two addresses listed for an Anghel Castnel, both in Romania.

We furthered searched the white pages of several Romanian phone directories (*www.whitepages.ro*) and the addresses associated with the name Anghel Castnel. This search provided one address for Bacau, which was the name of the city given by the perpetrator when completing the online purchase form. Someone by the name of Anghel Castnel was registered as living in an apartment located at the address in Romania where the merchandise was shipped. In steps two and three we (1) contacted the cruise line and also (2) the Romanian police.

A cruise line employee with the last name of Castnel may have had access to the personal information of passengers; this individual could have made the fraudulent purchase for shipment to himself or to a family member with the same last name. The U.S. certified letter to the "ACME" Cruise Lines, inquiring whether an Anghel Castnel or someone with the last name Castnel had worked on the cruise ship during the dates that Mr. Lapier and his family were aboard, or whether someone with that name had, at any time, been employed in any job position with the company, was never acknowledged.

We sent a copy of the chain of evidence we had obtained, together with all documentation of the searches, including a copy of the police report and the detailed notes from conversations with the fraud investigators, to the Romanian National Police Force. To this date, we have received no reply.

What effectively did we do in this case? This investigation may only have served as a catharsis for the victim; perhaps the cruise line took steps to secure their passenger's personal information; possibly they also extended our investigation with one of their own, and, maybe the Romanian National Police did, after all, follow up.

Regardless of the outcome, however, this example of an actual case illustrates several aspects of identity theft investigations. First, as in the Julie Blakely case, emphasis is placed on the importance of developing a plan, or strategy, before going forward with an investigation; second, the Internet was, again, a valuable tool for verifying the name and address of the shipment—the end of the trail where, as pointed out earlier, most identity theft investigations must begin; third, the case demonstrates the importance of careful and detailed documentation that may be used by others ultimately involved in the investigation, for example, the cruise line or the Romanian police.

Finally, this case shows that, despite their expressed needs for such information, the victims may never know their perpetrators, particularly when the case crosses foreign boundaries (i.e., legal jurisdictions). Victims report, however, that any investigation of ones' case serves as a catharsis, regardless of the outcome.

THE JANICE A. MACKLIN CASE: THE VICTIM WAS THE PERPETRATOR

Janice A. Macklin was a victim of identity theft: her former husband, who was then living in another state, was using her name and also had access to and was using her Internet addresses (Internet Protocol and e-mail) to commit auction fraud on the eBay Web site. Ms. Macklin first learned of the fraud when the eBay company closed her account owing to fraudulent transactions. Ms. Macklin had targeted her husband as the likely suspect because (1) he knew she had a registered eBay account and (2) he had previously been convicted of embezzlement.

Prior to contacting the MSU Crime Lab, Ms. Macklin had contested eBay's closing of her account and had also filed a complaint with the local police. The police, however, indicated they would not investigate this case. "Would we?" asked Ms. Macklin.

In addition to a voluntary background check and prior to opening a fraud file on an identity theft case, the Lab's standard procedure is to conduct a review of the victim's credit reports, which the victim obtains from each of the four credit reporting agencies—Experian, Equifax, TransUnion, and Innovis. Credit reports contain "red flags" for identity theft (discussed in Chapter 6), and, although infrequent, perpetrators have been known to use their own names to commit online frauds, claiming (when they are caught) that they are the victims of some impersonator who has stolen their identities and is using them. There is no objection, in our experience, by real victims to our background reviews; most victims, in fact, request that the reviews be conducted quickly so that the investigation can begin.

One "red flag" when reviewing a victim's credit reports is when sections or pages are missing or crossed off. Missing or crossed-off sections raise the question as to why the pages are modified —which raises the question as to whether information may have been omitted, either inadvertently or intentionally; if intentional, another question is "why?" Missing sections may contain aliases, addresses, or other information inconsistent with what a victim provides during the routinely conducted in-take interview. The routine check of Ms. Macklin's credit reports revealed missing pages, Ms. Macklin offered different explanations when questioned on two different occasions about the missing sections, and she failed to follow through on our repeated requests to provide the missing pages. The background check showed that Ms. Macklin uses, or at some time had used, several aliases; the report also revealed prior convictions for relatively minor traffic offenses. The report showed no theft or fraud-related arrests.

In cases such as this, where information obtained on a victim during the preinvestigation phase, or information provided personally by the victim, is inconsistent or questionable with what we know about identity theft (e.g., the use of alias names), the Lab procedure requires us to establish the reliability of the victim's responses to information given during the intake part of the process. Reliability is estimated by conducting two independent interviews by two different investigators who use the same questions, reframed, and randomly ordered. The interviews may involve only a few questions to clarify inconsistencies, and they may be conducted either in person or over the telephone.

Ms. Macklin's responses were inconsistent, both to questions about the missing credit history information and also the chain of events involving the auction fraud. Also of questionable accuracy was the claim by Ms. Macklin that her husband was able to access and use her Internet address. We, therefore, pursued further verification on details of the case.

The eBay fraud department cooperated. We learned that, on five different eBay auctions, a Janice A. Macklin had sold Playstation systems and accessories; the winners paid for their purchases through an online bank transfer system whereby money is automatically transferred from the bidder's bank account to the account of the eBay seller. In all the five cases, the bidders had paid the seller but, in return, had received no merchandise. With this information, we contacted the police department where Ms. Macklin had filed her identity theft complaint.

Although initially he had informed Ms. Macklin that her case could not be investigated owing to departmental understaffing, the police officer now sought and, subsequently, obtained a warrant to search the premises for identity theft impersonation evidence, namely, Playstation systems and accessories, and a computer that could be analyzed. The search produced the evidence, and the Internet Protocol (IP) and e-mail addresses traced to the computer located in Ms. Macklin's residence. Confronted with the evidence, Ms. Macklin admitted she was the perpetrator and not the victim; she was fined, ordered to pay restitution, and placed on probation.

What can be learned from this investigation? First, there are, indeed, perpetrators who claim to be victims; second, the routine background information obtained on a victim's claim can point to "red flags"; third, routine questions asked by two different interviewers at two different points in time concerning inconsistencies in background information can help establish the reliability of a victim's responses; fourth, cooperative fraud departments can provide the necessary evidence to pursue the investigation further; and fifth, under-resourced police departments, given sufficient evidence, can bring a case to closure. In the present case, Ms. Macklin claimed to be the victim; in the next case, the victim was charged as the criminal.

THE MARIA G. LOPEZ CASE: A CRIME OF FORGERY

The Lopez family was celebrating the Christmas holiday in the festive, traditional fashion of their beloved Mexico. Now, however, the Lopezes lived in the midwestern United States, where in the wintertime the wind chill was 20 degrees below zero and the snow, knee-deep. Mr. and Mrs. Lopez had secured good employment, and their children, Maria and Juan, had been accepted into the university. Their long-held dreams had come true. Moreover, the Lopez family had found a little three-bedroom house in a neighborhood where the residents took pride in their modest, well-maintained homes and manicured lawns. And now it was Christmas. This meant that as many as possible of the Lopez's extended family—or as many as could (or would) come to this cold climate—would gather together for a weeklong celebration.

It was during dinner on this Christmas Day that Officer Montange knocked at the side door. The Lopez family—aunts, uncles, cousins, and Grandma Lopez—were all seated around a long table in the big, warm kitchen, chatting and laughing, and enjoying the meal and each other's company. Honored by the thought that a police officer had taken the time to come to his home on Christmas Day to return Maria's purse stolen so long before, Mr. Lopez, without a moment's hesitation, invited the officer to join them—they would make room around the table and there was plenty of food. They would "set another plate."

But the officer had no purse to return; he came instead to arrest Maria Lopez for the crime of forgery. In front of her parents, grandmother, and other relatives, Maria was handcuffed and taken away in the patrol car;

arrested on Christmas Day, in her new country, for a crime she claimed she did not commit. The entire Lopez family was in shock.

The case history is shown in Exhibit 1.1.

EXHIBIT 1.1 *Maria Lopez Case History*

February 2004	Maria's purse containing driver's license and bank card stolen while checking out books from main university library.
March 9, 2004	Hispanic female identified by driver's license as Maria Lopez rents video game systems, games, and movies from video store.
March 19, 2004	Maria Lopez (purported impersonator) fails to return video store game systems, games, and movies. Manager contacts the company's other video stores to red flag the name "Maria Lopez." Manager discovers open accounts at each store, in the name of Maria Lopez. Manager tracks down Maria Lopez at the address on the rental form, which was taken from the driver's license. Maria Lopez (the victim) goes to the video store, explains to manager that her purse had been stolen, and claims her innocence. The manager recognizes that Maria Lopez (the victim) was, indeed, not the person who had rented the video equipment; manager then verifies error by comparing Maria's handwriting with the signature on the rental agreement.
March 21, 2004	Maria's (the victim) father now takes her to police station to file report on stolen purse and report the fraud incident.
March 21, 2004	Police department places a "red-flag alert" on Maria's driver's license record.
April 12, 2004	Manager of video store contacts police department to report a larceny of video game systems, games, and movies by someone impersonating another person. Manager's statement on police report: "The suspect must resemble Maria Lopez to some degree."

(continued)

EXHIBIT 1.1 *(continued)*

June 29, 2004	Hispanic female, identified by driver's license as Maria Lopez, attempts to cash a $900 check at a discount store. Suspicious cashier buzzes security who, in turn, calls police. Suspect hurriedly leaves store without driver's license or check, and drives out of the parking lot. Security gets vehicle description but not plate number. Cashier identifies the image on the driver's license as the person who presented the check. Police take check and driver's license and place them into evidence at police department.
August 15, 2004	Police officer attempts to contact Maria at residence given on driver's license; Mrs. Lopez (Maria's mother) believes officer is there about Maria's stolen purse, but Maria is in Texas; Mrs. Lopez gives officer telephone number to reach Maria in Texas.
August 15, 2004	Mrs. Lopez calls Maria in Texas about visit from police officer; Maria telephones police department, leaves name and telephone number for officer to return call. Officer does not return call.
September 10, 2004	According to police statement, officer drafts letter to Maria Lopez asking her to come in for an interview. The report states: "Suspect did not respond."
October 22, 2004	Officer contacts the prosecutor's office to obtain a subpoena. Subpoena to obtain check number and other information about the check goes out to the financial institution named on the check. Results reveal the check was fraudulently manufactured.
November 26, 2004	Officer contacts discount store; views videotape of suspect at counter attempting to cash check; security officer advises that the subject in the video is same as image on driver's license.
December 25, 2004	Maria Lopez is arrested at her home for forgery and attempt to use false document to obtain $900; Mr. Lopez (Maria's father) follows police car to jail; arranges to post bail; meanwhile, Maria is locked in jail.
January 12, 2004	Maria, out of jail on bail, makes appointment to meet an identity theft investigator at the MSU Identity Theft Crime and Research Lab.

EXHIBIT 1.1   *(continued)*

January 13, 2004	MSU investigator conducts routine background check and interviews Maria; requests copies of police reports, including the report made of her stolen purse as well as documents showing that a red flag was placed on her driver's license, and the name and address of video store manager. Investigator makes appointment with security to view discount store video.
January 14, 2005	Two MSU investigators, Maria Lopez, and security officer view video at discount store; video shows Hispanic female with long black hair, just like Maria's; the female, however, is taller than Maria. The female is pregnant.
January 15–17, 2005	Further investigation by the MSU Lab investigators revealed the following information:

- The discount store video of the person attempting to cash check showed only a side view; there was no frontal view to show the person's face.

- The security officer admitted to the Lab investigators that neither the check nor driver's license was preserved for fingerprinting; both check and license were handled several times by the cashier, the police officer, and the security officer.

- The video manager confirmed to the Lab investigators and Maria that the only common feature between the person who had rented the equipment and Maria was that both had long, black hair.

- The police acknowledged that they failed to see the "red flag" placed on Maria's driver's license record in March 2004.

- The security officer confirmed to the Lab investigators that the video of the female who had attempted to cash the check showed that she was obviously pregnant.

- Maria is not pregnant now, nor has she ever been pregnant.

(continued)

EXHIBIT 1.1   *(continued)*

Tues., Jan. 25, 2005	Maria appeared in district court for the preliminary hearing. Based on the above evidence together with notarized documents from both the video store manager and the security officer, Case Number 04-1973—Maria Lopez, ". . . was adjourned by the authority of the judge for good cause shown."

The perpetrator in this case has yet to be apprehended; now, however, largely because of the time and efforts of the investigators at our Identity Theft Lab, Maria's name has been cleared from the state's criminal databases—for crimes she did not commit.

Although she lost no money and was convicted of no crime, the emotional costs remain considerable. For Maria, the anguish of the pain suffered by her parents and grandmother, and the embarrassment of being arrested and handcuffed in the presence of her relatives, remains, to this day, a source of psychological distress.

Maria's case and the others above are only four of many that, since 1999, have been investigated by the MSU Crime Lab. No two cases are alike; nonetheless, they all involve some basic, common methods and procedures, which is what these cases intended to portray. The background check before beginning an investigation, the reliability interviews for inconsistent information, the development of a strategy (which becomes modified as the investigation progresses) all have been emphasized. The following chapters elaborate on other common aspects, including the several chapters that emphasize and illustrate the importance of using the Internet and the computer as primary twenty-first-century investigative tools. First, however, before embarking on any identity theft investigations, it is essential that one knows the crime and understands the criminal.

CHAPTER 2

KNOW THE CRIME AND UNDERSTAND THE CRIMINAL

THE CRIME DEFINED

What exactly is identity theft? Since the enactment of the Identity Theft and Assumption Deterrence Act in 1998, the crime of identity theft has continuously evolved as criminals find new ways to commit old crimes. The first thefts were of "personal" identities—the names, addresses, Social Security numbers, driver's license numbers, health care numbers, bank account, and credit card numbers, mother's maiden name (to obtain the original birth certificate for a complete identity takeover), and any other information related to or that would identify an individual. Perpetrators soon, however, learned that easy cash could also be had using "business" identities.

Business identities include the business name, address, telephone number, corporate credit card numbers, banking account numbers, Federal Employer Identification Number (FEIN), Treasury Number (TR), Tax Identification Number (TIN), Electronic Filing Identification Number (EFIN; Internal Revenue Service), Electronic Transmitter Identification Number (ETIN; Internal Revenue Service), e-business Web sites, URL addresses, and e-mail addresses. Criminals use business identities in the same way they use personal identities—to obtain loans, or open accounts for the fraudulent purchase of tools, equipment, and other merchandise, which are then sold in the black market.

IDENTITY THEFT IS A NETWORK CRIME

Neither personal identity thefts nor business identity thefts are committed by a single criminal operating alone; rather, identity thefts typically involve networks of individuals who are more or less organized and who operate in cells that perform different but interrelated functions. One mistake often made by law enforcement investigators is that of knocking on suspects' doors before gathering sufficient evidence to assess the scope of the crime. Only the "front" criminals are then apprehended—the cell members responsible for opening post boxes at (usually) private postal companies or whose task is to receive the deliveries of fraudulently ordered merchandise. Cell leaders and other members of the hierarchically organized network go undetected: depending on the size of the network, which usually also evolves to include increasing numbers of members, the front-end criminals often do not know the names of the cell leaders or the person who stole the list of identities or the place they were stolen from. The organizational structure with different cells performing different functions serves to layer the crime and also hide the most hardened criminals. Premature arrests of the front men (or women) send warnings that reverberate speedily throughout the network, and cell members flee to another state or go into hiding; nonetheless, the identity theft network remains intact and the identity frauds continue.

In one unusual case, the violent crimes task force of a large metropolitan police department investigating the theft of the identities of over 3000 executives in a major automobile manufacturing company chose not to arrest the front perpetrators; instead, for six weeks the detectives conducted surveillance and gathered information and only then apprehended what they determined to be the entire network. This book's author later analyzed the police reports using social network analysis; the purpose was to determine how the network evolved, operated, and was maintained. These details are presented here so that investigators can understand the crime and the criminal *before* conducting an investigation. A good place to begin is with the al Qaeda network, which is similar in many ways to identity theft networks.

THE AL QAEDA ANALOGY

Social science research has shown that individuals with similar interests, experiences, and characteristics gravitate to one another, which might help explain how crime networks originate and evolve. The structure and operations of identity theft networks are similar to most other crime organizations. The al Qaeda network is a prime example. In fact, the al Qaeda Training Manual[1] is a major text for courses taught at the MSU Crime and Research Lab to police officers, FBI agents, and business fraud investigators.

The al Qaeda Manual describes identities as being "falsified"; however, from congressional hearings on terrorists acts against the United States, it is known that terrorists conceal themselves and their activities using "stolen" identities—"real" identities are needed to verify the creditworthiness of the person who seeks to rent automobiles and apartments, obtain lines of credit from financial institutions and retail businesses, purchase services such as flight or truck driver training, and obtain driver's licenses, passports, and other forms of identification.

The following quotes from the al Qaeda Manual show how terrorists use stolen identities; they are statements that are applicable to all crime networks, including those involving identity crimes.

- "All documents of the undercover brother, such as identity cards and passports, should be falsified," p. 22.
- "When the undercover brother is traveling with a certain identity card or passport, he should know all pertinent information such as the name, profession, and place of residence," p. 22.

- "The brother who has special work status (commander, communication link, . . .) should have more than one identity card and passport. He should learn the contents of each, the nature of the (indicated) profession, and the dialect of the residence area listed in the document," p. 22.
- "When using an identity document in different names, not more than one such document should be carried at one time," p. 22.
- "The validity of the falsified travel documents should always be confirmed," p. 23.
- "It is preferable to rent apartments using false names," p. 26.
- "It is necessary to have at hand documents supporting the undercover (member). In the case of a physician, there should be an actual medical diploma, membership in the (medical) union, the government permit, and the rest of the routine procedures known in that country," p. 27.
- Those members going to a meeting with other brothers should ". . . Verify the proper cover for the documents he has with him," p. 61.
- For an assassination operation, ". . . falsified documents should be prepared for the participating individuals," and "The documents related to the operation should be hidden in a secure place and burned immediately after the operation . . .," p. 66.

As in the al Qaeda Manual, testimonies at U.S. Congressional hearings and in reports of such hearings also equate the term *false* identity with *stolen* identity. For example, James Woolsey, former head of the CIA, reported in the *New Republic* magazine[2] that agents of Osama bin Laden stole the identities of at least 12 western-educated young men who were murdered in 1990 to "move freely around the world using a *false* (emphasis added) identity." The extent to which a "real" identity is valued by the al Qaeda terrorists is revealed by the fact that the "Families of all 12 men also were killed and all their paperwork erased so nobody would stumble on bin Laden's lethal impostors."[3]

Former FBI Chief of the Terrorist Financial Review Group, Dennis Lormel, in testimony before the U.S. Congress and when referring to the use of false identities by terrorists, stated: "The stolen identity provides a cloak of anonymity for the subject while the groundwork is laid to carry out the crime . . ." and, "includes the rental of mail drops, post office boxes, apartments, office space, vehicles, and storage lockers as well as the activation of pagers, cellular telephones, and various utility services."[4]

Chief Lormel's testimony could have as well applied to identity theft networks, which also use stolen identities for all of the above-stated activities—the only difference between identity theft networks (and most other crime groups) and terrorists is the ulterior motive—to commit Jihad against the infidels versus traffic drugs, smuggle humans, launder money, support a drug habit, among others. Of course, terrorists do these things too, but the primary common denominator for terrorism and most or all crimes is the stolen identity.

Clearly, then, identity theft investigators must be knowledgeable about the identity theft networks and their operations. The following sections describe how one identity theft network originated and, within six weeks, evolved to include an estimated 45 perpetrators who operated together across three states and multiple legal jurisdictions (local, county, state) while committing credit card, retail account, telecommunications, and utilities frauds.

HOW NETWORKS EVOLVE, OPERATE, AND ARE MAINTAINED

On her last day of work at one of the world's largest automobile manufacturing companies in Detroit, a female contract worker printed and then stole a computerized list of over 3000 executives' names, home, and work addresses, Social Security numbers, payroll, and other personal identifying information. The perpetrator had been hired into the company by an outsourced staffing agency for a temporary, entry-level data processing job.

This woman, it was later learned, stole the identities in October and, in early December, the busiest times of the retail year when frauds are least likely to be detected, and began selling and otherwise distributing the identities to relatives, friends, and friends of friends. Together, these individuals coordinated to fraudulently purchase goods and services valued at thousands of dollars.

The theft of the 3000 identities was uncovered as executives whose names were on the stolen list began receiving notices that credit card and other account payments were past due. The local police department, which at the time did not have an identity theft unit, assigned a contingent of detectives to work full-time on what was considered a high-profile case. On the last day of a six-week intensive round-the-clock investigation, the detectives apprehended many but not all of the known perpetrators.

For purposes of the present illustration and because the complete report on the entire network of 45 perpetrators is considerably long, the details below are taken from police department and court records for only 28 of the perpetrators, including 16 males and 12 females. To protect the anonymity of those involved, the actual names contained in the police and court reports have been replaced with numbers. Therefore, the numbers in the exhibits represent the transgressors.

Sources of the Identity Thefts and How the Stolen Identities Were Used

The perpetrators committed innumerable frauds (Exhibit 2.1). To begin, the police records showed that, in addition to the theft of the 3000 executives' names, four other female perpetrators also were tasked with the job of stealing identities: one stole 800 names from the account records of a discount store where she was employed; a second perpetrator employed at another discount store stole credit card numbers and names from that company; a third female, employed by a telecommunication company, repeatedly stole an undetermined number of names from that source, and the fourth criminal stole payroll checks from the company she worked for.

EXHIBIT 2.1   *How Networks Are Maintained*

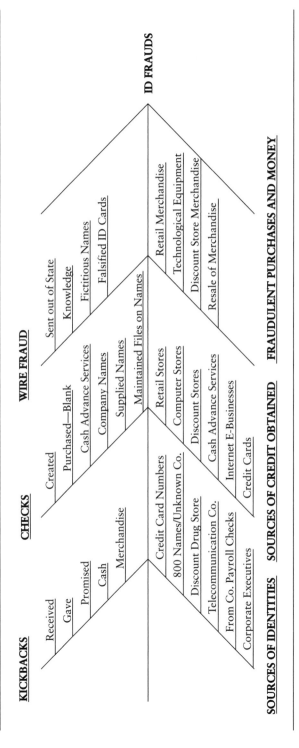

The five female perpetrators turned over the stolen identities to male members of the network, who used the personal information to obtain credit at retail, computer, and discount stores; cash from cash advance services and fraudulent wire services transactions; and credit cards, which they used for online purchases. Several female perpetrators purchased merchandise at retail and discount stores, and male members of one cell purchased expensive cameras, computers and computer games and systems, software, cell phones, and other technological equipment, most of which was resold on the street for cash.

Members of another cell were involved primarily in bank and check fraud. The ultimate search of their residences uncovered sophisticated printing, duplicating, desktop publishing, and other equipment and materials. These perpetrators created authentic-looking checks and also imprinted names and bank numbers on purchased blank checks. The names and addresses used were taken from the lists stolen by the group of five females; however, fictitious company names and addresses were used for some checks. This group of offenders, primarily in charge of printing, duplicating, and forging, maintained an organized file of the names and addresses used on the checks that they supplied to members of another cell who, in return, reimbursed these forgers with kickbacks of money and other favors.

In fact, the police records showed that most of the members of the network were very generous in sharing the fraudulently obtained money, merchandise, and stolen identities with one another. For example, they:

- Provided one another with names, Social Security numbers, and other not yet used (stolen) personal identifying information.
- Used a chain of communication to warn other members of a suspected police raid, such as when perpetrators became suspicious of UPS delivery-police impersonators.
- Opened post office boxes and shared post box addresses at various private postal businesses, for the delivery of fraudulent merchandise.
- Arranged for sites for other deliveries of merchandise, such as at the home of a relative or friend.

- Collected for one another, from post office boxes or any other arranged sites, the UPS, FedEx, or U.S. mail delivered merchandise.

The details obtained on this network revealed its composition: different offenders specialized in different crimes; groups of offenders worked together in cells that collaborated with one another on the crimes; and the offenses committed by members of one cell (e.g., check forging) facilitated crimes committed by members of related cells (e.g., check cashing).

The organizational structure and operations of this and other crime networks, including the al Qaeda terrorist group, are much the same as most businesses: employees with certain skills work in specific departments, where they perform specialized tasks, and the departments, all interrelated, work to achieve a common company goal, which is to generate income.

Thus, investigators of identity theft must be aware that, even though the theft of identities may be a one-person crime, the offense usually, if not always, is a larger operation, one that has evolved to include relatives, friends, friends of friends, and other potentially long-term, hardened, and dangerous criminals. Investigators must also know that the crimes have not ceased with the arrest of the front-end criminals who may not even know the names or locations of the cell leaders or the number of cells or members involved overall.

Fraudulent Merchandise Ordered and Methods of Delivery

For purposes of illustration, Exhibit 2.2 categorizes the merchandise deliveries into three subgroups: shipper, receiver, and merchandise delivered. Shipper is the company used by the perpetrators to transport the fraudulently ordered merchandise; receiver is the person the merchandise was shipped to; and merchandise simply refers to the types of purchases that were delivered.

For the crimes that required delivery of merchandise, the perpetrators used United Parcel Service (UPS), Federal Express (FedEx), and the U. S. Postal Service. United Parcel Service and FedEx deliveries were made not only to friends and relatives who knew the merchandise was fraudulent but also to unsuspecting parents, grandparents, and other family members. Merchandise was also delivered to U.S. Post Offices as well as to private post office services that were opened in the names of identity theft victims.

Exhibit 2.2 additionally shows the type of merchandise that was delivered; the majority of purchases by the male offenders was for technical equipment such as computers, DVD players, camcorders, cell phones, and others, and some of the female members purchased kitchen and other household items, and jewelry.

How Perpetrators Avoid Detection

Criminals, including the members of the network described earlier, conceal their fraudulent activities in at least three different ways (Exhibit 2.3). First, the members within and between the cells routinely communicated with one another; second, except in a few isolated, anomalous cases, these individuals had the merchandise delivered to locations other than their apartments and in names other than their own; and third, the perpetrators stored the merchandise, once delivered, at locations other than their own residences. Typically too, these individuals destroyed the shipping and other bills and documents related to the purchases and deliveries of the merchandise. Exhibits 2.4 through 2.8 show how the network evolved to increasingly include the above-described members and their respective cells (the Exhibits, however, do not show all the cells or all of the members of this network, because those details would simply be replications of the same or similar crimes committed by different offenders).

EXHIBIT 2.2 *Fraudulent Merchandise Orders: Shipper, Receiver, Types of Merchandise Ordered*

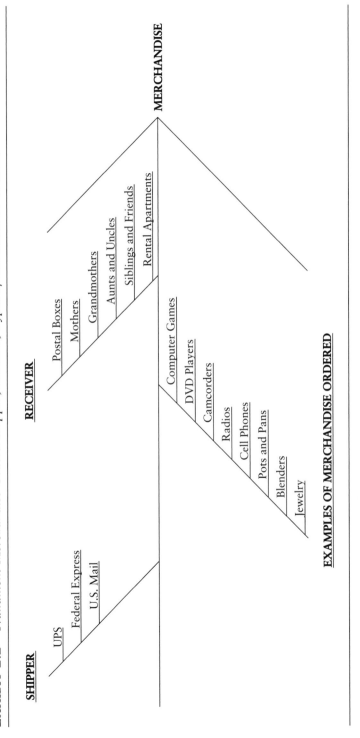

SHIPPER

UPS
Federal Express
U.S. Mail

RECEIVER

Postal Boxes
Mothers
Grandmothers
Aunts and Uncles
Siblings and Friends
Rental Apartments

MERCHANDISE

Computer Games
DVD Players
Camcorders
Radios
Cell Phones
Pots and Pans
Blenders
Jewelry

EXAMPLES OF MERCHANDISE ORDERED

EXHIBIT 2.3   *Avoiding Detection*

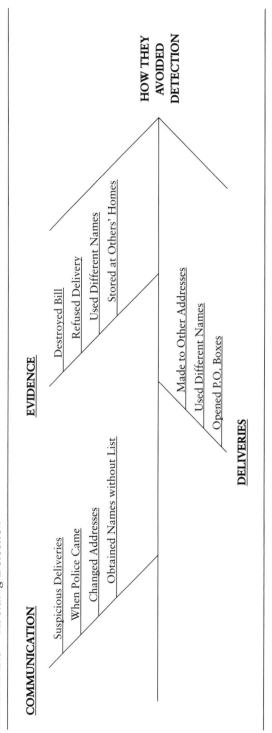

COMMUNICATION

Suspicious Deliveries

When Police Came

Changed Addresses

Obtained Names without List

EVIDENCE

Destroyed Bill

Refused Delivery

Used Different Names

Stored at Others' Homes

DELIVERIES

Made to Other Addresses

Used Different Names

Opened P.O. Boxes

HOW THEY AVOIDED DETECTION

EXHIBIT 2.4   *Identity Theft Network Starts with Person #20*

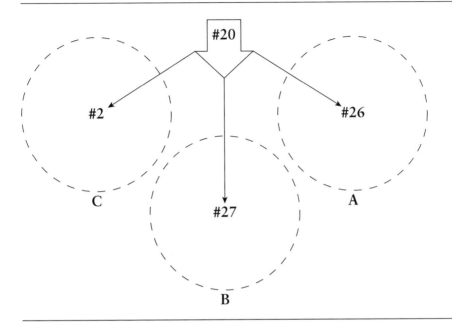

EXHIBIT 2.5   *Identity Theft Network Evolves: Cell #1*

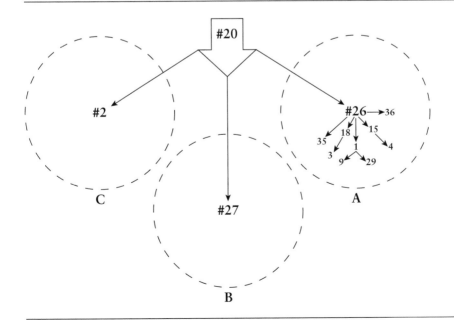

EXHIBIT 2.6   *Identity Theft Network Further Evolves: Cell #2*

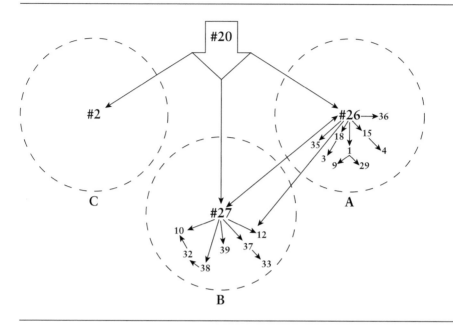

EXHIBIT 2.7   *Identity Theft Network Evolves: Cell #3*

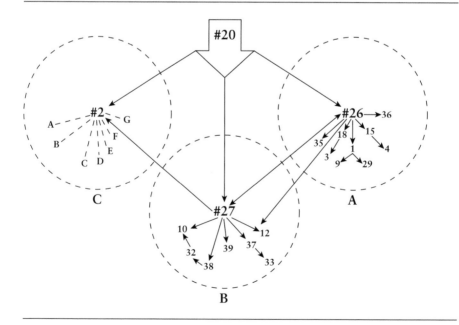

EXHIBIT 2.8   *Identity Theft Network Evolves: Cell #4*

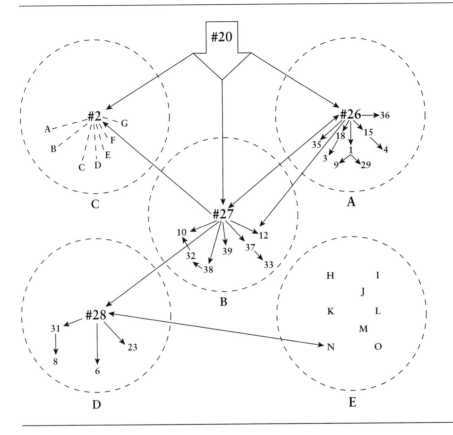

THE CRIMINAL NETWORK

The fraud began with the previously described 25-year-old female contract worker who was employed on a temporary basis by a large corporation that routinely uses contract workers during periods of high work overloads. This individual is noted in Exhibit 2.4 as person #20 (the numbers were assigned in the order in which the author coded the police records). In Exhibit 2.4, the circles and the letters (A, B, C) below them represent three cells of the network. The dotted lines that form the circles indicate permeable boundaries through which members of cells interact with one another. The arrows show the direction in which the stolen identities were passed along to members within or across cells.

As described earlier, on her last day of employment, #20 stole a computerized list of over 3000 names of corporate executives. The list contained the following information on each executive: age, gender, home and work addresses, Social Security number, salary, and other payroll information including costs for health care plans, savings, and retirement programs and other company benefits, as well as the amounts of federal and state income tax withholdings.

Subject #20 contacted three other subjects—#2, #26, and #27—giving each of them pages containing names (identities), which were torn from the computerized list. Subject #20 and the other three perpetrators shared common characteristics: Subject #2 was a relative of #20, and #26 and #27 were her close friends; these four people lived within a two-mile radius of one another; they were all in the same 20–30 age group. Of the four, one was a female—offender #20 who stole the list of names.

The paper trail of information from the police records showed that subjects #2, #26, and #27 worked together to commit a range of identity frauds—credit card, bank, retail account, telecommunications, and others. Each of these perpetrators also helped the network evolve by selling lists of names stolen from the various sources (described in Exhibit 2.1) to others.

For example, member #26 contacted and gave the names from his list of stolen identities (Exhibit 2.5) to other people (#1, #3, #4, #9, #15, #18, #29, #35, and #36). These new members included a sister and a nephew, two cousins, and several friends. Two of the friends were husband and wife. Each of these individuals collaborated with #26, the cell leader, in the fraud schemes using the victims' identities directly for in-store purchases or indirectly by ordering merchandise through the U.S. mail or over the Internet and by receiving the ordered shipments at postal addresses that were registered in the names of the victims.

Within cell A, there was evidence that #1 continued the flow of information (identities); also, not shown as arrows, #3 and #4, the husband and wife team, contacted #9, a friend, who agreed to open a post office mailbox for delivery of merchandise fraudulently obtained using the stolen identities. The husband and wife team also discussed the fraud scheme with a brother-in-law, #29, but there was no indication that either #9 or #29 perpetuated the flow of information or assumed any of the victims' identities for any purpose. However, with the contact between cell leader #26 and #27 (shown in Exhibit 2.6), the network continued to expand.

Exhibit 2.6 shows how member #27, perhaps more than any other member, was responsible for maintaining and perpetuating the network. To illustrate, in Exhibit 2.6 (cell B), member #27 first involved seven other people. The relationships within cell B were as follows: #10 was a friend who already had a list of names stolen from another company, that is, other than the executives' company. Members #10 and #27 together visited #10's uncle, to pick up false credit cards the uncle had made by forging #10's stolen list identities. Subject #32 was #10's mother.

Subject #27 promoted the continuous flow of identities across the network's cells through interactions with the leader, #20 (to, from time to time, obtain additional names from the executive list), and with cell leader #26 and, subsequently, cell leader #28 (described below). Police records also revealed that subject #27 gave a list of the executives' names to a friend who was in town, visiting from "Philly," which shows how networks extend into other states.

In addition to proliferating the system network through these social (and criminal) interactions, #27 creatively transformed the executives' personal information into documents that were then used to fraudulently obtain cash and goods. For example, the executives' names were included on counterfeit checks that were either cashed or used to purchase merchandise; he (and the other cell members) assumed the identities of the executives to obtain, activate, and use credit cards; #27 also used one executive's name and other information for a telephone company to "turn on a phone" for a friend, and used other executives' identities to purchase computers, camcorders, and digital video equipment through mail-order companies with instructions for delivery to his grandmother's home address.

Further, subject #27 was involved with the cell leader #2 (cell C) in a check kiting operation; they opened accounts at several banks, where they cashed checks before the funds were deposited to cover the drafts. The unique fraud tasks for cell C were to create counterfeit checks using the stolen identities provided by other key members of other cells. The letters A–G in cell C represent individuals who, according to the police records, were only indirectly affiliated with #2 and who were, purportedly, not implicated in the use of the stolen identities.

Exhibit 2.8 shows the continued evolution of the network: cell leader #27 gave a list of the executives' names to the new member #28. Member #28 and the others in cell D specialized in purchasing computers and selling them in the black market. Member #28 had the computers delivered to the addresses of member #31, who in turn also ordered computers, which he got delivered to member #8. In addition, member #28 had mail-ordered computers delivered to member #6 as well as to his own mother (#23), who was unaware of the fraud scheme. Member #28 also personally delivered at least one computer to cell leader #27.

Exhibit 2.8 also shows that member #28 became associated with a new cell E when he distributed stolen identities to an individual who became that cell's leader. These five cells and others not depicted here evolved and operated over a six-week period prior to the arrests, insofar as the theft and use of the executives' identities. (These offenders may have known one another and been operating together much longer in other crimes.)

For the criminal investigator, these real world data show that apparent suspects are likely operating in collaboration with numerous others and that it is imperative that covert surveillance be conducted until no new faces appear on the network crime scene. Not obvious in this chapter is the fact that the investigation began at the end of the trail, where the executive's credit reports (covered in Chapter 6) revealed the merchandise was delivered.

In summary, the information learned from this case can be practically applied to investigations of identity theft where:

- More than one person or a few people are likely to be involved.
- The number and types of crimes increase as the network evolves.
- Premature interviews with suspects can trigger a chain reaction of alerts throughout a network.
- Identity crimes are "layered" to protect the identities of key members—the leaders of the cell and also the names of individuals operating in other cells.

This "layering" of the crime is common across crime networks, which is one reason why identity thefts continue—the offenders conceal their own identities from members of the cells in their own network. The network organization, though loosely structured, is, to some extent, hierarchical in form so as to purposely protect the people in command. This knowledge of how crimes are layered is important for developing the investigative strategy.

THE LAYERING OF IDENTITY CRIMES

In identity theft networks, the leaders of the cells usually know one another; however, the members of a cell often do not know the names of either the leaders or members of other cells, and as a network evolves to include increasingly larger numbers of cells, even the cell leaders may not know one another. Perpetrators intentionally "layer" the crime, which is one way the networks are maintained.

In the above example, the police reports revealed that most members of the network did not know who stole the (original) list of executives' identities, the names of other cell leaders or members, the persons who created the counterfeit checks, or that there existed friends of friends from Philadelphia. Identity theft networks evolve especially rapidly to other states and countries when perpetrators sell stolen identities on the Internet.

For purposes of further instruction, Exhibits 2.9 through 2.13 depict the various ways in which perpetrators have layered other identity frauds. In Exhibit 2.9, for example, a clerk at a discount store distributed to three confederates an unknown quantity of customer names, addresses, and credit card numbers obtained using a card reader; the accomplices sold these identities on the street.

Exhibit 2.10 shows how in another unrelated case the crime itself is layered. A former bank employee accessed and stole the override codes and collaborated with a currently employed bank cashier and two other bank employees to open checking accounts using stolen identities. The bank employees overrode the bad checks they wrote to a discount store for the purchase of merchandise, which they later returned for cash, which, in turn, was distributed among the accomplices.

A third case, shown in Exhibit 2.11, involved a $1.3 million counterfeit check operation in which a bank check sorter (the network leader) had access to, and stole, blank checks, which he gave to a middleman who, in turn, distributed the checks to workers in four different states. Those workers distributed the checks to runners who cashed them. The percentages of cash proceeds were distributed across the network as follows: runners, 20%; workers, 20%; middleman, 30%; and the leader, 30%.

Exhibit 2.12 shows how, in another case, the Internet was used to commit auction fraud using stolen identities. Customers in Florida, California, Ohio, and North Carolina won the bids on an e-auction site for original artwork sold by "a lady in Detroit" who, in turn, transferred the cash to an account in Spain using a fraudulent Internet Protocol (IP) address (discussed in Chapters 3 and 9) that was traced to Utah.

Exhibit 2.13 shows how an employee of a business (1) staged a break-in and stole blank checks which he (2) sold to an accomplice for a one-time fee; the accomplice (3) sold the checks to another confederate for a larger fee, and (4) the confederate distributed the checks to runners, who cashed them for payouts that were split among all the members of the network except for the employee who stole the checks.

EXHIBIT 2.9 *Layering an Identity Theft Crime: The Card Reader Case*

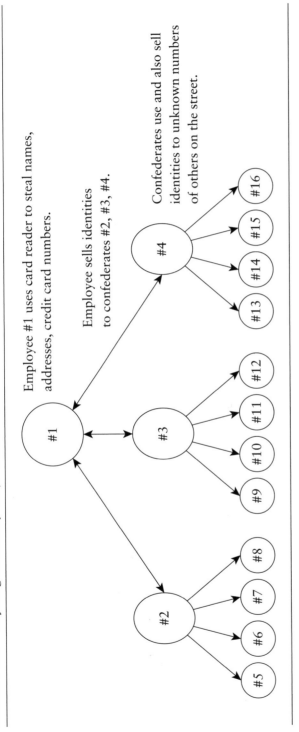

Employee #1 uses card reader to steal names, addresses, credit card numbers.

Employee sells identities to confederates #2, #3, #4.

Confederates use and also sell identities to unknown numbers of others on the street.

EXHIBIT 2.10 *Layering an Identity Theft Crime: The Theft of Override Codes*

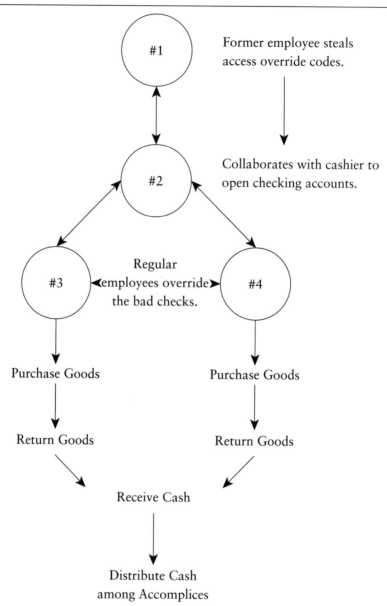

Exhibit 2.11 *Layering an Identity Theft Crime: Check Fraud and Identity Theft*

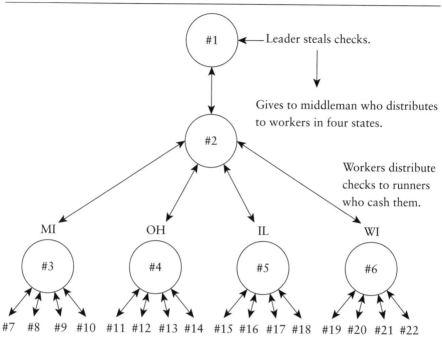

In each of these cases, stolen identities were used to commit crimes that were layered so that the leader or leaders would remain unknown to the other members of the network. Here again, the al Qaeda analogy is telling. Note the similarities with the identity theft networks.

For example, in the al Qaeda network, the layering of terrorist acts is carefully organized with specific instructions that, "Cell or cluster methods should be adopted by the Organization. It should be composed of many cells whose members do not know one another, so that if a cell member is caught the other cells would not be affected, and work would proceed normally."[5]

EXHIBIT 2.12 *Layering of an Identity Theft Crime: Auction Fraud and Identity Theft*

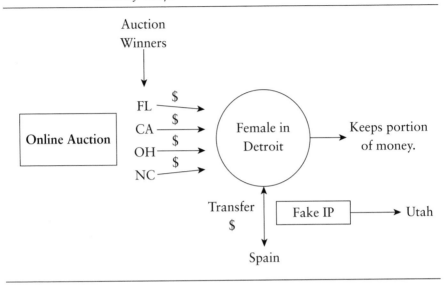

EXHIBIT 2.13 *Layering of an Identity Theft: Burglary, Check Fraud, and Identity Theft Crime*

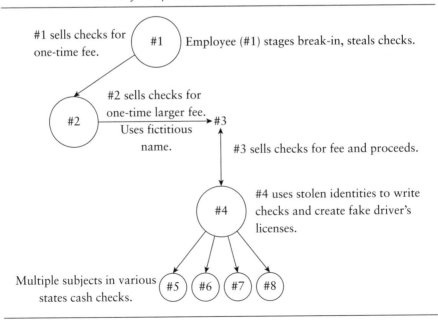

For al Qaeda, as is the case with other crime networks such as drug traffickers, and human smugglers, the organizational structure is intentionally designed to layer the crime. With identity theft networks, the organizational structure evolves on its own as network members obtain new lists of stolen identities that they then sell or give as kickbacks to relatives, friends, and other criminals.

Also, the al Qaeda network, as with other crime networks, further defines its organizational structure so that upper level members are protected. According to the al Qaeda manual, the members are to be subdivided into three groups—the overt member, the covert member, and the commander—and each group is to have its own security measures.[6] Identity theft networks that evolve on the street may be less sophisticated insofar as their organizational planning; however, each cell does have a leader and, as the above examples showed, there often also exist middlemen (or women).

In addition, much like al Qaeda and other organized crime networks, the members of identity theft networks perform specific tasks. For example, in case of raids and capture of infidels, different al Qaeda members are assigned to different tasks, such as who will:

- Engage the enemy with bullets.
- Flee with important documents.
- Specify escape routes.
- Make sure all members have left the scene.[7]

Similarly, in identity theft networks, criminals rely on specialized divisions of labor. In the identity theft network described above, one cell was responsible for making counterfeit checks; another conducted online credit card fraud; members of another cell were experts in wire fraud; one female group committed retail fraud at upscale clothing stores, while another female group used stolen credit cards to purchase goods at primarily discount stores; one cell was responsible for ordering technological equipment from e-businesses. When the network began with one contract worker, there were undoubtedly no such organizational plans; however, the cells evolved in great part because criminals gravitated to other criminals with similar interests and experiences, and different criminals had different backgrounds and had learned different ways of committing crimes.

Another similarity between the al Qaeda network and identity theft networks is the emphasis on teamwork. The al Qaeda manual states, "Almighty God says, 'And hold fast, all together, by the Rope which Allah (stretches out for you), and be not divided among yourselves.'"[8] Members of the above identity theft network warned one another of suspected police surveillance, made checks for members of other networks, purchased goods that they sold for money that was shared with one another, gave merchandise to one another for kickbacks, and, in general, worked as a team both within and between cells.

Understanding how crime networks are structured and operate is important for investigations. Whereas the source of most stolen identities is in the workplace, the sources of the criminal activities that use those stolen identities are in different locations and the crimes are committed by different individuals operating in mutual reciprocation. Where there is credit card fraud, there likely is also bank fraud, retail account fraud, utilities and telecommunications fraud, wire fraud, and so forth. Investigators must gather holistic facts before knocking on a suspect's door in an investigation.

In recent years, criminals have learned to use the Internet to layer the crimes by e-mailing stolen names, addresses, and credit card or Social Security numbers to accomplices in other states or, as in Exhibit 2.12, using online auctions. Perpetrators also set up fraudulent Web sites to obtain personal information from naïve "customers" or even create legitimate Web sites with superimposed pop-up windows to collect the personal information—a technique known as "phishing." Since perpetrators work online, investigators must go there too. It would be a serious mistake to overlook the Internet and computer for today's investigations, which is why, before opening a fraud file for investigation, the next two chapters show investigators how to prepare their computers for online investigations.

COMPUTER SECURITY FOR IDENTITY FRAUD INVESTIGATIONS

Identity fraud investigations require three primary tools: an automobile, a telephone, and a computer. It is not surprising that, in today's high-tech information era, of the three, the computer is the most used. Chapters 3 and 4, therefore, prepare the investigator, and the computer, for online investigations. These two chapters are written particularly for investigators who are new to the Internet.

Chapter 3 introduces computer security issues, provides an overview of especially useful security software programs as well as directions on where to find them on the Internet, and uses exercises and tutorials to help familiarize investigators new to the Internet with tools that prevent computer infections by viruses, parasites, worms, and other scumware.

Neither Chapter 3 nor the other chapters in this book are intended as "read throughs." The exercises, tutorials, and readings take time. Approach this chapter as a series of lessons that may take parts of several days to complete. *Do not skip the readings*—they contain important background information and sometimes materials for the exercises and tutorials.

GUIDELINES FOR DOWNLOADING AND INSTALLING SOFTWARE FROM THE INTERNET

Many types of useful and reliable computer software can be downloaded from the Internet free of charge. Examples are Grisoft's AVG Antivirus program and Ad-Aware, a software program that provides protection from advertisements, tracking activities, browser hijacking, and other intrusions. Many other types of freeware are introduced later in this chapter. Identity fraud investigations sometimes lead to questionable Web sites, the accessing of which could render one's computer susceptible to infection. Computer security, therefore, is imperative. Let us begin by reviewing the following terms and guidelines on downloading and installing computer software, in preparation for Exercise 3.1, where you will install security programs.

- Learn the difference between "freeware" and "shareware." Freeware is free; shareware is not. Shareware can be used for a trial period after which there is a charge.
- Conduct research on the product. From online searches of Internet directories such as Google or Yahoo! and from the vendor's Web site, locate, and carefully read third-party as well as customer reviews. Also visit the following Web sites for reliable reviews of security software:
    - CNET.com at *http://www.download.com/2001-20_4-0.html? tag=cnetfd.sb*
    - PC Magazine: *http://www.pcmag.com/category2/0,1738,2130,00.asp*
    - SnapFiles: *http://snapfiles.com*
    - ZDNet: *http://downloads-zdnet.com*
- At the vendor's Web site, read the product description, refund and privacy policies, and the directions for downloading and installing.
    - Also read the system requirements to determine if the program will work correctly on your computer's operating system (Microsoft, Macintosh, Lynx) and platforms such as Windows XP and Windows 95/98.

- Prior to installing software:
  - Close all other programs to avoid interference with proper installation.
  - If not already installed, download, and install a recent version of a reputable antivirus program (e.g., AVG Antivirus at *www.grisoft.com*, Norton, McAfee; for reviews, search Google: antivirus software reviews).
  - Update the antivirus software.
- Read the licensing agreement. Be aware that some software is available free for personal use while a fee is required for business use.
- Print and save registration information for future use, such as for reinstallation of the program on a new computer.
- Before installing software from the Internet, use the antivirus program to first scan the downloaded files.
- Before installing software, delete any software of the same type from the computer. For example, particularly in the case of firewall software, two different firewall programs are likely to interfere with each other. The result can affect a computer so that it functions slowly or perhaps even not at all, such as, for example, by preventing access to the Internet.
- Thus, for emphasis, when updating features of an operating system or a platform, such as Microsoft Windows, verify with that company's customer service department the compatibility of the to-be-installed software.

In addition to the above guidelines, and before beginning Exercise 3.1 on downloading and installing software, conduct a review of precautions developed by professionals at the CERT Coordination Center, an organization that conducts federally funded research, located at: *http://www.cert.org/homeusers/HomeComputerSecurity/#7. Do not skip this review*. When finished, begin Exercise 3.1.

EXERCISE 3.1   *A Lesson in Downloading and Installing Software*

Although different software may use different approaches for downloading and installing software, most programs today provide easy-to-understand instructions that guide the user through the process with simple clicks of the mouse to each "Next" step. Exercise 3.1 demonstrates how to configure a computer to download and install software, using as an example an evaluation copy of SSNDTECT, which is Social Security Number validation software. Using SSNDTECT, an investigator can verify the validity and also the state of issuance for Social Security numbers (assigned at this time, however, only through the year 1980). (Should SSNDTECT be offline when conducting this exercise, use any reputable freeware, such as one of those mentioned in the previous review.)

Step 1.

Create a folder (also called a *directory*) on the desktop for storing the software so that, once downloaded, the software will be easy to locate:

- Click on the *My Computer* icon located on the desktop.
- Click on the *C:* icon (your computer's hard drive).
- Under *File*, click on *New*.
- Then choose *Folder* from the menu. Name the folder as per your choice. Try "SSN Detect."
- Close by clicking on the "X" in the upper right corner of the monitor.
- Note: You may wish to create your new directory (folder) in the Programs file on the C: drive.

Step 2.

Type the following Uniform Resource Locator (URL) into the browser bar: *http://www.comserv-inc.com/downloads.html*

- Now at the Web site, click on the blue *SSNDTECT* link, which takes you to the registration page. You may choose to complete the entire form or only the required fields. When finished,
- Click on the *Continue* button.

Step 3.

On this page, review the terms of use and click on the link at the bottom of the page to begin the download of the evaluation software.

Step 4.

A "File Download" box appears. Click on *Save.* A "Save As box" appears. In the first box, select "C" for your hard drive. A list of all folders on your hard drive will appear.

Step 5.

Double-click on the folder you named *SSN Detect* to open it. To download, click on *Save.* Once the download is complete, close the browser.

Step 6.

Once again, click on the *My Computer* icon located on the desktop. Click on the C: icon (your computer's hard drive).

• Scroll down the list of folders until you find the one you named "SSN Detect."

• Double-click on the folder to view its contents.

Step 7.

Locate the file ending in ".exe" (COMSERV-SSNDTECT-3.0-Eval-Version.exe) and double-click on it.

• Type "C:\SSN Detect" to unzip the program in the folder you created earlier. Since the folder is open, you will see the files appear.

• Next to the Computer icon, double-click on *Setup.exe.* A Welcome Screen will appear. Click on the *Next* button located at the bottom of the screen.

• Click on the *Yes* button at the bottom of the License Agreement.

• Click on the *Next* button at the bottom of the Information Screen.

Step 8.

The next screen, Choose Destination Location, allows you to choose where you want to install the program. You may use the Default location simply by clicking on the *Next* button. Within a few seconds, the program is installed and ready to use.

Now that you know about the precautions involving software obtained from the Internet and also how to download the software into a newly created folder, it's time to go online to find and then download software programs designed especially for computer security.

COMPUTER SECURITY FOR ONLINE INVESTIGATIONS

Today, the computer is a standard tool used for fraud investigations and must, therefore, be as well tuned and maintained as any other type of crime fighting equipment. Written particularly for the new computer user/investigator, this section presents information on virus protection software, firewalls, and e-mail encryption programs.

Virus Protection Software

Antivirus software detects and eradicates viruses, which are simply software programs. Viruses destroy or otherwise compromise the computer operating system or data stored on a computer's hard drive. Some viruses replicate themselves and spread from computer to computer, and throughout a computer system, without doing much, or any, harm. Microsoft programs, files, and operating systems are especially vulnerable to threats by viruses, although Lynx and Macintosh are not immune.

Viruses are contracted most commonly by:

- Opening an e-mail attachment.
- Opening a Microsoft Word document.
- Opening a Microsoft Excel spreadsheet.
- Accessing a Web page containing malicious code.
- Exchanging files in newsgroups or chat rooms.
- Sharing infected floppy diskettes.
- Downloading files or software from the Internet.

It is difficult, if not impossible, to remain one step ahead of computer predators who write malicious and harmful virus programs. It *is* possible, however, to control the extent to which viruses, once contracted, can debilitate your computer. Employ the following tips for avoiding and controlling viruses:

- If you have not already done so, install an antivirus program now (use the steps above for downloading software). Because new viruses are so frequently discovered (as evidenced by ongoing notifications by software companies of the requirement and availability of new software patches), it is important to regularly update the software. Some software vendors include options for subscribing to e-mail alerts regarding new viruses.
- Refrain from opening e-mail attachments unless you are absolutely sure it is safe. Even e-mails sent from familiar addresses can be infected with a virus. Most antivirus programs provide an option by which attachments can be scanned before they are opened. As a courtesy to others when sending them attachments, inform the recipient of the attachment and its purpose.
- Scan all floppy diskettes before opening them.
- Download programs only from reputable Web sites.
- Regularly perform a computer backup of important files.
- Scan the computer daily for viruses, especially when using the computer for online investigations where tracking takes one into places that perpetrators frequent, such as chat rooms and questionable Web sites.

The two most popular antivirus programs are Norton (Symantec) and McAfee (Network Associates). Both vendors offer free trial versions of the software on their Web sites at:

1. Norton: *http://www.symantec.com*
2. McAfee: *http://www.mcafee.com*

Another help tool, especially for investigators new to computers, is the list of facts involving computer viruses, which can be found at *Computer Virus FAQ for New Users* at: *http://www.faqs.org/faqs/computer-virus/new-users*. *Read these FAQs now*. When finished, continue with the following instructions on firewalls.

Firewalls

Firewalls are software programs (or they may be a combination of both hardware and software) that prevent other computers from accessing a computer that is online. Firewalls can stop most, but not all, intruders. Because crime evolves with technology, as soon as new patches are developed to cover a computer's vulnerability, perpetrators find novel methods of intrusion. Also, some computers are more vulnerable than others.

For example, a computer connected to the Internet by broadband (DSL or cable) is more vulnerable to intrusion than the traditional dial-up connection. With a broadband connection, the Internet service provider (ISP) assigns each computer a unique Internet Protocol (IP) address. In contrast, a dial-up connection is assigned a different IP address each time it is connected to the Internet and is, therefore, less vulnerable than the constant broadband connection. (In Chapter 9, investigators learn how to trace IP addresses).

Some software programs, however, are available to disguise the computer's IP address when connected to the Internet while also blocking intruders. These programs, in addition to the security features, can also prevent infections that are caused by e-mail viruses and worms. One such program, "Zone Alarm," which is freeware for individuals and nonprofit organizations, is available at *http://www.zonelabs.com/store/content/home.jsp*. Although reputable, Zone Alarm, once installed, may be difficult to remove and may also interfere with a computer's operation *if another firewall already exists on the computer*. It is best to verify the compatibility of any software with the vendor before downloading and installing updates or new software.

Firewall security, relative to other security software, is more advanced. To be fully informed, *please now read* the *Home PC Firewall Guide* by Henry S. Markus at: *http://www.firewallguide.com*.

The Home PC Firewall Guide

After reading all about them, download and install a firewall (if not already installed on your computer) using the step-by-step instructions provided above for installing software. To locate a firewall program (software), use the CERT and other resources cited earlier in the chapter, and then continue to the topic of e-mail encoding.

E-mail Encryption Programs

E-mail is a major means of communication for individuals and businesses. Depending on the distance it travels, an e-mail message may be routed through dozens or even hundreds of servers. At any one of these junctions before reaching the intended recipient, an e-mail message can be intercepted and deleted, erased, or even replaced. E-mail encryption—the writing of a message in code—is the only known way to secure an e-mail message.

Unfortunately, there are fewer encryption programs than other types of security software, and the most common programs are somewhat difficult to implement. "Pretty Good Privacy," or PGP, is one well-known encryption program. For most people, the learning curve for PGP is not steep, but it takes time. Fortunately, the PGP instructions are clear and concise; with a little effort and practice, most individuals can learn how to use PGP to encode e-mail messages that only a recipient will be able to decipher. Of course, this means the recipient also knows how to use PGP (which is why the tutorial below recommends a partner). For new investigators, allocate plenty of time—a day or even days—to download, install, learn, and practice using PGP.

"Pretty Good Privacy" is free for noncommercial use and can be downloaded at *http://www.pgp.com*. The link to the free trial for the software is on the right side of the homepage. Take time now (or sometime before going on to the next section) to complete the encryption tutorial.

Encrypting E-mail Messages: A Tutorial

Conduct this tutorial with someone you communicate with using e-mail. Follow the PGP instructions (*http://www.pgp.com*) together on how to send encrypted e-mail. In addition to the PGP instructions given on that Web site, and especially for investigators new to the computer, additional and helpful beginner PGP instructions also can be located by searching Google. Go to *www.google.com*. In the Google textbox, type: pgp step-by-step instructions. After completing the PGP tutorial, and to reinforce what you have learned in this section, take time for the short reading titled *"Email – A Postcard Written in Pencil,"* by Lawrence R. Rogers of the Software Engineering Institute, Carnegie Mellon University and located at the CERT Web site: *http://www.cert.org/homeusers/ email_postcard.html*. When finished, continue with the next section on managing cookies.

ABOUT COOKIES

A cookie is a piece of data that is stored in a computer's browser the first time it visits a Web site. When returning at a later time to that Web site, the cookie activates and recalls from the previous visit the pages that were viewed or information that was typed into the textboxes on that Web site.

For example, if an individual types his or her name into a textbox on a Web site, upon returning to that site, that individual may be greeted by name and with a customized message. A "cookie" stores the information the individual types on a form, such as name and e-mail address.

Marketing firms use cookies to track the buying habits of consumers and also to tailor advertisements to individual Internet users. Most marketing firms also are data brokers: they compile and sell to others the personal data they collect from individuals on the Internet. In addition, merchants and financial institutions also use cookies on their Web sites, primarily to provide customers with personally customized shopping and banking experiences. The use of cookies is quite controversial; advocates of privacy rights oppose the planting of cookies on a computer without first obtaining approval. The concern is that, because of tracking by cookies, an individual cannot remain anonymous on the Internet.

An additional issue is that a large number of cookies stored on a hard drive will slow down the computer's performance. However, Microsoft Internet Explorer (IE) and Netscape provide practical and easy-to-implement solutions for cookie management. Exercise 3.2 is a lesson on how to manage the cookies on your computer's hard drive.

EXERCISE 3.2 *A Lesson in Managing Cookies*

For purposes of illustration, this exercise uses Microsoft IE 6.0. (To determine the version of IE on your computer: Click on *Help* on the browser toolbar. Then click on *About Internet Explorer* to find the version number. To close the window, click on *OK*.)

- **Step 1.** Click on *Tools* in the browser bar. Then, click on *Internet Options*.
- **Step 2.** Under the *General* tab, find the heading *Temporary Internet Files*. Click on *Delete Cookies*.
- **Step 3.** After the cookies are deleted, click on *Delete Files*.
- **Step 4.** Click on the *Settings* button. Under the heading *Temporary Internet Files Folder*, choose the amount of space you wish to allocate for storage of Web page visits.
- **Step 5.** Click on the *Privacy Tab* at the top of the box. Here you will find a slider bar. You may choose options ranging from Block All Cookies to Accept All Cookies. Slide the bar down to the second mark from the top for *High*.
- **Step 6.** Click on *Edit* at the bottom of the page under the heading *Web Sites*. Type in the exact Web addresses of the sites you will allow for placing cookies on your computer.
- **Step 7.** Click *OK*. Click *Apply*.

Voilà! You now can control your cookies while protecting your anonymity during online investigations. Do not be tempted, however, to move ahead in the book to the chapters on investigating: you must first learn how to configure a computer to preserve the chain of evidence you discover online, which is covered in Chapter 4.

Before moving on to Chapter 4, complete Chapter 3 by reading the following two articles about cookies:

1. *Cookie* by INT Media Group, Inc. at: *http://www.webopedia. com/TERM/c/cookie.html*
2. *Cookies* by Richard Lowe and Claudia Arevalo-Lowe at: *http:// internet-tips.net/Security/cookies.htm.*

Now continue on to Chapter 4 to learn how to configure your computer browser in preparation for Internet searches and for some hands-on practices with commonly used cyber-searches. (Later chapters introduce the *less* commonly known search tools.)

CONFIGURING THE COMPUTER AND INTRODUCTION TO CYBER-SEARCHING

With the computer now secured as per the guidelines in the previous chapter, one more task remains before preparing for the investigation (Chapter 5), which is to configure the computer to record the time, date, and place for each Web page that is visited during the course of the investigation. Called "preserving the chain of online evidence," this section shows how it is done.

CONFIGURE THE COMPUTER TO PRESERVE THE CHAIN OF EVIDENCE

Investigators who once were required to spend valuable time traversing locations in an automobile in search of information on perpetrators can now, in a matter of minutes, uncover the same information and more from a desktop computer in the precinct office. Especially in the case of identity theft, it would be a serious mistake to overlook the Internet for clues inasmuch as stolen identities are used online to apply for and use credit cards, open and access bank accounts, apply for telecommunication and utilities services, and conduct other transactions that once were handled in person over the counter. Though computer technology has wrought to simplify interactions, negotiations, and transactions in the information age, computers also are now commonly used for illegitimate and fraudulent purposes.

The Internet, with its billions of interconnections and abundance of information, has reduced the time fraud investigators spend on the street and in police cars. Information found on the Internet often provides police with sufficient evidence to obtain a search warrant or subpoena and to substantiate testimony, should a particular case be brought to trial. The credibility of the information retrieved from the Internet depends, in part, on preserving the chain of evidence in the sequential order in which it was found (the conduciveness of using Internet information for this purpose is discussed later). That is, the time, date, and place the information was found on the Internet must be documented on printouts of Web pages, which should be maintained systematically in the order retrieved. The first step, therefore, prior to opening a fraud file that sets the investigation in motion, is to configure the computer to print on each page the following details for evidence found while conducting Internet searches:

- The URL—the location on the Internet where the information was found.
- The time and date the information was retrieved.
- The number of pages contained in the search.
- The progression of the search, from one Web page to another.
- The progression of the search from one Web site to another.

Exercise 4.1 describes, in a series of steps, how to configure Internet Explorer, the most commonly used computer browser.

EXERCISE 4.1   *Configuring a Computer*

- **Step 1.** Add details to the top (header) and bottom (footer) of a printed Web page:

    A. On the Internet Explorer toolbar, click on *File*

    B. From the menu, click on *Page Setup*

    C. A gray box appears. Under the heading *Headers and Footers* there are textboxes for entering the information that can be added to printed Web page(s).

    D. Click *once* on the *?* located in the upper right corner of the gray box.

    E. Move the mouse down and click *once* on the heading *Headers and Footers*. A white box containing instructions on how to enter variables that will produce the printed information appears. Notice that all variables begin with an ampersand (&).

- **Step 2.** The Uniform Resource Locator (URL) and the date are two of the most important pieces of information to preserve on a printed Web page:

    A. In the textbox labeled *Header*, type: &u

    B. In the textbox labeled *Footer*, type: &D

    C. Click on the button *OK* under the *File* menu, and select *Print Preview* to review the header and footer information now displayed on the printed page.

- **Step 3.** Abbreviate the date format, and in the textbox labeled *Footer*, type: &d

- **Step 4.** Add the time of day to the footer by typing: &d &T. Note the *space* between the date and time (click on *Print Preview* to view).

- **Step 5.** Add a centered page number in the footer by typing: &d &T&bPage &p&b. Note the space between the words "Page" and &p. Center the page number by typing &b before the word "Page" and after &p.

(continued)

EXERCISE 4.1   *(continued)*

- **Step 6.** When printed, a single Web page may take several 8 1/2" × 11" sheets of paper. The total number of printed pages for a Web site can be added to the footer by typing: &d(space)&T&bPage(space)&p(space)of(space)&P&b.
- **Step 7.** Text or a combination of text and numbers, such as your name, department, or an exhibit number, can be added in the header. If more than one investigator is working on the case and using the same computer, it is recommended that the name be routinely changed. Add information to the header that is to appear on the printed page by entering it in the *Header* textbox: &u&b&bMSU ID Theft Lab. Everything typed after &b&b is right-justified.

The configured browser can preserve the process through which evidence was found on the Internet; the printed Web pages are the documents that will, eventually, comprise the "fraud file." The details on the printouts serve also as reference points for resuming interrupted searches as well as for coinvestigator ease and efficiency in following the trail of online searches performed throughout the course of the investigation.

Investigative searches should be conducted using more than one major search engine, since different engines employ unique features for indexing Web sites. Even when using the same search term, different engines can produce new and incremental information. The next section provides an overview of search engines with practice exercises that, for purposes of illustration, use commonly known cyber-searches. In subsequent chapters, investigators will be introduced to relatively uncommon cyber-searches.

ABOUT SEARCH ENGINES AND DIRECTORIES

Major search engines are of two types: crawler based and people powered. Crawler-based search engines automatically "crawl" or "spider" the World Wide Web in search of new Web pages and then include them in their directory indices. If a Web page changes, the search engine also detects the change and automatically updates the description of the Web page.

People-powered directories contain Web addresses and Web site descriptions submitted by editors, who approve and manually enter this information into the search directory. If the Web site changes, the editors must also update the directory index.

It is difficult to keep pace with the increasing numbers of Internet search engines and any list would not be comprehensive; however, Exhibit 4.1 lists some *common* search engines that do not necessarily contain the same information. Recommendations are to conduct the search using one or both of the major search engines (e.g., Google or Yahoo!) together with random searches using one or more of the others (listed in Exhibit 4.1).

Google is a crawler-based search engine, which is, for at least three reasons, a popular search tool:

1. Users can locate information by simply entering a search term or phrase in a single search box located at the top of the computer homepage.
2. Cached Web pages can be retrieved. Even after a Web site is removed from the Internet, Google stores the Web pages in its index, and these pages can continue to be retrieved and viewed in their original forms. An additional advantage in identity fraud investigations is that Google also caches older versions of current Web pages.
3. The Google search engine recognizes and can retrieve several different types of files, including:
   - Microsoft Word (doc)
   - Microsoft Excel (xls)
   - Microsoft PowerPoint (ppt)
   - Plain text files (txt, ans)
   - Adobe Acrobat Portable Document Format (pdf)
   - Microsoft Works (wks, wps, wdb)
   - Lotus 1-2-3 (wk1, wk2, wk3, wk4, wk5, wki, wks, wku)

- ◦ Microsoft Write (wri)
- ◦ Rich Text Format (rtf)
- ◦ Lotus WordPro (lwp)
- ◦ MacWrite (mw)

EXHIBIT 4.1   *Search Engines and Directories*

Major Crawler-Based Search Engines:

Google	*http://www.google.com*
Yahoo!	*http://search.yahoo.com/*
AltaVista	*http://www.altavista.com*
HotBot	*http://www.hotbot.com/*
MSN Search	*http://search.msn.com/*
Netscape Search	*http://channels.netscape.com/ns/search/default.jsp*
AOL Search	*http://search.aol.com/aolcom/index.jsp*
Teoma	*http://www.teoma.com*

Major People-Powered Directories:

Yahoo!	*http://dir.yahoo.com/*
Open Directory	*http://dmoz.org/*
LookSmart	*http://search.looksmart.com/*
Lycos	*http://www.lycos.com/*

Major Metacrawlers and Metasearch Engines:

Dogpile	*http://www.dogpile.com*
Vivisimo	*http://www.vivisimo.com*
Kartoo	*http://www.kartoo.com*
Mamma	*http://www.mamma.com*
Surfwax	*http://www.surfwax.com*
Excite	*http://www.excite.com/*
World Curry Guide	*http://web.curryguide.com/*
Infonetware RealTerm	*http://www.infonetware.com/*
Ithaki	*http://www.ithaki.net/indexu.htm*
MetaCrawler	*http://www.metacrawler.com/*
ProFusion	*http://www.profusion.com*
Query Server	*http://www.queryserver.com/web.htm*

Google contains many search features not reviewed here but these can be found at *http://www.google.com/intl/en/help/features.html#pdf*. It is worth while to spend some time at the Google Web site, because new search tools and efficiencies are continually introduced.

There are, however, many common searches that are conducted for most or all identity theft investigations, using many different search engines. Exercise 4.2 describes the (1) *type* of search, (2) specific *format* to use for the term that is entered into the textbox on the Web site, and (3) the *results* the search produces. The exercise uses Google, Yahoo, and Vivisimo Web sites. For Exercise 4.2, I suggest conducting the searches using your own personal information. Do not short-cut or skip this exercise, because the searches that are presented are used frequently in identity theft investigations.

EXERCISE 4.2   *Common Cyber-Searches*

Step 1. Search by telephone number:

Textbox format: 517-555-1212

Results produced: Address and maps of location

Also,

Textbox format: phonebook:first name last name+state

Note: Do not capitalize the word "phonebook," use spaces only between the first and last names.

Step 2. Search by first name, last name, and city:

Textbox format: First Name Last Name+City

Textbox format: Business name+City

Also use: +state or +country

Results produced: Address and maps of location

Note: Use the plus sign (+) for finding pages containing all words entered in the keyword textbox.

(continued)

Also, use the + sign between any two terms.

Example: flowerkisses+ebay

Results produced: links to a number of Web pages that refer to "Flower Kisses," a business once investigated for auction fraud. For example, click on the "cached" link on the first Web page listed.

Step 3. Search by an exact phrase:

Textbox format: "Any Name" (first and last, or business)

Example: "Bayan Elashi"

Results produced: Pages containing the words appearing together and matching the exact phrase as typed between the quotation marks.

Note: Enclose the phrase with quotation marks (" ").

Step 4. Search for specific type of file:

Textbox format: credit card number filetype:txt

Also can use other extensions: doc, pdf, ppt, and so on.

Note: Type the search term(s) and leave a space. After filetype: (no space), enter the type of file (extension) to find.

Results produced: Specific types of files containing the search term(s). When the pages containing the search term (in this example, credit card number) have been retrieved, spend some time visiting the Web pages. Searches using search terms specific to an identity theft investigation, using these simple search tools, can uncover a surprising amount of useful information about the case, because perpetrators communicate online.

Step 5. Search for a page *within* a Web site using a term and the Web address.

Textbox format: corporate fraud site:infosecurityinstitute.com

Or

Textbox format: Baker Hall site:www.msu.edu

Results produced: Searches of entire Web site for specific pages. *Note: Type the search term(s) and leave a space. After site: (no space), enter the URL of the Web site to search.*

Step 6. Number range search:

Textbox format: Computer $500.$1000

Results produced: Matches containing search terms and specified number range. *Search for a range of numbers by typing one period (.) between the numbers.*

Step 7. Specialized number searches:

- FedEx, UPS, USPS Package Tracking
- Vehicle Identification Number (VIN)
- UPC Code
- Airplane Registration Number
- Area Code

Type the number in the search box.

Step 8. Search for cached Web sites:

Textbox format: Search by keyword(s) and click on link "cached" within the retrieved Web pages.

Results produced: The version of the Web page indexed by Google, also:

- If an existing Web page has changed, the index may contain a snapshot of the page before the current changes were made.
- If the Web site has been removed from the Internet, the index may contain a snapshot of the entire site or some of the pages. (A later chapter describes the Wayback Machine for finding cached Web pages.)

Step 9. Search for Web pages that have links to Web sites:

Textbox format: link:www.bioport.com

Results produced: list of Web pages that have hyperlinks to the textbox search term

(continued)

EXERCISE 4.2   *(continued)*

The Yahoo! Search Features are similar to those used by Google. Yahoo! began in 1994 as a people-powered directory but now uses crawl technology to locate and list Web sites and Web pages and also to cache copies of discontinued pages in an index. Continue this exercise at *www.yahoo.com* by conducting the following searches on any name or topic of interest:

Step 10. Use the plus sign (+) between search words entered into the textbox to find all of the Web pages containing these words.

Step 11. Use quotation marks (" ") to find pages containing words that appear together and that match exactly the word (or term) enclosed by the quotation marks.

Step 12. Find specific file types, such as:

- htm, html – Standard HTML
- pdf – Adobe PDF
- xls – Microsoft Excel
- ppt – Microsoft PowerPoint
- doc – Microsoft Word
- txt – Plain Text Format

Step 13. For specialized number searches: simply enter the number into the textbox.

- Aircraft Registration Number
- Area Code
- Flight Tracker Number
- Packing Tracking Number
- Vehicle Identification Number
- Zip Code

Yahoo!, in addition to the above search technology, also provides a unique search tool for locating names, profiles, e-mail addresses, and telephone numbers of members listed in its member directory. Going now to *http://members.yahoo.com,*

Step 14. Search for Real World Phone or E-mail Listings:

  Textbox format: First Name (optional) and Last Name

  Results produced: E-mail and street addresses, phone number and map of location. (Recall from Chapter 1 using this Web site to locate Anghel Castnel.)

Step 15. Advanced Search

  Textbox format: Screen name, real name, or e-mail address

  Results produced: Profile and/or picture

In addition to the crawl technology employed by Google and Yahoo! search engines, clustering engines, or meta-search engines, are used by Vivisimo to simultaneously query several other search engines. Continuing at *http://www.vivisimo.com,* type the information as above into the textbox at the top of the page:

Step 16. Use the plus sign (+) for finding pages containing all the words.

Step 17. Use quotation marks (" ") to find pages containing the words appearing together and matching the exact phrase as typed between the quotation marks.

  Example A. In the textbox, type: fake id

  The results, sorted and categorized, are listed on the top left side of the Web page. Continue on this Web page with Example B.

  Example B. Search for a specific text within the "fake id" clustered search results:

- Type the following keyword in the textbox on the lower left side of the screen: template

- Click on the red GO button.

  Results produced: Web sites containing the words "fake id" are displayed and, within those sites, only those pages are shown that contain the word "template." To go where perpetrators sometimes go, take time now to visit and explore some of these sites.

The previous section reviewed only three search engines and only a few features that are common for most investigations. Most search engines provide their own tutorials to introduce users to the respective unique features. Before preparing for the investigation in Chapter 5:

- *Take time now* to become acquainted with the numerous possibilities provided by the different search engines listed in Exhibit 4.1.
- *Then also take time* to explore *http://searchenginewatch.com/links/index.php*, a valuable source for the latest information on new search engines.
- When finished with exploring the various search engines, continue on to Chapter 5 to understand the victim and then begin the investigation.

CHAPTER 5

UNDERSTAND THE VICTIM, THEN PREPARE FOR THE INVESTIGATION

While it is imperative that investigators understand dynamics of the crime under investigation, it is equally important to understand the crime from the victim's perspective. The discussion in Chapter 1 of "real world cases" provided some insights into the impact of identity theft on victims; Chapter 5 provides additional information, such as how people learn of the identity theft and the specific steps they must take to prevent further abuse. Chapter 5 actually begins the investigation, because the chapter describes the important documents that victims must obtain and also analyze for evidence of fraud. This first stage of an investigation is sometimes referred to as "opening the fraud file," because these evidentiary documents are the first to be filed in the fraud folder.

HOW PEOPLE LEARN OF THE IDENTITY THEFT

Chapter 1 described how three victims learned of their identity thefts; Julie Ann Blakely was denied employment, Ray C. Lapier discovered fraudulent charges on his credit card statement, and Maria G. Lopez was arrested on Christmas Day 2004 for a crime she did not commit. (Recall that Janice A. Macklin was discovered to be the perpetrator and not the victim she claimed to be.) These three incidents describe some of the common ways in which individuals learn that they have been victimized. There are also other examples of how people learn of their identity thefts.

In one case, a young couple discovered the theft when denied a home equity loan. The investigation by researchers at the MSU Crime Lab revealed that an offender had been using the husband's Social Security number for nearly nine years. How did this happen?

The perpetrator repeatedly used the victim's SSN over a period of time to obtain loans from various financial institutions located in different states across the country. The perpetrator lived on these loans, making payments on monthly balances with subsequent, additional loans. The perpetrator also used some of the money to purchase and then sell cars for a profit. Over a period of time, the offender's payments were frequently delinquent until, eventually, the credit rating associated with the victim's SSN was so low that the perpetrator could obtain no further lines of credit. Neither, of course, could the assigned owner of the SSN—the victim.

In other cases, a victim may receive a telephone call from the fraud department of a credit card company inquiring about that individual's application for a credit card. One identity theft red flag known to credit card companies is the listing of a new address on a new application for credit. The red flag occurs when this new address does not match the address on the credit report and also when the purported applicant has lived at the "previous" address for a number of years. The new address, of course, is where the fraudulently applied for credit card will be mailed; the previous address listed on the credit report is actually the victim's current address. This new address may appear to be a street address but often is a post box address, usually located at a private post office. Even when legitimate, however, the street address may be the location of a rented or perhaps a vacant apartment or building used by the perpetrators for deliveries of fraudulently ordered merchandise.

Other times, victims learn of their identity thefts when they are contacted by representatives of collection agencies who impose themselves on the victims, causing, sometimes, considerable, additional emotional duress.

Victims may also discover the theft themselves, when they find unauthorized, long-distance telephone calls on their monthly statements. Most identity theft criminals, in addition to commiting credit card, bank, and retail account fraud, also commit telecommunications fraud. This is because criminals often use only one telephone number and one cell phone for one "job" and replace them both when planning the next crime.

In these cases of long-distance phone calls, neither the victims nor their investigators should attempt to trace the telephone numbers by calling them; one phone call could alert an entire identity theft network, preempting any access to gather information on either the offenders or the crime.

In addition to the above examples, victims also report being contacted by retail stores demanding payments for checks written without sufficient funds, or by their banks to cover overdrawn accounts. Nearly as common as credit card fraud, bank fraud occurs when perpetrators use a victim's name, address, and bank account numbers to withdraw money from checking and savings account. One very sad case involved a couple who had saved their money for many years and had resolved all outstanding debts in preparation for retirement. Over a three-day holiday weekend, an identity thief withdrew large sums of cash from the couple's retirement account. The victims discovered the theft the day after the holiday when they used their ATM card to obtain cash for purchases they had planned.

Of course, there are many other ways, as well, that victims learn of the identity thefts, such as when they are denied the use of their credit cards at a restaurant or retail business or when applying for an automobile loan or a student loan. Unfortunately, student identity theft is being reported with increasing frequency. Perpetrators know that Social Security numbers are issued at birth and not used for many years, usually until 15 or 16 years later when the teen applies for a driver's permit or license or begins the first job. During the 15 or so years, therefore, the offender lives quite well by obtaining fraudulents loans, opening credit card and retail accounts for purchasing merchandise to sell in the black market. Ironically, even though the birth date of the assigned owner of the SSN is listed on the personal section of every credit report, credit reporting agencies have no mechanism for matching SSNs with birth dates. So what is a victim to do? This is the first question asked of identity theft investigators. The steps below describe the steps a victim must take before the investigation can begin. Read each step carefully. The victim plays an important role in helping the investigator resolve the identity theft crimes, beginning with the filing of a police report, by contacting each of the four credit reporting agencies, and also by obtaining other pertinent information that may provide evidence of the crime.

STEPS THE VICTIM MUST TAKE IMMEDIATELY AND SUBSEQUENTLY

Step 1. File a Police Report

The victim, or someone given the power of attorney if the victim is incapacitated by the crime or for another reason, must first file a police report of the identity theft and any fraud that has been committed—credit card, bank, retail account, or any other. Technically, that is, for legal purposes, without a police report there is no crime. Moreover, as shown in Step 2, the victim must provide a copy of the police report to the credit reporting agencies when requesting an extended seven-year alert on the credit files (versus the 90-day alert the credit agencies would otherwise record). Additionally, when seeking to reconcile fraudulent accounts, victims may be requested to provide businesses and financial institutions with copies of the police report.

In past years, and as recent as 2004, victims in some states report encountering difficulties when attempting to file a police report: police officers would simply not take the complaint of the victim. Many victims have reported to our Lab claims by police officers that identity theft was not a crime; other officers have told victims that they could not take a complaint because the case would not be investigated anyway. Police officers simply did not (and many still do not) know the crime. The explanation may be that most police departments are under-resourced which leaves officers hard pressed to address even the more serious crimes, such as child kidnappings and homicides.

Times, however, have changed. Identity theft is now related to most crimes and can no longer be underestimated or overlooked; wherever there is a methamphetamine lab there also are stolen identities; wherever there is drug trafficking, human smuggling of women, children, or illegal immigrants, and terrorism, there too one can find stolen identities. And, of course, wherever there are bank frauds, credit card frauds, retail account, auction, wire, telecommunications, and any other frauds, stolen identities also are involved.

The crime of identity theft has exploded to the extent that it now undermines not only the economy but also the security of the United States. Police departments, though lagging behind the learning curve, are now, with increasing frequency, developing best practices for working with victims and managing identity theft cases. Today, fewer victims complain of being unable to file a police report. But isolated instances still exist. When these occur, we urge victims to be persistent: identity theft is a federal offense punishable by fines and imprisonment. Citizens have the rights and privileges for reporting crimes that have been committed against them. And victims need copies of the police report to resolve their credit issues and sometimes even to be exonerated from crimes they did not commit.

Step 2. Contact the Credit Reporting Agencies

The victim's second responsibility, after the filing of a police report, and one that cannot be assumed by the police officer or business fraud investigator, is to file an alert with each of the credit reporting agencies. Before opening an account or granting a loan, a merchant or bank officer will obtain a copy of the applicant's credit report so as to establish the applicant's credit worthiness. A fraud alert on the victim's credit file will inform the merchant or loan officer that an identity theft has occurred and that applications for accounts or loans should be carefully screened. Alerts are usually placed on the credit file for 90 days.

However, although the credit agencies do not make it well known, victims may file a "seven-year" alert or even a "permanent" alert; such requests must usually be made in the form of a written statement and include evidence of the individuals' identity, such as a copy of the driver's license, Social Security card, and a copy of a recent utilities, telephone, or other statements, so as to verify the current and correct address, and a copy of the police report. Exhibit 5.1 provides the contact information for each of the three credit reporting agencies that are recognized by the Federal Trade Commission—Experian, Equifax, TransUnion—as well as the information for a fourth credit agency, Innovis.

Innovis, like Experian, Equifax, and Trans Union is a data broker; Innovis also claims to be a credit reporting agency. Innovis maintains a database of credit histories on U.S. citizens and also provides these credit histories to merchants and financial institutions. Victims may, therefore, wish to verify the accuracy of their information contained in the Innovis credit database. Innovis also places fraud alerts on credit files and provides the victim with a free credit report. A real person answers the phone.

When requesting the placement of the fraud alert on the credit file, victims may request a free credit report. Credit agencies do not share database information, so each of the four credit reports are likely to contain somewhat different information. The details on these credit reports are needed to conduct the investigation.

A word of caution: As shown in Exhibit 5.1, victims can "one-stop shop" to both place a fraud alert and obtain copies of credit reports, but there is only ONE legitimate Web site where this can be done: *www .annualcreditreport.com.* Be very careful to use the correct terms as there

EXHIBIT 5.1   *Credit Agency Contacts for Fraud Alerts and to Obtain Credit Reports**

Contact: *www.annualcreditreport.com,* or for consumers who do not use the Internet,

    Phone: 1-877-322-8228, or

    Write to: Annual Credit Report Request Service, P.O. Box 105281, Atlanta, GA 30348-5281, or

    To contact a specific credit agency:

EQUIFAX – www.equifax.com

    To order your credit report: 1-800-685-1111 or write:
    P.O. Box 740241, Atlanta, GA 30374-0241

    For Fraud Alerts: 1-800-525-6285 or write:
    P.O. Box 740241, Atlanta, GA 30374-0241
    Hearing impaired call 1-800-255-0056 and ask the operator to call the Auto Disclosure Line at 1-800-685-1111 to request a copy of your report.

EXPERIAN – www.experian.com

    To order your credit report: 1-888-397-3742 or write:
    P.O. Box 2002, Allen, TX 75013

    For Fraud Alerts: 1-888-397-3742 and write:
    P.O. Box 9530, Allen, TX 75013

TRANS UNION – www.transunion.com

    To order your credit report: 1-800-888-4213 or write:
    P.O. Box 1000, Chester, PA 19022

    For Fraud Alerts: 1-800-680-7289 and write:
    Fraud Victim Assistance Division, P.O. Box 6790, Fullerton, CA 92634

INNOVIS – www.innovis.com

    To order your credit report: 1-800-457-0247 or write:
    Innovis Consumer Assistance
    P.O. Box 1358, Columbus, OH 43216-1358

    For Fraud Alerts: 1-800-457-0247

---

*Innovis, like Experian, Equifax, and Trans Union is a data broker; Innovis also claims to be a credit reporting agency. Innovis maintains a database of credit histories on U.S. citizens and also provides these credit histories to merchants and financial institutions. Victims may, therefore, wish to verify the accuracy of their information contained in the Innovis credit database. Innovis also places fraud alerts on credit files and provides the victim with a free credit report. A real person answers the phone.

now are many Web sites that offer free credit reports as part of promotional packages for purchases. Note the language at the *annualcreditreport .com* Web site: victims can obtain a free copy every 12 months from EACH of the three credit agencies, Experian, Equifax, and TransUnion.

Step 3. Make Other Contacts

In addition to filing a police report and placing the alerts on the files of the credit reporting agencies, victims may have to make a number of other contacts. For example, if the victim's bank account was accessed or if the fraud involved the use of the victim's credit card, those financial institutions should be immediately contacted. Victims of bank and credit card fraud often ask the questions, "Should I change banks?" or "Should I change credit card companies?" The answer to both questions is, "No." Why not? Because there is no bank, credit card company, or other business that is immune from the threats of identity theft. What victims must do, however, is (1) cancel current accounts and open new ones with different account numbers and (2) place different passwords on each account.

Another important contact may be the Social Security Administration, if the Social Security number (SSN) was used in the fraud. Victims also often ask if they should request a change of SSN. The answer is, again, "No." A new SSN can be compromised just like the current one was. The victim should, rather, follow the steps outlined in Step 6 on protecting the future flow of personal information.

In addition to the above contacts, if the identity theft involved fraudulent or stolen checks or check blanks, the victim should contact each of the check verification companies. For contact information for these companies, refer to Exhibit 5.2.

Further, and depending on the type of identity fraud committed, one or more other contacts should be made. For example, the Federal Communications Commission (FCC) should be notified of identity thefts involving phone services; the Internal Revenue Service (IRS) should be informed in cases of any frauds involving tax documents or the fraudulent filing of

EXHIBIT 5.2   *Check Verification Contacts*

Certigy Inc.: 1-800-437-5120

International Check Services: 1-800-526-5380

TeleCheck: 1-800-710-9898

SCAN: 1-800-262-7771

CheckRite: 1-800-766-2748

Chex Systems: 1-800-428-9623

CheckCenter CrossCheck: 1-800-843-0760

National Check Fraud Service: 1-843-571-2143

tax returns; the Department of Motor Vehicles in your state is the authority to notify if the driver's license was used; for identity theft involving investments, the contact is the Securities and Exchange Commission (SEC); for thefts using another's ATM or debit card, the issuing financial institution is the appropriate contact; and for thefts involving stolen mail, the contact is the U.S. Postal Service. Complete addresses, toll-free telephone numbers, and e-mail addresses for the federal agencies can be found at the MSU Identity Theft Crime Lab Web site, *www.cj.msu.edu/ ~outreach/identity,* click on the "Victim's" button. For victims who do not use the Internet, complete contact information for all of these sources can be found in the Identity Theft Victim's Assistance Guide (at a negligible cost of $3.95) and also at the Web site of the Federal Trade Commission (FTC), *www.ftc.gov.*

Step 4. Additional Preinvestigation Tasks

When making the above contacts, it is the victim's responsibility to obtain information for the fraud file, and those documents specifically needed are the credit reports from each of the credit agencies and statements from credit card companies, banks, retail stores, or other institutions or businesses where the victim's identity was fraudulently used to purchase merchandise or services or to obtain cash or loans.

Credit Agency Reports. The investigator reviews these reports when "authenticating" the case (Chapter 6) prior to the investigation and later again at the onset of the investigation to identify red flags related to the identity fraud.

Other Agencies, Businesses, and Financial Institutions. The victim also has access to copies of any documents related to the identity theft from any businesses or financial institutions, such as the fraudulent application made by a perpetrator for a credit card or retail account, telephone or utilities services, loans, mortgages, student loans, driver's license, or any other fraudulent act.

In the past, investigators in fraud departments refused or were reluctant to provide the victim with any information about the fraudulent transaction. The only way to obtain a copy of a fraudulent credit card application, for example, which contains information valuable for an investigation (see Chapter 6), was for a police officer to obtain a search warrant; but to obtain a search warrant, a police officer must be investigating the case—and most did not do this. In the past, neither victims nor their investigators were able to obtain the evidence they needed to track the perpetrators. Now, however, these obstructions to obtaining the needed information have been removed through recent amendments to the Fair and Accurate Credit Transactions Act (FACTA) of 2003 that allows either the victim or a police officer access to any documents without first obtaining a search warrant.

According to FACTA, Section 151(e):

". . . 30 days after the date of receipt of a request from a victim . . . a business entity that has provided credit to, provided for consideration products, goods, or services to, accepted payment from, or otherwise entered into a commercial transaction for consideration with, a person who has allegedly made unauthorized use of the means of identification of the victim, shall provide a copy of application and business transaction records in the control of the business entity, whether maintained by the business entity or by another person on behalf of the business entity, evidencing any transaction alleged to be a result of identity theft to—(A) the victim; (B) any law enforcement agency or officer specified by the victim in such a request; or (C) a law enforcement agency investigating the identity theft and authorized by the victim to take receipt of records provided under this subsection." A copy of FACTA is available for download from the FTC Web site at *www.ftc.gov*; click on the FACTA link in the right sidebar.

What FACTA means for victims is that they must no longer rely on police departments, who may be unable to help with an investigation, nor must victims rely on a business's fraud investigator who, without higher-level authorization, would previously not divulge information on the fraud. The victim, of course, must provide the business or financial institution with a letter of evidence of his or her identity. For the convenience of the investigator (police officer or victim), Exhibit 5.3 presents a template of one such letter. Note: it is recommended that the letter be sent using certified mail.

EXHIBIT 5.3   *Facta Template for Letter to Businesses*

Date

Name of Director, Owner, or Manager of the Business
Name of Business
Street Address
City, State, Zip Code

Dear Mr./Mrs._____:

RE: *IDENTITY THEFT VICTIM: TYPE COMPLETE NAME*

On *month/date/year* I learned I was a victim of identity theft when . . . *here describe the complete circumstances* (e.g., I discovered unauthorized charges on my monthly credit card statement; checks had been cashed using my bank account number; long distance charges were reported on my telephone bill; an account had been opened at your store and charges fraudulently made to my name; a loan had been processed using my name and Social Security number; a collections agency called to inquire about a past due payment on an account I never opened, etc.). *Include if you know it, the*

(continued)

EXHIBIT 5.3   *(continued)*

date of the fraudulent transaction, the amount of money lost (if any), and the credit card number, bank account number, retail account number, or other relevant information. Enclosed for your information is a copy of the police report documenting the identity theft and the above identity fraud.

The purpose of this letter is to respectfully request from you copies of all documents pertaining to this transaction that fraudulently used my name, address, Social Security number (and...*here list any other personal identifying information*). Specifically, under amendments to the Fair and Accurate Credit Transactions Act (FACTA) of 2003, not later than 30 days after the receipt of this request:

"a business entity that has provided credit to, provided for consideration products, goods, or services to, accepted payment from, or otherwise entered into a commercial transaction for consideration with, a person who has allegedly made unauthorized use of the means of identification of the victim, shall provide a copy of application and business transaction records in the control of the business entity, whether maintained by the business entity or by another person on behalf of the business entity, evidencing any transaction alleged to be a result of identity theft to the victim" (Sec. 151(e)).

As proof of positive identification, enclosed are copies of my:
- Social Security card,
- Driver's license,
- Recent utilities statement, to verify correct address, and
- Statement showing the fraud activity (if there is one).

<u>Please mail all business transaction records to the address below within the 30-day limit according to the FACTA.</u> Thank you.

Sincerely,
Signature in pen

First, Middle, Last Name	Checklist of Copies Enclosed:
Complete Mailing Address	___ Police report
City, State, Zip Code	___ Social Security card
	___ Driver's license
Home Phone: xxx-xxx-xxxx	___ Utilities statement
Office Phone: xxx-xxx-xxxx	___ Statements showing the fraud activity (if any, e.g., credit card, bank, telephone)

Up to this point in the preinvestigation phase, the victim has taken several steps preliminary to the investigation: he or she has (1) filed a police report to document evidence of the crime; (2) placed fraud alerts on the credit files to prevent further abuse; (3) notified the respective businesses or financial institutions (e.g., retail stores, banks, credit card companies); and (4) requested from those businesses the copies of financial transactions that used the victim's personal identifying information. Only two tasks now remain: the victim must (1) complete the investigator's "intake" form (to document details of the crime for the fraud folder) and also take steps to (2) protect the future flow of personal identifying information.

Step 5. The "Intake" Form: Additional Documents for the Fraud File

Victims are known to have more facts about a crime committed against them than anyone else would have. Identity crimes are no exception: investigators in the MSU Identity Theft Crime and Research Lab repeatedly find that victims know more than they initially think they do about their identity thefts. For example, only a victim knows the details of recent visits to a physician or a hospital (where identity thefts frequently occur), a mother's maiden name, services (e.g., telephone, utilities) applied for, the number and type of credit cards owned, the types and locations of loans obtained, and other information that the investigator must verify against the credit report history. The completion of an "intake" form, therefore, in which victims document these details, is essential for the investigation. This "form" is composed of information the victim gathers, using the checklist presented in Exhibit 5.4.

The victim's role in the investigation is essential. Only the victim can obtain some of the documents and information that will point to leads and direct the investigation to each successive stage. The victim, therefore, must be involved as an investigator The advantage of victim involvement is for the investigation itself, but also, victims who become involved feel less helpless, more in control, and are less likely to suffer

EXHIBIT 5.4   *Victim's Intake Form*

Use the following checklist to describe the fraudulent activities that were conducted using your personal identifying information and to also provide additional details that may help the investigation. First complete the personal section below.

PERSONAL SECTION

NAME (First, Middle, Last)_____

STREET ADDRESS _____

MAILING ADDRESS (IF DIFFERENT FROM STREET ADDRESS) _____

_____

CITY, STATE, ZIP _____

HOME PHONE (____) _____

WORK PHONE (____) _____

SOCIAL SECURITY NUMBER _____

DATE OF BIRTH _____
                    Month   Date   Year

PREVIOUS ADDRESS _____

DATE AT PREVIOUS ADDRESS _____
                                  M/D/Year   to   M/D/Year

NAME AND PHONE NUMBER OF POLICE OFFICER WHO TOOK YOUR COMPLAINT

Officer's Name _____

_____

_____

Telephone Number _____

DESCRIPTION OF THE FRAUD(S)

In the section below and on the reverse side of this page, provide a complete description of the circumstances surrounding the identity theft and the frauds that were committed using your stolen identity. Include: the date you

EXHIBIT 5.4   *(continued)*

first learned of the fraud, whether or not you know who committed the fraud, the names and addresses (if available) of any suspects, the name(s) of the bank, credit card company, or other businesses or financial institutions involved, account numbers, total loss incurred, the date of the fraudulent application, address on the application, and method of applying (e.g., in person, Internet, telephone, mail). Use additional pages as necessary.

FOR YOUR OWN RECORDS AND ALSO TO FACILITATE THE INVESTIGATION OF THIS CASE, OBTAIN AND DELIVER TO THE POLICE OFFICER THE FOLLOWING DOCUMENTS:

1. Credit reports from all four credit report agencies,

2. Financial statements and documents from all accounts that show fraudulent activity, including copies of any in-store videotapes,

    a. Bank

    b. Credit card

    c. Retail account

    d. Telephone

    e. Utilities

    f. Other

3. Photocopy of Social Security card,

4. Photocopy of driver's license, and

5. From the Social Security administration: Obtain to review for accuracy a copy of your work history.

PROVIDE A SAMPLE OF YOUR HANDWRITING BY WRITING THE FOLLOWING SENTENCE IN THE SPACE PROVIDED BELOW:

"The O-zone was labeled Ymn134, but the A-zone was Ylktuv85."

_____

_____

_____

_____

(continued)

EXHIBIT 5.4   *(continued)*

NOW WRITE YOUR NAME (FIRST, MIDDLE, LAST)

_____

_____

ALSO, PRINT YOUR NAME (FIRST, MIDDLE, LAST)

_____

Do you have any medical condition that would affect your handwriting?
____Yes ____No

*IN THE SPACE BELOW AND ON THE REVERSE SIDE OF THIS PAGE
PROVIDE ANY INFORMATION YOU MAY HAVE ON:*

1. Reports of identity theft at your place of employment

2. Reports of identity theft at place of previous employment

3. Reports of identity theft at any other places you frequent now or
    have frequented in the recent past (e.g., health club, medical office,
    insurance company, school or university attended, any other)

CHECKLIST OF DETAILS TO HELP THE POLICE INVESTIGATION

Trace your activities for the past three months. Use your calendar, check-
book, and any other sources that would help you to remember your activities during this time. Use the checklist below and separate sheets of paper to
document details for each of the following items. For each item, include
names, addresses, and telephone numbers.

_____Business services applied for (e.g., cell phone, utilities, loans, mort-
       gages, credit cards, other): provide names, addresses, and telephone
       numbers.

_____Medical information: physicians, clinics, pharmacies, hospitals visited.

_____Financial information: make a list of all business names and addresses
       where you used your credit card, retail account card, ATM card,
       health card, and any other financial transaction cards you own.

_____Social Security number: list the dates (if known) and names of places
       where you provided your Social Security number.

_____Suspect locations: List the name and addresses of any locations where
       you think your personal information may have been stolen and
       describe the reason for your suspicion.

EXHIBIT 5.4   *(continued)*

_____ Suspects: List the names and addresses (if known) of any suspects, provide descriptions (if available), and also describe the reason for your suspicion.

Please carry a notebook to jot down any information that, in the days ahead, you may recall about the identity theft, circumstances surrounding the identity fraud, or any other information that may potentially be relevant for this investigation. The information you provide will be held in strict confidence to be used only for purposes of the investigation of your identity theft.

severe emotional consequences. As stated in the beginning of this book in the "Message to the Lay Investigator," the victim plays a valuable role as "research assistant" for either the business or private investigator or the police officer who, eventually, can obtain a search warrant or subpoena, or make an arrest based on the cumulative evidence.

Step 6. Protect the Future Flow of Personal Information

Throughout the investigation, the victim may help in many ways, such as by obtaining information (in addition to the above reports and documents), maintaining the fraud file, placing telephone calls, and especially by performing online searches as well as other tasks that would facilitate and speed up the investigation. At this point, however, the victim must take steps to protect the flow of future personal information.

Exhibit 5.5 presents a checklist of the many things a victim should and should not do. The first security precaution in Exhibit 5.5 is to obtain and review each of the four credit agency reports for red flags, such as evidence of any unauthorized accounts and, in the personal section, the listing of incorrect addresses, mother's maiden name, or alias names never used by the victim.

An amendment to the Fair Credit Reporting Act (FCRA) requires each of the three of the credit agencies—Experian, Equifax, and Trans Union—to provide consumers with one free credit report each 12 months. As discussed earlier, these three credit agencies have collaborated to provide consumers who use the Internet with a single, convenient online source located at *www.annualcreditreport.com*. It is worth repeating that many other so-called "free" credit report Web sites have surfaced to lure people into purchasing other credit history products and services. Do not fall for them. Be very careful to use the correct Internet address. Consumers who do not use the Internet may request a free credit report by phone: 1-877-322-8228 or by writing to: Annual Credit Report Request Service, P.O. Box 105281, Atlanta, GA 30348-5281. Ironically, to request the report by mail, the consumer must first download and complete the Annual Credit Report Request Form, which can be found online at *www.annualcreditreport.com*. However, consumers may also call the above toll-free number to request that the form be mailed.

The Innovis credit agency is not included in the federal statutes as being required to provide free credit reports; however, Innovis does send a free credit report to victims who call them to place a fraud alert on their Innovis credit file. Others who wish to routinely analyze their Innovis credit reports for red flags may have to pay a fee, depending on the state of residence. For details, consumers will find a link on the Innovis homepage at *www.innovis.com*. Consumers who call Innovis (contact information is presented in Exhibit 5.1) will be pleasantly surprised to be greeted by a real person!

It was also mentioned earlier that the credit reporting agencies do not share information, and this means that each credit report may contain different information. When contacting *annualcreditreport.com*, consumers may request an aggregated report—a summary of collective information from all three agencies; or, consumers may request a report from each credit agency, which is recommended, such as at different time intervals throughout the year.

EXHIBIT 5.5   *Protect the Future Flow of Information*

Use the following checklist to record the date and steps that you have taken to protect your personal information and to help prevent future revictimization.

Routinely analyze your credit report for red flags: changes of address, new accounts opened, incorrect information on the personal section, such as incorrect mother's maiden name or aliases of your name (also see Chapter 6 for how to analyze a credit report).

Date Completed

___ Month 1: Obtain the Experian credit report   _____

___ Month 4: Obtain the Equifax credit report   _____

___ Month 7: Obtain the Trans Union credit report   _____

___ Month 10: Obtain the Innovis credit report   _____

___ PLACE PASSWORDS on all financial accounts   _____

___ Create a safe place in your home for personal papers   _____

___ Install a U.S. Post Office mailbox that can be locked   _____

___ Carry only necessary credit cards   _____

___ OPTOUT of unsolicited preapproved credit cards[1]   _____

___ OPTOUT of national mailing lists and e-mail[2]   _____

___ REGISTER phone numbers with FTC REGISTRY[3]   _____

ROUTINELY:

___ KNOW dates that bank, credit card, and other financial statements arrive

___ REVIEW bank and credit card statements promptly upon receipt

___ Evaluate telephone and utilities statements for unauthorized charges

___ Provide your Social Security number for financial transactions only

___ TAKE outgoing mail to post office

___ PROMPTLY remove mail from mailbox (or use a locked or P.O. box)

___ SHRED mail and address labels—barcodes on magazines and so on sometimes carry personal identifying information

___ SHOP with online merchants you know

___ CHECK the Better Business Bureau's Web site when online shopping

___ WATCH the gas stations—use inside pumps[4]

(continued)

EXHIBIT 5.5   *(continued)*

___ USE your bank's (or other safe) ATM

___ SHRED plastic hotel keys (many contain credit card numbers and other personal information)

A FEW "DO NOTs"

___ CARRY Social Security card[5]

___ GIVE personal information over phone unless you initiate the call

___ Give personal information when using cell or other portable phones[6]

___ ANSWER unsolicited e-mail requests for personal information

___ OPEN e-mail attachments, unless you know the sender

___ GIVE anyone your mother's maiden name[7]

___ USE as part of a password: address, date of birth, part of Social Security number, or mother's maiden name

___ GIVE bank account or Social Security numbers to online merchants

___ LINK checking and savings accounts (access to checking provides possible access to savings—check with your bank).

———

[1]Call 1-888-567-8688 or, for Experian, 1-800-407-1088. Note, however, opting out is often only temporary, sometimes for only six months or until such time as the company updates its database with information, including perhaps your name and identifying information, purchased from another data broker. Opting out, therefore, is recommended as a routine maintenance task, performed biannually or when solicitations resume.

[2]Write a letter to: Mail Preference Service
Attention: Department 5779087
Direct Marketing Association
Post Office Box 282
Carmel, NY 10512

For telemarketers: Telephone Preference Service
Attention: Department 5779137
Direct Marketing Association
Carmel, NY 10512

For e-mail: *http://www.dmaconsumers.org/consumers/
optoutform_emps.shtml*

EXHIBIT 5.5 *(continued)*

[3]The telephone number for the Federal Trade Commission Do Not Call Registry is: 1-888-382-1222.

[4]Perpetrators have been known to insert card readers into credit card machines at end pumps, usually those out of view of the inside cashier.

[5]Seniors balk at this one, understandably; they need to carry Medicaid and Medicare cards in cases of emergency. For security, use a lightweight shoulder bag with a strap that crosses over the chest; unisex bags can be found at travel stores.

[6]Calls made on cell phones and other portable phones can be easily intercepted by cars driving by on the street or even by neighbors, such as through baby monitors or other electronic equipment.

[7]Contrary to what many people believe, the mother's maiden name is not necessary for financial transactions with any bank or credit card company; the mother's maiden name is used only as a password. The mother's maiden name is the sole piece of information needed by a perpetrator for a complete identity takeover, in addition to the victim's name, address, and date of birth. Once an identity has been assumed, the perpetrator can obtain a passport or driver's license, access Social Security information, and conduct financial transactions. For a password, use anything but a mother's maiden name. The best rule of thumb is to leave your mother out of it, already.

Not included on the checklist in Exhibit 5.5 are steps that can be taken to prevent the theft of identities from the workplace, where the majority of identity thefts occur. A recently published book, *Preventing Identity Theft in Your Business,* cites evidence to document the fact that the majority of identity thefts are now known to occur in the workplace.[1] Victims of identity theft can provide a valuable service to coworkers and customers at their places of employment by raising the awareness of identity thefts that are committed by dishonest workers or by outside criminals collaborating with insiders. Unfortunately, therefore, victims have limited methods to prevent further victimization. The burden largely falls on business managers to secure the job sites. Nonetheless, some identities are stolen from dumpsters, mailboxes, home and auto robberies, and by purse and wallet snatchers, so there are some steps individuals can take to protect themselves.

In summary, Chapter 5 showed the important role of the victim in obtaining information that is necessary to the identity theft investigation. The victim has "opened the fraud file" by obtaining these reports and documents that are pertinent to the case. If a police officer is investigating the case, he or she will first "authenticate" the information provided by the victim on the "intake" and other forms.

CHAPTER 6

AUTHENTICATE, THEN INVESTIGATE

THE AUTHENTICATION

The investigation begins with the "authentication" of the identity theft, which is conducted using the information provided by the victim on the intake form and found on each of the four credit reports. Authentication simply means verifying the identity theft claims before launching full-scale into the investigation. Unfortunately for the real victims who already are stressed by the situation, perpetrators have been known to use their own names and other personal information to apply for credit and to then file police reports claiming to be victims. Investigators who do not first verify the legitimacy of an identity theft claim may find themselves working for the criminal and not for the victim. How does this happen?

It occurs because many merchants do not verify the creditworthiness of their customers. For example, credit checks are not always conducted for the online purchases of merchandise from large department and discount stores, nor are credit checks conducted for most online auctions of goods that a perpetrator may never deliver. Further, the level of accepted creditworthiness varies between merchants and depends on the amount of the purchase; even though lacking in creditability, a perpetrator posing as a victim can commit identity fraud.

89

In the authentication stage, the investigator examines the credit reports and other documents including the victim's intake form, looking for specific red flags. In our experience at the MSU Identity Theft Crime and Research Lab, we have yet to meet a victim who, when the situation has been explained, fails to understand the need for such authentication, which involves a thorough analysis of the victim's credit reports, and an interview with the victim to clarify any discrepancies on those reports or on the intake form.

Review the Victim's Credit Reports

The victim's credit reports normally contain considerable information that could point the direction of the investigation. Exhibit 6.1 uses fictitious names in an example of a credit report. For the authentication purposes, the investigator reviews the credit report for: (1) alias names, accuracy of (2) driver's license number, date of birth, spouses first name and any other information in the personal section on the first page of the report, (3) correctness of present address, and (4) the numbers of residences listed in past two to three years.

The first red flag for identity theft is the listing of many aliases on a credit report. Exhibit 6.1 lists eight aliases for the name "Dennis Yarnell." These aliases may have found their way onto the credit report through the fraudulent use of the victim's Social Security number—the name, address, and any other personal information listed on the application follows the Social Security number (SSN), that is, the SSN is the key piece of information and any other information is assigned to the SSN. However, honest individuals may choose to use different variations of their name, so the investigator must verify with the victim the legitimacy of the aliases listed on the credit report. In most identity theft cases, a victim's credit report will show several variations of a name that the victim has never used.

EXHIBIT 6.1 *Example of a Credit Report*

ABC Credit Bureau

ABC Credit Bureau collects information about you from merchants, landlords, lenders, businesses, public records, and other reliable sources. We provide information about you to potential lenders, businesses, and employers. We also provide information to companies who will send you preapproved credit applications or insurance offers.

Personal Identifying Information

<u>Name:</u>

Yarnell Dennis	Yarnell Allen Dennis
Y. Dennis	Y. Allen Dennis
Y.A. Dennis	Dennis Yarnell
Yarnell Dennise	Yarnell Dennison

Social Security Number: 123-45-6789   **Date of Birth** August 21, 1964

Driver's License Number: D0566003926111   **Spouse's First Name:** Mary

Residences:

Current: 2775 S. Diamond Bar Blvd., #212
Diamond Bar, CA 91765

Previous: 497 Linden Blvd., #B2
Brooklyn, NY 11203

Employers:

Current: St. Joseph Hospital
1100 W. Stewart Dr.
Orange, CA 92868

Previous: St. Nicholas Hospital
1700 Bensonhurst Dr.
Brooklyn, NY 11203

(continued)

EXHIBIT 6.1   *(continued)*

Credit History

The following accounts may contain information that could have an adverse affect on your ability to obtain credit. This information stays on your report for seven years from the date the delinquency was reported, depending upon the state laws that are applicable. Information from public records, such as bankruptcy, may also be listed with your credit accounts.

Source: Capital One
    P.O. Box 2222
    Austin, TX
	Account# 116090665412 . . . .

Date Opened: January 2000	Date Last Reported: July 2001
Type: Revolving-Credit Card	Most Owed: $9,523
Responsibility: Joint with N. Abraham	Credit Limit: $10,000
Balance: $9,523	Status: 90 days past due

Source: American Collection
    P.O. Box 411
    Los Angeles, CA
	Account# 021569 . . . .

Date Opened: February 2000	Date Opened: June 2001
Responsibility: Individual	Most Owed: $2,435
Balance: $2,235	Status: 150 days past due
Original Creditor: GTE Company of California	

The following accounts have been reported to us and will not have an adverse affect on your ability to obtain credit.

Source:Yourbank.com	Account# 60228781015804 . . . .
Date Opened: May 2001	Date Last Reported: July 2001
Type: Revolving	Terms: Combined Credit Plan
Monthly Payment: $35	Balance: $4,852
Credit Limit: $5,000	Most Owed: $4,852
Responsibility: Individual	Status: Never late-prior 1 month from last update
Source: Hi-Lo Credit Corp.	Account# 900010619 . . . .
Date Opened: July 1989	Date Last Reported: June 1995
Type: Installment	Terms: 60 months
Monthly Payment: $0	Responsibility: Individual
Original Loan Amount: $10,500	Status: Paid

EXHIBIT 6.1　*(continued)*

The following is a list of all requests (authorized by you) to review your credit bureau report. These inquiries will remain on your report for two years.

Source:	Date of Request:
Metropolitan Bank	October 2001
Advanta Bank Corporation	October 2001
Citibank N.A.	September 2001
Wachovia Bank	August 2001
Bank of America	August 2001
Capital Financial Services	July 2001
American Collection Agency	July 2001
Yourbank.com	June 2001
Capital Financial Services	June 2001
GTE Company of California	May 2001

You did not authorize the following companies to view your credit bureau report. However, we offer credit information about you to credit companies who want to offer you preapproved credit cards; a potential investor for accessing the risk of current obligations; your current creditors so that they may monitor your accounts; a potential employer; and businesses who think you might be interested in learning about their goods and services. These inquiries are not part of the credit report requested and provided to others. Only you can view the inquiries.

Source:	Date of Request:
National Auto Insurance	August 2001
Abacus Marketing	May 2001
Associates-Texaco	January 2001
Michigan National Bank	October 2001
American Express	February 2000

Dispute Statements

Consumer Statement: ID Fraud Victim Alert: Fraudulent applications may be submitted in my name using correct personal information. Do not extend credit without first contacting me personally and verifying all application information at home at (517) 555-1212.

Date reported 10/01.

The investigator must also verify the current address as well as the number of past addresses. Criminals often move around the country, and their residential locations find their way, through various databases and data brokers, onto their credit reports. Of course, many honest individuals also move around and may reside at more than one residence. However, authentication—the evaluation of information for deciding whether or not this is an authentic identity theft case—relies on the combination of aggregated information and not just on past addresses.

The second red flag on a credit report, for authentication purposes, is missing or torn-off pages or blackened-out sections. Victims of identity theft, in our experience, do not alter their credit reports. Consider as suspicious any intentionally omitted information.

Interview the Victim

A "reliability" interview is conducted whenever a credit report review reveals inconsistencies or inaccuracies with what the victim has reported on the intake form or in discussions about the identity theft. Chapter 1 introduced the interview when describing the Janice A. Macklin case, in which Janice claimed to be a victim but later admitted she was the perpetrator.

Prepare for the interview by developing a set of questions based on the discovered anomalies. Use these questions, randomly ordered, in two different interviews on two different days and conducted by two different investigators, who will later compare responses. The cross-comparing interview method is not foolproof, but the response of most honest individuals is likely to be more consistent across interviewers relative to responses provided by someone wishing to conceal information.

In the hundreds of files that have been reviewed or investigated at the MSU Lab, only a few have been found to be questionable, and, from discussions with police officers in identity investigation training courses conducted at police academies across the country, we have learned that the majority of complaints are by legitimate victims of identity theft.

The crime of identity theft, however, continues to evolve as offenders discover and use new approaches that other offenders copycat until learning about another new twist. The perpetrator posing as a victim is one such example, perplexing both victims and investigators.

THE INVESTIGATION

The trail of an identity fraud investigation may take different turns as the case unfolds, depending on the type of fraud that has been committed. For example, the investigation of cases would differ where stolen identities were used to traffic drugs or smuggle humans versus when stolen identities are used to commit credit card, bank, retail account, and other frauds. Nonetheless, there also are standardized procedures that are common to *all* investigations involving the fraudulent use of a victim's identity, including the following activities that are detailed below:

- Analyze the victim's credit reports for fraudulent activity.
    - Chronologically order the fraudulent activities using a flip chart.
- Analyze the credit card, bank loan, retail account, and other account statements.
- Conduct surveillance.
- Go online: Begin the investigation at the "end of the trail" (discussed below), using the Internet.
- Create a flow chart of information as it is discovered.

In addition to the above standard tasks, and because the Internet has become a major source of communication among the members of identity theft networks, most if not all identity theft investigations will involve the tracing of Internet and e-mail addresses (Chapters 9 and 10). Members of identity theft networks use message boards and meet in chat rooms (Chapter 8), where they discuss issues and objectives, brainstorm tactics, make plans, and transmit warnings. Perpetrators of identity frauds have become increasingly sophisticated in the use of the Internet, which is why the Internet is an important tool for all investigators.

To elaborate on the steps above and for purposes of illustration and consistency in the following chapters, I will use the example of credit card fraud, which is the crime most frequently committed using stolen identities.

Analyze the Credit Reports—Experian, Equifax, Trans Union, and Innovis

The investigator now conducts a detailed analysis of the credit reports for evidence of the fraud; this exercise is in contrast to the above analysis of the credit reports for identifying inconsistencies with information a victim previously provided on the intake form or in discussions with the investigator. As the four credit reporting agencies do not share their information with one another, it is important to obtain and analyze independent copies from each credit agency. Each credit report contains several sections, and each section contains information potentially useful for tracking the perpetrators.

Exhibit 6.1, for example, shows two major sections, the personal history and the credit history. And within the credit history sections, several subsections list:

- Accounts that may adversely affect one's ability to obtain credit
- Information that is unlikely to have adverse affects
- Names of businesses the victim authorized to access a credit report
- Names of companies that, without the victim's knowledge, accessed one or more credit reports
- Dispute sections for victims' statements, such as for fraud alerts

In addition, some credit reports may contain sections containing

- Public records on civil judgments, tax liens, foreclosures, bankruptcies, and the amounts, dates, times, and places where the actions were filed

All parts of a credit report are equally important for information each may contain on the identity theft. The detailed analysis begins with the personal section.

First, examine the personal section for alias names. As mentioned earlier, offenders use variations of a victim's real name, and these aliases will show up on the credit report as a result of any financial transaction that was conducted using that alias. Make a note in the fraud file of all aliases listed on the credit reports.

Second, the personal section contains the "present" address and also the previous address. The "present" address listed on the fraudulent application is where the credit card or merchandise will be delivered. This is known as the "end of the trail" (versus the beginning of the trail, which is where the identity was stolen and which rarely is known). As mentioned earlier when identity theft has occurred, the "previous" address shown on the credit report is actually the victim's current address.

Third, working together with the victim, the investigator must now analyze the section showing the credit history so as to identify any unauthorized accounts opened in the victim's name. Only the victim can know which accounts he or she authorized. In the case of credit card fraud but also bank fraud, retail account fraud, telecommunications and other fraud, there may be one or many unauthorized accounts. List these accounts on a large flip chart using a black marker to clearly print in chronological order all of the following details associated with the fraudulent activity:

- Name of financial institution where credit card, loan, or other fraud was committed, or the retail store where merchandise was purchased.
- Date of the fraudulent activity.
- Amount of the loan, purchase, or loss incurred from each transaction.

The purpose for creating this ordered list is to help visualize patterns of fraud activity. Update this chart with information that may be uncovered as the investigation progresses. Post the sheets of the flip chart on a wall for easy visibility and access to all coinvestigators of the case.

Fourth, analyze the section of the credit report that shows businesses that have, without authorization from the victim, obtained a credit report from the credit agency. The business may be legitimate: credit card companies, for example, purchase credit agency reports on consumers to identify those individuals who are creditworthy and who could, therefore, be included on a list for preapproved credit card mailings or other promotions.

However, even though a business may be an entity legitimately registered with a state, it may nonetheless be operating as a front for purposes of obtaining credit information on potential victims, or it may be a legitimate business that did not authorize that a victim's credit report be obtained but where, instead, an employee-perpetrator used a business's pass code to obtain a report from a credit agency. *All businesses listed on the "unauthorized" access section of the credit report must be investigated as the potential source of the identity theft.*

Analyze Credit Card, Bank Loan, Retail Account, and Other Financial Statements

Fraudulent applications usually contain some legitimate information, such as the current address where the merchandise or credit cards are sent; a telephone number where the perpetrator can receive calls of verification from merchants or financial institutions; and sometimes the perpetrators even list the name of the victim's employer and the employer's address, and even the name of the victim's bank and bank account numbers. Therefore, now conduct a thorough analysis of the fraudulent applications—credit card, bank loan, retail account, or others. Recall from Chapter 5, in the pre-investigation phase, that the victim obtained these reports under the Fair and Accurate Credit Act and these documents are now part of the fraud file. Chronologically order any fraudulent activity on the flip chart described above.

Next, place a telephone call to the fraud department of the credit card company (bank or retail store) where the perpetrator made the application for credit. Solicit the cooperation of a fraud investigator to search the company database or hard copy files for other applications made around the same time and that have similar handwriting, if made in person or submitted through the mail, or that contain information similar to that reported on the fraud victim's application.

From experience, valuable information can be uncovered from comparisons of information on application forms. In fact, even bogus information can be "good" information, leading, for example, to the geographical vicinity of the identity theft network or even to the workplace from which the identity or list of identities was stolen.

In one case, a cooperative fraud investigator of a large credit card company took the time to manually search through files containing hundreds of applications submitted in writing in the year 2001. He looked for names that were common across the applications, such as previous or past employer or names given as references, and for common addresses. This investigator soon discovered, among many of the applications, a more common denominator—identical handwriting. The same perpetrator had mailed to the same credit card company dozens of hand-written applications for credit cards using the names and Social Security numbers stolen from victims.

Upon further analysis, the information written on these applications revealed some other interesting commonalities and other findings:

- The perpetrators appeared to have been working from both ends of an alphabetized list of names: the last names of the applicants for many of the applications began with the letters "A," "B," "C," "D," and then jumped to "S," "T," and "W."
- The "previous" addresses on all of the applications, it was later learned, were actually the victims' "present" addresses.
- Most of the "present" addresses listed on the applications were for commercial postal boxes, including Postal Center Plus; Mail Boxes; Postal Depot and the Village Postmark. These post offices were all located in neighboring suburbs of Los Angeles, CA.

- The post office addresses listed on the applications as "present" addresses were written to look like apartment numbers, instead of P.O. Box numbers as is legally required.
- The "present" address listed on one application was also the address listed for the nearest relative on another application.
- The address of the nearest relative on one of the applications was also listed as the address of the nearest relative on two other applications.
- The address of the nearest relative on one application was used as the "present" address on two different applications.
- With only one exception, the "present" and "previous" employers were all legitimate businesses.
- The addresses listed for relatives and employers were located in close proximity to one another in the same geographical area.
- As the case unfolded, it was discovered that the victims resided in multiple states across the country, from the East to the West Coasts.
- The perpetrators appeared to be familiar with companies and major streets and avenues in at least two large cities—one located in California and the other in Minnesota—they used these names and addresses for (purported) previous employers and references.
- The perpetrators used transformations of information, such as the names of major and well-known *avenues* that were listed instead as *streets*.

From the above-aggregated information, many things were learned that would not have been known without the cooperation of the credit card company fraud investigator and the collaborative analysis of the application blanks by the MSU Lab researchers:

- The names and numbers of the many victims, most who had not yet learned they were victims of identity theft
- The geographical locations of the operation in California and Minnesota
- Addresses that would be targeted for surveillance

- The likelihood that the perpetrators obtained the list of names from an alphabetized database
- Knowledge that the particular database was sufficiently comprehensive to include the correct names and addresses of employers
- Information pointing to the theft from a national database, since the victims' addresses were nationwide

When all of the credit reports, credit card or other applications and any and all documents pertaining to the theft have been analyzed, it is then time to begin the surveillance of postal, apartment, or other addresses. It is also time to begin the online investigation. Considerable literature exists on the latest techniques and tools for conducting surveillance, such as the various recommended types of vehicles to use as covers and other information. *Investigating Identity Theft* does not cover those surveillance techniques. However, with practice and patience, most anyone can obtain considerable information, such as jotting down license plate numbers of automobiles at suspect addresses. Under no circumstances, however, should a lay investigator approach a suspect, and it is far too early in the investigation for an officer to start knocking on suspects' doors.

At this point, the foundation of the case has begun to be formed. Online searches of the Internet can now help to provide information that may reveal the structure of an identity theft network and the source of the identity theft.

Go Online: To the End of the Trail

Identity theft investigations usually begin at the "end of the trail," at the "present" address listed on the credit card or other application, which as described above is often a private post office. Present addresses, however, could also be those of apartments, houses, or even vacant buildings. Whatever the address, when a victim's Social Security number is used for fraudulent applications, the "present" address listed on that application will follow the SSN that is used in the transaction. As also discussed above, that present address will, therefore, appear on the credit report. An online investigation begins by locating the address and printing a map of the directions to the present address—the place of delivery for the fraudulently applied for credit cards or merchandise ordered using the victim's identifying information.

Considerable additional information on the present address should also be obtained at this time, such as, for example, the name of the owner of the apartment building or residence, if it is not a post office; this information can be found through Internet searches of public records. In fact, in some states, the online public records report the size of the lot and show graphically the architectural descriptions of the building located on the lot including the number and size of the rooms in the building and even the locations of the entrances and exits. (Researchers at the MSU Crime Lab, investigating an identity theft case in Texas, stumbled upon such detailed property information for subjects involved in the infocomcorp case described in the "Forward" section of this book.) Property information, whether it be for an apartment complex, residential building, or a post office, is valuable for conducting surveillance and also for the search and seizure operation that may eventually be conducted. Online searches for end of the trail locations and their descriptions are, however, only the beginning of the investigation. If the stolen identity was used to commit auction fraud, online bank fraud, or other online crime, and particularly later in an investigation when a suspect's computer has been seized during a search of the premises, the investigation involves the tracking of Internet addresses—Internet Protocol (IP), Uniform Resource Locator (URL), and e-mail; these topics are covered in Chapters 9 and 10. Even without the suspect's computer, Internet addresses received by a victim, such as in crimes of phishing or other online scams (where perpetrators posing as authentic businesses solicit personal identifying information), can be traced.

Chapter 7 provides a step-by-step case example of how the Internet was used in one identity theft investigation. Before Chapter 7, however, it is now time to create a flowchart of information uncovered thus far so as to increment in an orderly fashion the information already listed on the above created flip chart sheets.

Create a Flow Chart (or Lists)

Post another large flip chart sheet of paper in a visible location for easy access by all coinvestigators. Use a black marker to clearly chart the flow (or make a list) of new information that has been uncovered. The flow chart may be composed of several large sheets with several subsections. Using, for example, the credit card application illustration above, one sheet may use arrowhead lines to show the flow of information from St. Paul to California to chart the locations of the postal sites and their proximities to one another, or to simply list the states of all victims. Although software is available to geographically map and show the distance between locations, manual mapping by an investigator of suspect residences, postal offices, victims' addresses and other locations can provide deeper insights into the case and trigger ideas that would not be formed from using a software package. The flowchart need not be a piece of art or take considerable time. The idea is to get the information down visually on paper where it can be evaluated by one or more investigators during the investigation while evidence unfolds.

These flip charts, flowcharts and/or lists that document the chronological order of activity, and the computer printouts produced from the Internet searches of addresses and other information, must all be routinely maintained in the order in which the information was discovered to be used as evidence for potential search warrants, subpoenas, and trial court testimonies.

CHAPTER 7

IDENTITY FRAUD INVESTIGATION: A CASE EXAMPLE

THE INTERNET: A PREDOMINANT TOOL FOR IDENTITY FRAUD INVESTIGATIONS

This chapter explains how the Internet is used to conduct identity fraud investigations. Although each identity theft case differs from the other, most share some common characteristics that provide the basis for common Internet searches for information. This chapter leads the investigator through some of those common searches; also included is a list (Appendix A) of hundreds of Web sites that have been found to be equally useful in fraud investigations but, owing to space limitations, these cannot be dealt with in this book.

An identity fraud investigation, as noted in earlier chapters, usually begins at the end of the trail—the designated delivery site for the fraudulently ordered credit cards and merchandise. The investigation usually begins, therefore, by searching Web sites for information about this location. Thereafter, however, the sequential steps taken by an investigation depend on several factors. For example, information found on one Web site may be a lead that directs the investigator to conduct a search of another Web site that, in turn, reveals another clue that points to a search of another site, and so on. With each new lead and each successive search of cyberspace, the investigation gains momentum.

In addition to this self-perpetuating process, the trail taken in an investigation depends on the investigator's skills, abilities, and experiences. Those who already have experience investigating crimes and who already have knowledge of the Internet will find more information faster than others less skilled. With practice, however, almost anyone can learn these skills and become proficient at using the Internet to solve crimes. Regardless of levels of proficiency, investigators who arrive at the same solution may not necessarily have followed the same path in reaching it—the efficiency and speed in solving a case comes with experience in knowing where on the Internet to search for information.

Many Web sites come and go while many others remain on the Internet much longer. From time to time, Web sites also change faces—new features, colors, layouts, and by adding new and deleting old information. Most Web sites also go offline from time to time for purposes of routine maintenance or to update the site's information. Upon finding a "page cannot be found" message, novices may conclude that the site is gone; however, the (new) investigator who later returns to that Web site will likely find it back online.

Investigators who learn to use the Internet as a primary tool will soon discover that a Web site may be registered under two or more Internet addresses (the URLs), and that some Web sites are moved around the Internet, usually by registering under similar but slightly different domain names, and sometimes also by changing Internet Service Providers. Terrorist groups and other organized crime networks often use this practice in an attempt to conceal their cyber-whereabouts. With experience, Internet investigators learn of these and other ways Web sites are changed or manipulated.

INTRODUCTION TO THE CASE EXAMPLE

The case described in the following text demonstrates several issues inherent in all identity theft investigations. First, the case shows the train of thought of one investigator who used the Internet to locate information on many Web sites, beginning with a site that provided a lead for the search of another site that triggered ideas for subsequent searches of yet other sites. As an investigator, you may have not conducted the same searches in the same sequential order, or perhaps you would have conducted the same searches but used other Web sites.

In addition to demonstrating the flow of one investigation, this case also demonstrates the problems involved in determining legal jurisdiction—the court district where a criminal case would be assigned for trial. Most identity theft cases involve multiple jurisdictions, which is why prosecutions of identity theft are difficult and, sometimes, impossible. Identities stolen in one state may be used to commit fraud in multiple other states or countries. One current and prime example is the theft of identities of U.S. citizens by identity theft networks with cell members located in the country of Romania, who are applying for fraudulent credit cards from financial institutions in Canada and using these credit cards to order merchandise from companies worldwide.

In this case, the perpetrators are operating globally across several jurisdictions and will require the collaboration of law enforcement agencies from these countries. The Federal Trade Commission recommends that victims file an identity theft complaint with law enforcement in the city or county where they reside, where the identity theft occurred, or where the identity was or is being used. In most cases, victims do not know where the identity was stolen and although the location where the identity was used is revealed on the credit card application or statement (or retail, telephone, or other account statements), the legal jurisdiction in which a warrant would be obtained or an offender arraigned is yet another, usually unclear, matter. Thus, in the past, the most a victim could do would be to take steps to prevent further abuse and accept the fact that the perpetrators may never be caught and convicted. Now, however, greater advances can be made by using the Internet to track the activities and locations of perpetrators across cyberspace where there are no legal jurisdictions that would require the often cumbersome, costly, and time-consuming involvement of multiple law enforcement agencies.

Another point the case makes, in addition to the issues involving the way a search may be conducted and the jurisdictional problems, is that identity theft perpetrators typically use a mail drop (private post office), rented or vacant apartment or building, or residence other than their own, for the delivery of fraudulently ordered credit cards and merchandise (which is usually sold on the street, in the black market). On the reports of the four credit agencies, this address becomes the victim's "new" current address. Recall from a previous chapter that the Social Security number (SSN) is an individual's *prime identifier* so that when a credit card, loan, or retail application is made using that SSN, the address provided on that application follows the SSN. Thus, the "current" address on an application blank shows up also on the credit report, and it is at this address where most identity fraud investigations begin.

A fourth and final, but most important, point is the importance of cooperation between the victims and the investigators. This case illustrates how a large identity theft network was uncovered due to the cooperation between the victim, a fraud investigator, the manager of a private post office, and, ultimately, a police officer.

This case is presented not only to illustrate the previous and other points as the case unfolds but it also is intended as a "hands-on" exercise. Readers who are serious about identity theft investigating, and especially those new to the Internet, are encouraged to visit each Web site in each of the steps below as if investigating this case from the beginning.

Also, while working through the case, make note of the important information produced through the above-mentioned valuable collaborations. Note especially, as in the final paragraphs, the lead role of law enforcement officers whose ultimate responsibility is to bring the case to court.

Finally, in this chapter as well in the others that follow, if unable to retrieve a Web site during a search recall that sites are taken down for maintenance and modifications. In these instances, visit the site again later or use the prime URL. For example: *www.thiscase.com* is a prime URL that takes you to the index or homepage of the Web site whereas *www.thiscase.com/photo/digital* is the prime URL that takes you to pages within the Web site. If a Web site has been modified, it is sometimes necessary to go first to the prime or index page—the homepage—and examine that page for words or references that will lead you to the information you seek.

BACKGROUND: CASE EXAMPLE

Donavon Adams (fictitious name) received a telephone call from the Fraud Department of CapitalOne Finance located in Dallas, Texas. It had been determined by the Fraud Department that an imposter had used Mr. Adams' personal identifying information—name, address, Social Security number—to obtain a credit card over the Internet. (Exhibit 7.1 shows the first page of the application.)

The perpetrator(s) used the victim's correct name and Social Security number; however, the date of birth and mother's maiden name did not match those of the victim. According to the application, Mr. Adams had moved from Illinois to California. The perpetrators had given CapitalOne a new mailing address for the delivery of the credit card. The application showed that Mr. Adams' Illinois address was a previous address. In reality, Mr. Adams works in Florida, where, in addition to the Illinois address, he maintains a temporary residence, but the Florida address did not appear on the application.

CapitalOne mailed the credit card to Donavon Adams' *new* address supplied by the perpetrator on the fraudulent credit card application:

14050 Cherry Avenue
Moreno Valley, CA 92551

1. Verify the Address

For the following Internet searches, type the bolded terms exactly as presented; do not leave spaces where none are shown; use commas where shown; use abbreviations as shown.

EXHIBIT 7.1 *Platinum Card Application*

Please complete the five easy steps below, and we will have a response for you in 30 seconds.

Step 1: Application Information

Before completing your credit card application, you should be able to answer **"Yes"** to each of the following statements by checking the boxes:

- ☑ Yes, my credit history is clear of bankruptcy.
- ☑ Yes, I am **not** currently past due on any of my accounts.
- ☑ Yes, I have **not** applied for a Capital One credit card in the last 45 days.

Step 2: Personal Information

Name (First, MI, Last)	Donavon A. Adams
Current Address:	14050 Cherry Avenue
City:	Moreno Valley State: CA Zip: 92551
Home Phone:	(909) 825-9728
Work Phone:	(909) 788-3000
Previous Address:	163 Chancy Lane
City:	Chicago State: IL Zip: 60626
Social Security Number:	123–45–6789 Date of Birth: 12 / 16 / 1968
Mother's Maiden Name:	Larsen
Reenter Mother's Maiden Name:	Larsen
E-mail Address:	

Step 3: Your Employment and Financial Information

Are you self-employed?	○ Yes ○ No
Are you retired?	○ Yes ○ No
Do you own a car?	○ Yes ○ No

Go to: *Yahoo!Maps* (See Appendix A under the category "Maps" for a listing of many other maps.)

In the browser bar, type: *http://maps.yahoo.com/*

To enlarge the window to cover the entire screen, click once on the box in the upper right corner of the browser bar.

Type the street address: **14050 Cherry Avenue**

Type the city and state: **Moreno Valley, CA**

Click on: *Get Map*

A message at the top of the page states: "14050 Cherry Avenue could not be found." This seems strange; CapitalOne mailed the credit card to the Cherry Avenue address, but the credit card had not been returned to the credit card company because of an incorrect address. Let us not drop this "address" line of inquiry. We must determine the location of Cherry Avenue.

2. Locate Cherry Avenue

Go to: *http://yellowpages.superpages.com/* (See Appendix A under "Directories.")

Scroll down the page and click on the link: *Verizon Super Pages-Yellow Pages*

To enlarge the window to cover the entire screen, click once on the box in the upper right corner of the browser bar.

At the top right side of the page under the heading, *Search by Distance*, click on the link: *Use Advanced Search to Search by: Street Address*

Type the *Street* address: **14050 Cherry Avenue**

Leave the *City* field blank.

Choose the *State* from the drop-down menu: **California**

Click on the *Find It* button.

Scroll down the page. Under the heading, *All Categories*, and sub-heading, *Travel & Transportations*, click on the link: *Receiving & Forwarding*

Post Box Plus
14050 Cherry Avenue, Suite R
Fontana, CA 92337
 To view the telephone number, click on the link: *phone*
Telephone: (909) 356-1555
From the above search it is learned that Donavon Adams' imposter used a commercial postal box service in Fontana, California, to receive the credit card sent from CapitalOne Finance. In this case, the imposter requested the credit card be delivered to a nonexistent street in *Moreno Valley*. The perpetrator even used the correct Moreno Valley zip code on the application. However, Post Box Plus does not have an office in Moreno Valley, but it does have one in nearby Fontana. The U.S. Postal Service delivered the credit card on the basis of the street address, which is located in Fontana.

 In many cases, identity thieves receive their stolen merchandise or credit cards at a commercial post office, at empty houses or apartments, or at abandoned businesses or factories. The criminals follow the delivery dates on the Internet using the package tracking capabilities provided by the U.S. Postal Service, FedEx, UPS, and various vendors. On the date of delivery, the thieves go to the particular location and intercept the mail or the package.

 The next step is to locate the county in which the postal center is located. For all identity fraud cases, there are two primary reasons for determining the *counties* in which illegal activity has occurred: (1) to determine legal jurisdiction and (2) to search the Internet for supporting records, many of which are publicly available county level documents.

 Thus, determine the corresponding county for the Fontana, CA, drop box.

3. Locate the County

 Go to: *National Association of Counties Web Site* (Appendix A under County Locator)

Type: *www.naco.org*

Enlarge the window to cover the entire screen.

At the bar on the top of the left side of the screen, click on the button: **Counties**

Then, click on the link: **Data and Demographics**

Under *Search counties by*, select the link to: **city search**

In the textbox, enter the city: **Fontana**

Click on the *Search* button.

The first entry shows that Fontana is located in San Bernardino County. Next, consider other information shown on the fraudulent credit card application. The perpetrator(s) listed two telephone numbers:

1. Business: (909) 788-3000
2. Home: (909) 825-9728

The next step is to match the telephone numbers with addresses. (Even though these numbers may be bogus, recall from Chapter 6 another case in which an investigator found many different applications made in the name of different victims and that contained similar or same street, employer, and other information. Although some of this information was bogus, the similarities across applications provided valuable patterns of information.)

4. Verify the Telephone Numbers

Go to: *www.yellowbook.com* (See Appendix A under "Directories.")

On the right side of the page under the heading *Yellow Book Tools*, click on the link: *phone number*

In the textbox, type the *Business* telephone number: **(909) 788-3000**

Click on the *Find It!* button.

The business telephone number on the credit card application traces to Riverside Community Hospital in four California cities—Costa Mesa, Orange, Riverside, and Placentia. When the original search was conducted, the address below was the only address associated with the telephone number:

Riverside Community Hospital
4445 Magnolia Ave.
Riverside, CA 92501

Click once on the *Back* arrow located in the upper left corner of
the screen.

Type the *Home* telephone number: (909) 825-9728

Click on the *Find It!* button.

No match was found for this number, indicating the number may be:
(a) newly registered and thus not yet on the Internet, (b) unlisted, (c) a
bogus number, (d) out-of-service, or (e) a cell phone number.

The perpetrator claimed Donavon Adams works at Riverside Community Hospital. Have you ever tried locating someone who works at a
large hospital or a medical facility? If so, you may agree that it can be
difficult: each medical specialty within a hospital is a somewhat independent organization of its own where employees come and go and
where central telephone directories may not yet be updated with new
employees' names, which is why perpetrators use the names of large
hospitals on their fraudulent applications.

Even though the business address was found, the home telephone
number did not trace to any address. Nonetheless, the area code and
first three digits will narrow down the location, type of service, and the
service provider. Realizing that the home number also may be bogus,
recall from Chapter 6 and above that an evaluation of all aggregated information can reveal patterns of activity or information related to the
crime and the criminals. Do not, therefore, skip these or other seemingly
minor details.

5. Find the Location Based upon the Area Code and First Three Digits

Go to *FoneFinder:* At: *www.fonefinder.net*

Enter the area code: **909**

Enter the prefix: **825**

Click on the *Search by Number* button.

The *home* phone number is a **Pacific Bell telephone** number located in **Colton, CA.** It is an unlisted landline telephone number.

Note the "FAQ" link at the bottom of this screen. Click on this link to translate the information in the "Telco Type" column. The acronym RBOC means it is a Regional Bell Operating Company, like Pacific Bell or Bell Atlantic.

The next step is to determine the corresponding counties in which the cities of Colton (the purported home telephone number) and Riverside (the purported employer) are located. At this point, it is useful to start pinpointing locations on a large map of California and, later, on maps of other states that are shown to be involved.

6. Locate the County

> Go to: *US County Resources at RootsWeb.* At: *http://resources .rootsweb.com/USA/*
> Enter the *City*: **Colton**
> Enter the *State*: **CA**
> Colton is in **San Bernardino County, CA.**

Donavon Adams' purported *home* telephone number on the CapitalOne credit card application traces to Colton, San Bernardino County, California.

Now locate also the county associated with Donavon's purported employer. Use the back arrow to return to the homepage.

> Enter the *City*: **Riverside**
> Enter the *State*: **CA**

Several counties are listed for Riverside; further searches of each county can uncover potentially useful information that could be matched to the applications of other victims, thereby linking one perpetrator to more than one criminal offense and ultimately revealing the operation of a larger network. At the time of the present case, only one county was listed for the City of Riverside—Riverside County.

Donavon Adams' purported *employer*, Riverside Community Hospital, is located in Riverside County, California.

The problem of determining jurisdiction is evident. Summarized below are the several states, cities, and counties involved in this case:

a. CapitalOne, located in Dallas, Texas, issued the credit card. Although rare, the credit card company may choose to file the complaint and initiate an investigation by law enforcement. In Donavon Adams' case, CapitalOne did not file a complaint. They chose to turn the case over to their internal fraud investigator.

b. The victim's permanent residence is in Illinois.

c. The victim maintains a temporary residence in Florida.

d. The victim's identity was used in connection with:

- Fontana, San Bernardino County, California (drop box where CapitalOne credit card was mailed).
- Riverside, Riverside County, California (victim's purported employer on credit card application).
- Colton, San Bernardino County, California (victim's purported home telephone number on credit card application).

Mr. Adams must determine where to file a complaint. He contacted two of the appropriate California Police Departments. Both were uncertain which department had the jurisdiction. In addition, Mr. Adams was informed that his case would not be investigated owing to lack of personnel, the overwhelming number of identity theft complaints already on file, and the high incidences of more serious crimes in their districts.

Donavon Adams immediately filed a complaint with the local police department in Illinois. Unfortunately, the local detective was preoccupied with investigating another crime and was of little help. *It is important to mention that the victim is often the best source for clues.* Most victims are willing to contact creditors, request information, and forward their findings to the investigating officer. And, increasingly, because of FACTA, company fraud investigators are willing to provide both victims and police departments with information related to the case.

In this case, which occurred before FACTA, Donavon Adams contacted the CapitalOne investigator for more information regarding the Colton, California telephone number 909-825-9728 (home telephone number given on the credit card application). The investigator informed Mr. Adams that he knew the name and address of the person associated with the telephone number. Although he could not divulge the name, he gave Mr. Adams the following address:

800 E. Washington St., Apt. 733
Colton, California

The investigator then volunteered information that could be an important break in the case: the address was used in 1998 in another identity theft case. At that time, according to the investigator, the perpetrators used a CapitalOne credit card to purchase jewelry over the Internet.

From this new information it is determined that (1) the *home* telephone number given on the credit card application is a legitimate number; (2) the telephone number traces to a specific apartment number; (3) the perpetrator has a history (from 1998) of identity theft crimes; (4) the perpetrator is connected to the Post Box Plus drop in Fontana, CA.

Knowledge of the address does not mean the perpetrator still resides there, and any number of people may reside at the same address. Nonetheless, the next step is to find the name of the apartment building and a contact telephone number. Most apartment buildings or complexes are named to distinguish them from others in the same area. There is usually a specific contact name and/or telephone number for obtaining rental information.

7. Find Information on a Specific Address

> Go to *Search Bug* at: *www.searchbug.com*
> Under the heading *Find a Company*, click on the circle preceding
>   **Type.**
> In the first textbox type: **apartment**
> Type the *City*: **Colton**
> From the drop-down menu, choose the state: **CA**

Click on the *Find* button.

Under *Most Popular Yellow Page Categories*, click on the link:
  Apartments

Scroll down the page to find the address. The listing appears in the center of the page. The name of the apartment building is:

Nova Pointe Apartments
800 East Washington Street
Colton, CA 92324

A telephone number also is listed: **(909) 824-7660**

Click on the *Nova Pointe Apartments*.

From this page one can obtain a **map** of the location and also **directions** to Nova Pointe Apartments, information that is useful for contacting management or for purposes of surveillance of the building or apartment or for obtaining plate numbers of cars in the Nova Pointe parking lot, possibly even the parking space assigned apartment number 733.

We wish to obtain information on the management or ownership of the Nova Pointe Apartments. The following search leads to Web sites within sites within other sites, and so on; this is referred to as "deep level" searching for Web sites and pages within Web sites that would not be uncovered directly from a general search from the index (home) page of any search engine.

Also, no two search engines are alike, and there may be great differences in the results each engine retrieves; however, as one delves deeper into the World Wide Web by following hyperlinks found within Web sites, the pages within sites become increasingly remote, or hidden. For practice and to introduce you to differences in search engines, the following search uses an engine not previously used above.

Go to *Query Server* at: *www.queryserver.com*

In the search field, enter: *nova pointe apartments colton ca*

Click on *Search*.

Under *Result Categories* a list of three hyperlinks is shown. Exploring those links leads eventually to Steadfast Companies.

Click on the hyperlink for *Steadfast Companies*.

The results return two hyperlinks.

> Click on the first link: *Steadfast Companies*
> Exploring this site,
> At the top of the page, click on: *MultiFamily*
> On the submenu on the right sidebar, click on: *View Properties*
> Click on: *State of California*
> Scroll down to see that Nova Pointe Apartments in Colton, CA, is a Steadfast property.
> Who owns Steadfast, that is, Nova Pointe Apartments?
> On the left sidebar, click on: *About Us*
> View the right sidebar: Here you find links that lead to names and detailed biographies on the Steadfast executives and also an organization chart of the Steadfast Company.
> We wish to find the contact information.
> On the left sidebar, click on: *Contact Us*

The street and e-mail addresses and fax and telephone numbers of Steadfast Companies are:

> **Steadfast Companies**
> 20411 S.W. Birch St.
> Suite 200
> Newport Beach, CA 92660
> **Phone:** 949.852.0700
> **Fax:** 949.852.0143
> **E-mail us:** *info@steadfastcompanies.com*

If the Colton Police Department was investigating this case, they could contact:

- The manager of Nova Pointe Apartments in person or by telephone.
- One of the executives of Steadfast Companies.
- The occupants of apartment number 733.

Mr. Adams made a business trip to California. He first contacted the Fontana Police Department because the drop box is located in that department's legal jurisdiction (refer to search #2 above.) Mr. Adams and a detective went to the Post Box Plus office located at South Ridge Plaza, 14050 Cherry Avenue, in Fontana.

The office manager cooperated fully and provided Mr. Adams and the detective with a wealth of information ranging from physical descriptions of the perpetrators to photocopies of the driver's license and MasterCard that were used as identification used to apply for the rental of the post office box:

- A young woman named Maureen Graham and her male companion originally opened the post office box. As a personal reference, they gave the name of Shelly Larkin, Archibald Ave., Ontario, California. According to the manager, three people receive mail in this box. Their names are Donavon Adams, Maureen Graham, and Martin Graham.
- A photocopy of a Michigan driver's license used as identification to open the post office box account contained the following information:
    - Picture of Black female
    - Driver's License number: A 820 427 607 ??? (last three digits were undecipherable)
    - Maureen Graham
    - 3185 Stem Lane
    - Mount Morris, MI 48458-2654
    - Expiration: 10-2?-2002
- A photocopy of the credit card used to open the box showed the following name and information:
    - Maureen Graham
    - MasterCard number: 5416-5100-0440-7020
    - Expiration: 04-03-2002
- Photocopies of four envelopes currently in the postal box. The envelopes were addressed as follows:
    - TO: Donavon Adams, Apt. R113, 14050 Cherry Ave., Fontana, CA 92337

FROM: Associates National Bank, P. O. Box 15687, Wilmington, DE 19850-5687. Postmarked South Bend, Indiana; first class, presorted, Permit No. 67

- TO: Donavon Adams, 14050 Cherry Ave., R 113, Fontana, California 92337
  FROM: Metropolitan Bank & Trust, 22901 Millcreek Blvd., Highland Hills, OH 44122. Postmarked 04-28-01 in CLV, OH
- TO: Donavon Adams, 14050 Cherry Ave., Apt. R-113, Fontana, CA 92337
  FROM: First Hawaiian Bank, Consumer Service Center, P. O. Box 2400, Honolulu, HI. Postmarked in Honolulu, HI on 04-30-01
- TO: Martin Graham
  FROM: CapitalOne

The post office manager provided the following descriptions of the persons posing as Maureen Graham, Maureen's male companion, and Donavon Adams:

- Maureen Graham
  - Race: Black
  - Gender: Female
  - Height: Approximately 5'2"
  - Age: 16–19 years old
  - Weight: Thin
  - "Maureen looked like a street urchin; unkempt hair—short, black—barely brushed; ungroomed, no makeup, no glasses, wore a flannel shirt, expressed no emotion; looked like a walking zombie; did not speak; did not make eye contact with me; was accompanied by a Black male. She has visited the post office a few times."
- Maureen Graham's male companion
  - Race: Black
  - Age: Late 20s to early 30s
  - Height: Approximately 6'1" or 6'2"

- ○ Weight: Thin
- ○ Hair: Black
- ○ "Brushed out, bushy hair. Unkempt appearance; wore flannel shirt, no glasses, no earrings; Black male did all the talking and told "Maureen" what information to show as identification; answered all the questions as well; paid the fee for the rental; acted as a pimp—someone who has possession of and tells another what to do and when. The Black man spoke with a Black accent—Black slant, and did not have a foreign accent."
- Donavon Adams
  - ○ Race: Black (Note: The real Mr. Adams is Caucasian.)
  - ○ Age: Late 30s to early 40s
  - ○ Height: Approximately 6'1"
  - ○ Weight: Slender for his height. Approximately 180 lbs.
  - ○ Hair: Black
  - ○ "Hair is short, professionally cut; no glasses; had no accent whatsoever—Black or foreign; as if he had lived in California all his life; exceptionally well groomed; expensive clothes; shoes shined; seemed sophisticated in both speech and dress. Came into the post office alone on two occasions."

The manager called Mr. Adams a few days later with more information. "The person posing as Donavon Adams came into the post office again and paid cash to renew the post office box. He was driving a black, compact, hatchback car with the license plate number DL4BGL____ (last three letters or numbers were blocked off on the plate)." Further, "The impersonator refused to give any identification when asked. He receives the TV Guide as well as merchandise from the Consumer Service Center, 1400 N. Fruit Ridge Avenue, Terre Haute, Indiana, also mail from Columbia House."

The Fontana detective used the police proprietary data system to verify the authenticity of the Michigan driver's license number: it was invalid. The State of California Attorney General's office refused to trace the license plate because, it was explained, there were nearly 1000 potential matches and the time involved would be too great. More was learned, however, from the information obtained at the post office.

Recall a MasterCard in the name of Maureen Graham was used to open the post office box in Fontana, CA, where Donavon Adams' CapitalOne credit card and various merchandise were mailed. The Illinois detective assigned to Mr. Adams' case used a police proprietary search system to trace the MasterCard to People's Bank in Bridgeport, Connecticut. (The sequence of numbers listed on a credit card provides the following information: type of card [Master, Visa, etc.], issuing bank [CapitalOne, CitiCorp, etc.], and the customer number.)

Mr. Adams contacted the People's Bank fraud investigator and learned that the numbers on the credit card had, at one time, been authentic: Maureen Graham had been a victim of identity theft. Her identity was stolen in 1998. At that time, People's Bank had mailed the credit card to a Maureen Graham at the following address, which had been listed on that fraudulent MasterCard application:

> 2355 Foothill Blvd.
> La Verne, California 91750

The next step is to trace the Foothill Blvd. address. The following query also demonstrates how perpetrators use stolen identities for primary frauds and then secondary frauds.

8. Verify the Address

> Go to *Maildrop Guide* at: *www.maildropguide.com*
> In the *search by* drop-down menu, select: *city*
> Enter the city: *la verne*
> Click on *Go.*

The name and address of the mail drop are:

> Mail Boxes Etc.
> 2355 Foothill Blvd.
> La Verne, CA

Center the curser over the name Mail Boxes Etc. and then click on the hyperlink to find the telephone and fax numbers:

Telephone: (909) 392-0524
Fax: (909) 392-9609

The perpetrators used a drop box at Mail Boxes Etc. to receive a credit card from People's Bank, in the name of another victim— Maureen Graham. Then, this stolen MasterCard was used to open up yet another drop box, in another nearby city, in which yet another (Mr. Adam's) fraudulent (CapitalOne) credit card and various merchandise were received. The case at this point illustrates how thieves use identities for *primary* and *secondary* frauds:

- The perpetrators use the victim's identity for the *primary* purpose of obtaining goods, money, and services.
- Once the victim takes action to stop credit from being issued (as in Chapter 5), the perpetrators use the identity for *secondary* purposes, such as for identification for renting postal mail drops.
- The perpetrators then steal and fraudulently use the identity of a new victim, using the newly opened mail drop to receive goods, money, and services, and the cycle continues.

This case now involves another city, another county, and, to complicate matters for possible future prosecutions of the case, another legal jurisdiction. We must also, therefore, locate the county in which the city of La Verne is located.

9. Locate the County

Locate the county for the city of La Verne, California.
To conduct the search, return to search #6, Locate the County.
La Verne is located in Los Angeles County, California

Another city, state, county, and victim are now associated with Mr. Adams' case. Although no conclusive evidence exists, it appears likely that Mr. Adams' identity has fallen into the hands of a network operating in several states. There are two confirmed victims; the name, Maureen Graham, is associated with two cases: her own and Donavon Adams' (case):

- The victims reside in different states.
- Mail drops are used in both the cases.
- The disparity in appearance and behavior between Donavon Adam's (the imposter) imposter and Maureen Graham (the imposter) suggests a multilevel (layered) identity fraud operation: Donavon Adams is described by the post manager as sophisticated in both speech and dress; on the other hand, Maureen is described as a street urchin who neither spoke nor made eye contact and who only followed the instructions of her male companion.
- The perpetrators are not novices; they used addresses in several counties, making it virtually impossible to determine jurisdiction, thus limiting the likelihood of apprehension and, hence, prosecution.
- The network is efficient and well established; the perpetrators have operated for at least three years (Maureen Graham's stolen identity was first noticed in 1998 and Mr. Adams' stolen identity was first discovered in the year 2000).

Continuing the investigation, recall that the post office box in Fontana, California was opened in the name of Maureen Graham who used as identification, in addition to the MasterCard, a State of Michigan driver's license with an address in the city of Mount Morris. The next step is to learn more about the Mount Morris address—exactly where it is, who resides in and rents or owns any apartment, residence, or other building located at that address, and any other information that could be uncovered from leads followed from sequential and deep-level searches of Web sites.

10. Verify the Address

Go to *Yahoo!Map* at: *http://maps.yahoo.com/*
Type the street address: **3185 Stem Lane**

Type the city and state: **Mount Morris, MI**
Click on the *Get Map* button.

Yahoo shows that the house number does not exist. However, the street name, city, and state are correct. Stem Lane is a very small street in a residential area south of I-475. The nearest primary road is West Coldwater Road that runs east and west and is located directly south of Stem Lane.

On the left side of the map in the *Zoom In* box, click on the number *5*. This map shows that Stem Lane is a few miles northwest of Flint, Michigan. The dark tan area indicates that Mount Morris and Flint are located in the same county.

The Michigan driver's license used by Maureen Graham (impersonator) to open the post office box in Fontana, CA, denoted a zip code of 48458-2654. *The last four digits are important because they point to specific addresses*, in this case, addresses on Stem Lane in Mount Morris, MI. The next step is to interpret the zip code.

11. Interpret the +4 Portion of the Zip Code

Go to *City/State/Zip Code Association* at: *http://zip4.usps.com/ zip4/welcome.jsp*
Click on the tab at the top: *Search by Address*
In the first Address textbox, type the street name: *Stem Lane*
Type the City: *Mount Morris*
From the State drop-down menu select: *Michigan*
Click on the *Submit* button.
The house numbers on Stem Lane range from 6100 through 6299.
Click on a *Mailing Industry Information* link on the right side of the page:
Stem Lane is located in Genesee County.

The +4 (2654) used on the driver's license corresponds to even house numbers ranging from 6100 through 6198 (see the first entry on the screen). Why did the perpetrators choose an obscure street in a small community when a much larger city (Flint) is nearby? It seems unlikely that the perpetrators used the +4 by accident. This information is potentially helpful in the investigation because it may indicate that the perpetrators may:

- Have an intimate knowledge of the area.
- Have a worker (cell member) located there.
- Have stolen the identity of a Mount Morris resident.
- Be receiving fraudulent credit cards or merchandise at the Stem Lane address.

A search can be performed to locate the names of residents at specific addresses on Stem Lane.

12. Locate Residents

Go to *White Pages.com-Find a Person* at: *http://www.whitepages. com/person*

At the top of the screen (in the purple), click on the *Reverse Address* tab.

Leave the Street Number blank.

Enter the Street Name: **Stem Lane**

Type the City: **Mount Morris**

Choose *Michigan* from the state drop-down menu.

Click on the *Search* button.

The search reveals sixteen residences with listed telephone numbers on Stem Lane and the first ten listings 1–10.

Since the zip+4 points to residences ending with even numbers ranging from 6100 through 6198, the search can be narrowed to those fitting this even number criterion. The next step would be to search the county records to find information about the individuals residing in these households. Since we cannot use fictitious names to illustrate how to find information on the court records of real people, the following section describes how an investigator would conduct such a search for information on a case under investigation.

13. Find County Records Pertaining to Residents

There are no standards for the design of county Web sites, which means that the investigator must spend some time exploring the layout of any given site for the state of interest. There also are no statewide standards for the type of information that a county designates as "public domain." Nonetheless, an incredible amount of information is available on the Internet for the investigator who takes the time to conduct deep-level searches of the World Wide Web. The following examples use sites from the State of Michigan to show how to peruse a government Web site.

> Go to *Genesee County, Michigan Register of Deeds Instrument Search* at: *www.co.genesee.mi.us/rod/Navigate.asp?SimpleSearch.x=82&SimpleSearch.y=10*

Or, to trace back this link to the homepage, use the primary URL:

> Go to: *www.co.genesee.mi.us/*
> Click on *county offices* (left sidebar).
> Click on *Register of Deeds* (right sidebar).
> Click on *Instrument Search* (bottom of page).

Here, by simply typing in an individual's first and last name, one can find records of deeds for properties, when and where the deeds were filed, the subdivisions in which the properties are located, the names of any previous owners of the property, the names of the financial institutions where mortgages were obtained, and other related details.

Similarly,

> Go to *Genesee County, Michigan Death, and Marriage Record Search by Name* at: *www.co.genesee.mi.us/vitalrec/Navigate.asp?SimpleSearch.x=94&SimpleSearch.y=17*

And now, for practice in surfing a Web site, backtrack from this long link. To initiate the search:

> Go to: *www.co.genesee.mi.us*
> Click on *List of Services* (center of page).

Now follow the links to the Web Services Simple Search Menu where you can enter a first and last name to obtain marriage names, dates, and places.

The types of state records pertaining to residents are too numerous to list; however, an investigator with little practice can quickly learn to efficiently navigate Web sites to locate the information they need for a case. Following the State of Michigan examples above, the two Web sites mentioned in the following text are examples of many Web sites in many states that are available to the public and that provide potentially useful information for identity fraud cases.

14. Find State Records Pertaining to Residents

The URLs for the following Web sites take you directly to the search screen where you enter the name of a person.

> Go to *Michigan Department of Treasury Money Quest-Unclaimed Property Search* at: *www.michigan.gov/treasury/0,1607,7-121-1748_1876_1912-7924--,00.html*

A search of this site lists names of individuals who have unclaimed property. To examine the site, enter any common last name (e.g., Anderson) in the search field; when on a Web site, click on any hyperlinks and also any other tabs to further explore that site.

> Go to *Michigan Department of Corrections – OTIS* at: *www.state.mi.us/mdoc/asp/otis2.html*

This site provides the names of offenders incarcerated or released from the State of Michigan Department of Corrections. To explore the site, enter any common last name (e.g., Anderson) in the search field; then click on the hyperlink at the top of each column on the screen. For example, by clicking on each of the blue *Offender Numbers*, you may view the inmate's record. Some of the convictions are for charges such as retail fraud, attempted murder, manufacture of cocaine, carjacking, and identity theft.

It is impossible to publish in one book the many different searches that are conducted in the course of an investigation, however, the above are examples of searches commonly conducted for any identity theft case and Appendix A presents hundreds of other search sites. These Web sites and their addresses may change or be modified, and new ones continue to appear. Learning where and when to go to a site takes practice and the trail of sites visited will determine what was uncovered at the last site. Briefly reconsider the above case, and how the investigation followed from one address on a MasterCard used to rent a mail drop in California was traced to a little town in Michigan and from there to county records listing names and, eventually, to a criminal database.

Repeatedly I have mentioned that identity theft investigations usually begin where the merchandise is delivered or where the information on credit card, retail account, telephone or other statements (now obtainable by the victim as per FACTA) reveals that illegal activity has taken place. The above simple searches have shown that the city, county, and state records are especially valuable resources for leads from search terms derived from such application blanks or other documents or records

In the case mentioned, envelopes containing credit cards continued to arrive at the Fontana mail drop; the fraud investigators of the many banks, who also were victims, were contacted and many of them provided incremental information that uncovered dozens of victims located in Minnesota, Kansas, Illinois, New York, Indiana, Pennsylvania, Massachusetts, and other states. The credit cards and fraudulently ordered merchandise all went to California mail drops. Mr. Adams did not lose a penny; in this case, the credit card companies and the merchants were the financial victims.

The U.S. Secret Service (USSS) normally investigates frauds that involve substantial losses of money; however, this agency also investigates credit card frauds when evidence exists to show the existence of a larger pattern that crosses multiple legal jurisdictions. In the present case, given all of the many states where the victims resided, the California locations of the perpetrators, the multiple states in which the banks were located, and the numerous locations of the retailers where merchandise was fraudulently obtained—at least 75 different jurisdictions were involved.

The volume of information in this case, obtained primarily through Internet searches and printed as described in Chapter 4 to preserve the chain of order retrieved, were turned over to the USSS, who eventually resolved the case. It is emphasized that this case could not have been solved without the help of police officers, bank fraud investigators, and the postal manager who, when asked, were fully cooperative in providing proprietary information that would become the bases for further searches and more findings.

In conclusion, Chapter 7 introduced common search hyperlinks, and Appendix A provides a list of hundreds more. These are but a microcosm of what can be found among the 8,168,684,336 sites (as of today, September 25, 2005) contained on the Internet. Next, in Chapter 8, I invite the investigator on a walk through the World Wide Web where we will visit other Web sites, including some of those that perpetrators may frequent.

CHAPTER 8

A WALK THROUGH THE WORLD WIDE WEB

In Chapter 7, investigators conducted online searches common to most or all identity theft cases. Chapter 8 takes the investigator to the inner sanctum of the cyber-world, to dark-sided, suspect, and less-common sites that perpetrators are known to frequent.

The primary purpose of this chapter is to provide investigators with additional hands-on experience in digging deeper into the World Wide Web as well as to provide insights into the types of sites that can be used for fraud investigations. Each subsection in Chapter 8 is an "exercise." Do not rush through the many Web sites you now will be introduced to. Rather, take considerable time to visit each page within each site. Most certainly, you will return to many of them later while investigating identity thefts. We will first use the *Wayback Machine* to take you to archived Web sites that can no longer be found using common searches.

WALKING THROUGH THE WEB TO ARCHIVED SITES

The files cached by Google and Yahoo! disappear over time as Web sites are changed, discontinued, or removed by their owners (or by federal agencies). Nonetheless, as is true with the hard drive on a computer, digital evidence can also remain on a server on the Internet. There is a way

131

to find these hidden Web pages or Web sites. The tool to use is the Internet Archive's WayBack Machine. Let us go there.

Internet Archive (http://www.archive.org)

> In the textbox labeled *Wayback Machine*, type: **taleban.com**
> Click on the button: **TAKE ME BACK**
> Under the heading **1998**, click on the date: **Dec 12, 1998**

This Web site was "taken down" after September 11, 2001.

> Click on the last link on the left side of the page: **HOW TO CONTACT US**
> The address and telephone number are in Flushing, New York. This is the contact information for the Afghan Taleban Mission to the United Nations.

Pages dated from 1998 through March 2, 2001 are intact. After March 2001, the site was hacked. Take time now to explore some of these pages, which should still exist unless someone has now reformatted the server or taken other steps to completely wipe these pages.

WALKING THROUGH THE WEB TO GENERAL INFORMATION SITES

The Internet contains hundreds of Web sites owned and used by perpetrators. For example, the terrorists of 9/11 operated and communicated with one another through several Web sites. Perpetrators—terrorists who also are identity thieves—and others know how and where to find the sites they need, which is why investigators must learn about them and also go where these perpetrators go. The sites listed in the following sections are not known by this author to be perpetrator's sites, but that is not to say that perpetrators do not visit them. Let us start with ATM fraud and Anarchist Central.

ATM fraud is committed using a stolen identity—the password that allows access to a bank account. And, for credit card fraud, the perpetrator needs a valid card number. Let us now take a walk through a few Web sites devoted to these topics.

ATM Fraud

Go to Anarchist Central (http://www.geocities.com/M_STANLEY_00/)

> Click on the RED book: **Anarchist Cookbook**
> Click on the chapter: **Carding and Fraud**
> Click on: **ATM Fraud**

The pages in this Web site contain a brief history of ATM machines as well as practical advice about "breaking into" them. What other information can be found on this Web site? *Take time now* to explore some of the links within links for this site. When finished, continue on to another (underground?) Web site that certainly can be useful for identity theft investigations.

Credit Card Validating and Password Stealing Software

Go to CardCheck (http://xequte.com/cardcheck/)

> This site provides free software for validating credit card numbers.
> At the bottom of the page, click on: To download without providing your e-mail address

Notice that you may download the software and even make a donation . . . if you wish.

John the Ripper Password Cracker (http://www.openwall.com/)

> Here you can find free password retrieving software.
> Nothing needs to be said about this self-explanatory Web site.

Fake Identification

The World Wide Web is replete with sites selling fake IDs, including the following, rather well-known, site that advertises authentic products created by master gurus:

Fake ID Guru (http://www.fakeidguru.com/)

> The Fake ID Guru sells novelty IDs for USA, Canada, and Australia.
>
> In the right top corner under **resources,** the following comment is seen "Please mail us with your shipping address and name for a free sample so we can show you how impressive our high quality cards really are. We are absolutely positive you will be impressed with our product and after all seeing is believing. We can think of no better way to prove our product to new customers."
>
> In the lower right corner are **Top 10 Novelty IDs** based on customer sales.
>
> At the top of page in the light blue bar, click on: **US samples**
>
> From the drop-down menu, select: **MICHIGAN (or some other state)**
>
> On the left side of the page, click on: **Contact Us**

Scroll down to the FAQ paragraph: "Are you the cops? NO, are you? We are not even located in the countries that we produce novelty IDs of. Try your luck with a novelty ID site with a mailing address in the USA if you want to deal with cops."

Who is this "fakeidguru"? Let us explore.

Go to Sam Spade (http://www.samspade.org)

> In the textbox next to the DO STUFF button, type: **fakeidguru.com**
>
> Click on the button: **DO STUFF**
>
> The Registrant of this site was Osman Abdullah in Cairo, Egypt, until it was changed on October 12, 2004. At that time, the registrant's telephone number was the fax number of the Four Seasons Hotel in Cairo. The registrant is now listed as Claasen Felix in DE (Germany).
>
> The Web site was registered by easyDNS Technologies Inc. on September 26, 2003. The domain name record expires on September 26, 2006.
>
> The site is hosted on a server named "fast ids." Let us explore further.

Go now to Netcraft (http://news.netcraft.com)

> In the textbox on the left side of the page, type: **fakeidguru.com**
>
> Click on the button: **Search**
>
> According to Netcraft, the IP address is: **203.98.176.136**
>
> Click on the country: the Web site is hosted from a server in **Hong Kong.**
>
> Under the heading, *Netblock Owner*, click on the second link: **New World Telephone**
>
> Scroll down to the next page to find fakeidguru.com. Notice the owner of this Web site is "unknown."

However, by visiting the "About Us" link (on the fakeidguru site) one learns that the gurus are "Highly Skilled Artists and Masters of our trade." Take time now to peruse this site. Visit the FAQs, click on the question, "Do your novelty cards say 'government' on them?" Interesting response, don't you agree?

Considerable more information can be found on the Web about the "gurus." *Take some time now* to explore on your own. Use some of the common searches introduced in Chapter 7 or select others from the categories listed in Appendix A. Then later on come back to these mini-exercises and to *www.shadowcrew.com* once operated by a, now famous and indicted, identity theft network.

THE SHADOWCREW: AN IDENTITY THEFT NETWORK

October 28, 2004 – Department of Justice Press Release:

- Indictment of 19 persons who are alleged to be the founders, moderators, and operators of *www.shadowcrew.com*
- Twenty-one persons arrested in the United States as well as a number of persons arrested in foreign countries
- Nearly 4000 members worldwide

- Trafficked in stolen identity documents (driver's licenses, passports, and Social Security cards), credit cards, debit cards, and bank account numbers

Their other specialties included computer hacking.

> Type in the browser bar: *http://www.google.com*
> Click on the link: **Groups**
> Click on the last link: **Browse all of Usenet**
> In the third column, click on: **alt**
> In the first column, click on: **alt.2600**
> In the middle column, click on: **alt.2600.fake-id**
> At the top of the screen, click on: **about this group**
> From the Archive menu, select the last link for Nov 2004: **44**
> Scroll down to the message from the offshore crew shown in Exhibit 8.1.

Note the *Shadow* hyperlink at the top of this brief message that said only "new day." There was also a *show options* link that disclosed the e-mail client that was used to send the message, which was Yahoo!'s (free) hotmail. Exhibit 8.2 shows the page retrieved when clicking on the *show options* link.

At one time, before the Federal indictments of the shadowcrew, this author stumbled upon the shadowcrew Web site while investigating

---

EXHIBIT 8.1   *Offshore Crew Message*

<u>Shadow</u>

1. offshore crew   Nov 3 2004, 7:39 pm   <u>Show Options</u>

offshorecrew.biz

new day - 1 message - 1 author

EXHIBIT 8.2 *Show Options Link*

Newsgroups: **alt.2600.fake-id**

From: **offshorec...@hotmail.com (offshore crew)** - Find messages by this author

Date: **3 Nov 2004 15:39:40 -0800**

Local: **Wed, Nov 3 2004 7:39 pm**

Subject: **shadow**

Reply to Author I Forward I Print I Individual Message I Show original I Report Abuse

another identity theft case, and I explored the links that provided the following sample of menus:

- Discussion Forums
- The Lounge
- Identification
- Cyberspace
- Credit, E-Currencies, Checks, and Bank Accounts
- Qualification
- Tutorials and How-To's
- Auction Forum
- Vendors and Reviews

Return for a minute to Exhibit 8.1. When clicking on the *Shadow* link in this e-mail message, the viewer was directed *from* the current shadow-crew.com Web site *to* a new offshorecrew.biz site. The offshorecrew.biz Web site was identical to shadowcrew.com—homepage title, discussion forums, colors, layout, links—all were the same. The Shadowcrew, after their indictments, were operating under a new domain name. Or were they? According to some other Web sites, Offshorecrew was a sting operation intended to trap Shadowcrew customers who were dealing in stolen identities and related frauds. The point made here, however, is (from Chapter 7) of the method used by criminals (or sting operators) to create mirrored Web sites.

Since the indictments by the Department of Justice, the offshorecrew and shadowcrew Web sites were taken offline. What information, if any, can now be found about these criminal Web sites? Let us, again, go exploring.

Sam Spade can help.

> In the browser bar, type: *www.samspade.org*
> In the first textbox, type: **offshorecrew.biz**
> Click on: **Do Stuff**

Summary: The domain name, offshorecrew.biz, was registered on November 1, 2004, which was just a few days after the press release by the Department of Justice on the shadowcrew indictments. No wonder it was a "new day" (as per the message of Nov 3, 2004, which could be viewed by clicking on the *shadow* link as described above).

The registrant, administrative contact, billing contact, and technical contact is shown as Tony Stiller, Apt. 6-144, El Dorado, Panama. The contact telephone number is listed as (507) 226-5320.

Questions that an investigator might ask are, "Is this an authentic new identity theft Web site?," "Is Tony Stiller part of the operation or an innocent technical contact?," "Is the name 'Tony Stiller' a real or fictitious name?," "Is this a 'sting' site set up to entrap buyers of stolen identities?," and so on.

These questions, among others, are examples of thoughts that might be triggered by information found on a Web site that suggests the next step, which, in turn, leads to sequential and subsequent trails that an investigation takes. The challenge for new Internet investigators is to spend adequate time on a Web site so as to extract all the available, pertinent information. The tendency for some may be to rush on to the next example or exercise, before exploring all that is available. Taking one more step on the offshorecrew.biz case, let us trace Mr. Stiller's telephone number (to give the reader another Web source to be used for investigations).

This time, let us use Vivisimo.

> In the browser bar, type: *www.vivisimo.com*

In the textbox at the top of the page, type the telephone number:
507-226-5320
Click on the button: **Search**
Click on the link: **1. Welcome to the San Lorenzo Project**

Summary: The contact telephone number for the registrant of off-shorecrew.biz is the fax number for the San Lorenzo Project located in the Panama Canal. Apparently the offshorecrew.biz did not want to receive any telephone calls. Let us explore further:

Go to *www.netcraft.com* (again, for practice)
In the search field in the left sidebar, type: *www.shadowcrew.com*
Here is the old IP address and other information on shadowcrew.

Note at the top right, however, the statement: "This domain is parked, pending renewal, or has expired." Of course, we now know it was parked—as was the entire shadowcrew.

Now go, again, to: **www.archive.org**
In the search field at the top of the page, type: *www.shadowcrew.com*
Click on the Sept 03, 2002 link.

Here is an old shadowcrew homepage. Compare the menu on the left sidebar with the earlier description. Given the time and interest to search at deeper levels, considerable other information on the shadow-crew identity theft network that likely remains hidden somewhere beneath the surface of the World Wide Web can be unearthed. Take time now to return to and explore Google's many usenet links, perhaps beginning with the *alt.* Groups. Then follow the next trail for a final walk through another suspicious Web site.

THEFT OF A BUSINESS IDENTITY—THE NAME OF A REPUTABLE HOSPITAL

Investigators who use the Internet for fraud investigations frequently stumble upon suspicious activities, undoubtedly because, with experience, investigators learn to detect suspicious looking Web sites or statements made on them. The situation described in the following text is one happened upon by investigators at the MSU Identity Theft Lab when investigating another identity theft case. Although the trail is somewhat long, and it may appear confusing at times, I urge you to follow along until the end to see what can be easily uncovered when using the Internet as a search tool.

Type in the browser bar: *http://www.google.com*

Click on the link: **Groups**

Click on the last link: **Browse all of Usenet**

In the third column, click on: **alt**

In the *Directory Search* textbox in the upper right corner, type: **alt.drugs.dealers.playground.bert-hoff**

Click the button, *Directory Search*

Click on the link, **alt.drugs.dealers.playground.bert-hoff**

In the *Search this Group* textbox located in the upper right corner, type: **oxycontin**

Click on the button, *Search this Group*

Find the posting dated October 16, 2004.

Click on the thread subject: **morphine oxycontin dilaudid legally easily from your doctor, and read the posted e-mail messages:**

"... I"ve been trying to get someone to write **oxycontin** for my fibro and none of these cold hearted doctors even cared that i was ready to kill myself because the ..."

Oct 16 2004, 10:07 pm by Aaron Walsh – 1 message – 1 author Summary: Obtain meds without a physical examination by completing an online form.

At the end of the message, click on the hyperlink: *www.pmrs .netfirms.com*

Under the heading, **Announcements**, click on the green link: **Congratulations to Dr. Webster!**

Scroll back up to the top of the page. In the yellow area is the name: **Contoso Hospital**

Click on: **About the Hospital**

Click on: **Staff List**

Click on: **Hospital Services**

Click on: **Pain Medicine Referral Form**

Place the mouse on "*contacting us first*" and this time use the "*right*" click on the mouse.

Now select *properties* to view the e-mail address: **mail to:** pmrs44@yahoo.com

Now scroll to the bottom of the same page to the copyright information. Place the mouse over the green letters *PMRS*. The e-mail address is: **jepke11@yahoo.com**

Summary:

- The site is hosted by a free Web hosting company (*www.netfirms .com*).
- The contact e-mail addresses are Yahoo! accounts.
- The Web site seems disjointed with little information about PMRS other than the online form. The name of a hospital, Contoso Hospital, appears at the top of one Web page.
- The site claims to be an Intranet site (an in-house Web site for employees), but it is an Internet site.

This is suspicious. Now:

Type in the browser bar: *http://www.google.com*

In the textbox, type: **Contoso Hospital**

Click on: **Search**

Click on the link: **About the hospital**

In the browser bar, backspace until the URL reads: *http://www .sharepointsample.com/*

Hit **Enter** on the keyboard or click on **GO** in the browser bar.

Summary: <u>This is a Microsoft Web page for downloading Web design templates for use with Microsoft FrontPage software!</u>

Click on the green button: **Hospital**

Click on the link: **Hospital sample site for FrontPage**

Summary: This is the exact Web page found on the PMRS Web site with the exception of an additional navigation link on the left side of the page (Pain Medicine Referral Form) and the copyright statement at the bottom of that page.

> Type in the browser bar: *http://networksolutions.com*
> In the menu bar at the bottom of the page, click on the link: **Whois**
> Under the heading "Enter a Search Term" type: **netfirms.com**
> Click on the button: **Search**

Summary: Netfirms.com is a Web hosting service registered in Ontario, Canada. The Web site in question, *www.pmrs.netfirms.com*, is sitting on their server.

> At the bottom of the page, next to **DMOZ**, click on the link: **1 listing**
> Next to the **URL** label, click on the link: *www.netfirms.com*
> Scroll to the bottom of the page and click on: **Contact Us**

Summary: Contact information provided for Canada and Buffalo, New York offices of Netfirms.

Web sites come and go, as we saw in the shadowcrew.com case; the above site may also be "parked," eventually. When that happens, the above trail will change, but as was also seen in shadowcrew.com, information remains hidden in cyberspace and can be found by experienced online investigators.

Practiced investigators can find credible information that, when documented by date, time, and cyberplace to preserve the chain of evidence, the trail taken by the investigator can provide evidence sufficient for a search warrant subpoena or arrest. At this time, the investigator turns the file over to a police officer who has authority to submit affidavits and warrants for approval and to conduct searches and seizures. However, the lay investigator's role does not end here. The investigator can continue to assist the police office with continued online searches and, sometimes, also with the search and seizure of suspects' properties. Chapter 11 briefly describes the investigator's role as police research assistants. Before then, however, Chapters 9 and 10 provide exercises on tracing Internet addresses, which are tasks routinely conducted at some point in most or all identity theft cases.

CHAPTER 9

TRACING IP ADDRESSES AND URLS ACROSS THE WWW

The goals of fraud investigations are to gather sufficient evidence to obtain an information search warrant or subpoena and ultimately to provide substantiating evidence that will hold up as evidence in a court of law. Fraud investigators who are called upon to give expert witness testimony would know the appropriate terms and definitions associated with online investigations and also be capable of providing documents showing the chain of evidence for when, where, and how the testimonial information was uncovered and preserved during the cyber-searches. Investigators on the witness stand may also be called upon to demonstrate their expert knowledge of how they used the computer and Internet to produce the evidentiary documents. Attorneys, juries, and judges will, undoubtedly, call into question the expertise of investigators whose testimonies fall short of basic Internet concepts, which is what this chapter is all about.

The chapter first presents an overview of Internet Protocol (IP) and Uniform Resource Locator (URL) addresses, defines these and other related terms, and then provides an exercise demonstrating how to track these Internet addresses. Next, the investigator is taken to several interesting Web sites, collects information on the locations of the traced Internet addresses, and is shown (in Exhibit 9.1 on page 152) how to interpret the record of information for a given Web site. The chapter also includes several exercises to introduce investigators to Web sites commonly used for investigations, including a revisit of the Wayback Machine to search for cached Web sites.

THE IP ADDRESS

Each computer is associated with three Internet addresses: (1) Internet Protocol, (2) Uniform Resource Locator, and (3) e-mail (covered in Chapter 10). Internet addresses can be easily traced to reveal valuable information about the activities of an identity thief. The "Internet Protocol," or IP, is a computer's unique identification number, analogous to a telephone number.

Example: 124.11.12.12:

- 124 is equivalent to a telephone area code.
- 11.12.12 is the actual number of the computer, assigned by the telecommunications company.

Example: http://216.239.57.99 = *http://www.google.com*

Unless you already know it, complete Exercise 9.1 to identify your computer's IP address.

EXERCISE 9.1   *What Is YOUR Computer's IP Address?*

- In Windows 2000 or XP: Click on the "start" button in the lower left-hand corner of your computer screen; select "run"; type the letters "cmd" (for command) in the box; at the DOS prompt, type "ipconfig."
- In Windows 95/98: Start > Run > winipcfg
- On the Macintosh: Apple Menu > Control Panels > TCP/IP Control Panel
- On Mac OS X: Open "System Preferences" > under "Internet and Network" > "Network"
- Or just go to google.com and, in the textbox, type: find IP address

Static versus Dynamic IP Addresses

An IP address can be either "static" or "dynamic." Investigators must know that, depending on its type, an IP address may not provide substantiating evidence in a court case. For example, a static IP address of a computer is one that does not change each time the user logs on to the Internet. An e-mail message, therefore, could be traced to this particular computer. The IP addresses for computers connected to local area networks (LANs) are likely to be static. Computers located in schools and businesses are likely to have static addresses.

Alternatively, some computers access the Internet through dial-up connections. For these computers, the Internet Service Provider (ISP)— a company that provides access to the Internet for a monthly fee— assigns a different, or "dynamic," IP address each time the user logs on to the Internet. One way to find out if your computer has a dynamic IP address is to log on to the Internet, check the IP address, and log out; then, sometime later, reconnect and check again. In the meantime, if another computer somewhere has been assigned your IP number, you will have a new IP address. Your dynamic IP address will be within a "block" of other assigned IP addresses. For example, some Internet service providers allocate to large apartment complexes a range of IP addresses for tenant subscribers, and whenever a user logs into the Internet, an IP address within that range is assigned to the computer.

The distinction between static and dynamic IP addresses can be critical in a court proceeding when, for example, an investigator must provide evidence about a computer that was seized in an identity theft case involving an online credit card fraud. It may be difficult to trace an IP address obtained from the Internet Service Provider to a certain computer if the IP address is dynamic.

In addition, the length of time for which information is saved on the ISP's server (which is a computer with a large hard drive) depends on the type of IP address. For static IP addresses, the data may remain on the server for days, weeks, or months; however, the data logs for dynamic IP addresses are only temporary, usually remaining for only a few days. Even if the testimony does not refer to a specific IP address, the entire outcome of a case can rest on the extent to which expert knowledge is demonstrated by an investigator who does or does not know the difference between static and dynamic addresses. Some tips to remember for the witness stand, therefore, are that IP addresses:

- Are traced to computers, and not to people
- Only can get one closer to the crime
- Can narrow down the suspect list

But:

- Some perpetrators, those who are one step ahead of the law, may use dynamic IP addresses to avoid detection.
- IP addresses can be falsified.

Nonetheless:

- IP addresses can make or break a case because the log files of the ISP's server record the connections made by one computer to others.
- The hard drive on a personal computer can also be analyzed to reconfirm the evidence of those connections.

Two recent cases illustrate the importance of IP addresses in an investigation. In the first case, an online auction fraud, the suspect's computer was identified through the ISP because the Internet service was provided through a local area network, making the IP address static; in the second case, however, although the IP address designation was dynamic, the ISP's records seized the next day showed the user had not logged off for a long period of time that happened to coincide with the timing of online credit card applications across the country.

Although linking a computer and an IP address to a crime does not link the owner or primary user of the computer to that crime, the information can provide further evidence that could lead to another facet of the investigation. In many respects, online investigations are no different than on-site investigations: one piece of evidence leads to the next, which leads to another, and so on. A major difference, however, is speed. Even though online crimes can be carried out with a few simple keystrokes and a click of the mouse, those keyed letters and that click may lead to a piece of information critical to a case, and similarly the investigator can traverse cyberspace much more quickly than telephoning or traveling to locations in search of information that is available online. In summary, the Internet Protocol is one identifying address for a computer. Another is the Universal Resource Locator.

THE UNIVERSAL RESOURCE LOCATOR

Every Web page on the Internet has a unique Universal Resource Locator (URL). So, in addition to the IP address of your computer, if you have a Web site, you will also have a URL address.

Here is a URL address for a Web site we have used previously and will also use below and in the following chapter: *http://www.samspade.org*. The http:// indicates the format for a Web site and *www.samspade.org* is the actual address. Samspade is the site's domain name.

Let us take a look at this site: go to the menu bar at the top of your computer's Internet browser program and type in the Sam Spade URL: *http://www.samspade.org*. (Note: The Sam Spade Web site, as is true with most Web sites, is routinely updated, during which time the Web site is offline. If you are greeted with a message when going to samspade.org stating, "This Page Cannot Be Displayed," return again later as this site soon will be back online.) Next, in the field labeled "Do Stuff," type in your computer's IP address and hit the "Do Stuff" button. Now, what is the URL address that comes up?

You will see an extension after the .org/ that may look something like this: .org/t/lookat?a=35.10.45.118 (or whatever the IP address is for your computer). The extension after the main address refers to a page on a Web site.

Why do we need to know this? Consider again the courtroom testimony after a long and intensive investigation, a great part of which may have been conducted using the Internet. An investigator's credibility can quickly be revealed to a jury by a few simple questions asked by the defense attorney, which is why, incidentally, it also is important to know the difference between the terms "World Wide Web" and "Internet."

The World Wide Web versus the Internet

The "World Wide Web," or WWW, refers to the millions of Web sites in cyberspace. How many are there? Well, the number increases, perhaps exponentially, every day as Web site technology becomes easier to use and more and more people use computers. Let us go to the bottom of the page at *www.google.com* for a good estimate of the number of pages on the WWW today—as of this writing, August 7, 2005, there are 8,168,684,336 Web pages.

The word "Internet," in contrast, refers to the infrastructure—the copper and fiber optical cables that carry data between computers and servers worldwide. Think of the Internet as the *physical* technology and the World Wide Web as *virtual* reality. The URL, then, is a WWW marker, which relies on connections made possible through the Internet. Now let us practice tracing IP and URL addresses.

EXERCISE 9.2   *Tracing IP Addresses and URLs across the WWW*

Internet Protocol (IP) addresses and their associated URLs can be traced through one of the following five Regional Internet Registries—nonprofit organizations within specific regions of the world responsible for allocating Internet resources, registering services, and coordinating activities that support the operation of the global Internet:

- American Registry for Internet Numbers (ARIN),
- Asian Pacific Network Information Center (APNIC),
- Latin American and Caribbean Information Center (LACNIC),
- Reseaux IP Europeens (RIPE) Network Coordination Center, and the
- African Network Information Center (AFRINIC).

All these Regional Internet Registries (RIRs) receive their address blocks from the Internet Assigned Numbers' Authority (IANA), and each RIR maintains a database of the IP numbers within their region.

The RIRs manage IP addresses for the following groups of users:

- Internet Service Providers (ISPs) who are allocated blocks of IP addresses that they, in turn, sell to their customers.

- End-users who can be allocated blocks of IP addresses for use within their internal networks; these addresses cannot be used or sold outside of the end-user organization.

The ARIN service region includes Canada, the United States, and several islands in the Caribbean Sea and North Atlantic Ocean; however, ARIN can be used to perform all IP search inquiries. If the IP address is outside of the ARIN region, ARIN refers users to the correct RIR database. Using ARIN:

- Type the following URL into the browser bar: *http://www.arin.net*

- Type the numeric IP address 35.8.10.26 in the textbox located at the top of the right side of the ARIN homepage.

- Click on Search Whois.

The returned results show that Michigan State University has been assigned a block of IP addresses, including 35.8.10.26. What if, however, the IP address is unknown? The ARIN registry can also be searched for the known URLs. In the Whois textbox, type: Michigan State University.

The results show all of the IP addresses assigned to Michigan State University, including, as you will see if you peruse the list, the block of addresses that include 35.8.10.26.

Now let us use APNIC, which is responsible for distributing and registering Internet addresses for the entire Asia Pacific region:

- Type the following URL into the browser bar: *http://www.apnic.net*

- Type the numeric IP address 35.8.10.26 in the textbox located at center page.

- Click on Search Whois.

(continued)

EXERCISE 9.2   *(continued)*

Since Michigan State University is out of the APNIC region, the returned message directs the investigator to either the ARIN or the RIPE Registries:

35.0.0.0 - 35.255.255.255

IANA-NETBLOCK-35

This network range is not allocated to APNIC.

If your whois search has returned this message, then you have searched the APNIC whois database for an address that is allocated by another Regional Internet Registry (RIR). Please search the other RIRs at *whois.arin.net* or *whois.ripe.net* for more information about that range.

In addition to Regional Internet Registries described in Exercise 9.2, the four tools listed below are also useful for tracing IP and URL addresses. Of the four, All Net Tools and Geek Tools will also trace routes taken by e-mails or other packets of information across the Internet to a recipient. Traceroute software looks up and displays the names and IP addresses of each machine (server) along the path from origination to destination hosts. Most online fraud investigations make use of both Whois technology and traceroute technology:

- Network Solutions (*http://www.networksolutions.com*)—Whois – Search by IP address or domain name; All Net Tools (*www.allnettools.com/toolbox*)—Whois – Search by IP address or domain name—Traceroute; Geek Tools (*www.geektools.com*)—Whois – Search by IP address or domain name—Traceroute

- SamSpade (*www.samspade.org*)—Whois – Search by IP address or domain name

Samspade is an especially useful resource for obtaining detailed Whois information. For example:

> Go to *www.samspade.org*
> In the "Do Stuff:" field, type: *www.msu.edu*
> Click on "Do Stuff"

The results return considerable information that can be used to track down the owner of a domain name and Web site, contact information for whoever maintains the site, contact information for the owner of the IP address, and other potentially useful evidence for an investigation. See Exhibit 9.1 on how to interpret Whois records using, as an example, the record retrieved by SamSpade for Michigan State University.

The next section lists additional search tools for identity theft investigations.

OTHER SEARCH TOOLS

For each of the search tools listed below, try the related exercises to view the useful types of information an investigator may need for an identity theft case:

- IANA – Country Code Top Level Domains (*http://www.iana.org/cctld/cctld-whois.htm*): Lists country code top-level domains (ccTLDs). These domain codes end with two letters, such as .uk (United Kingdom), identifying a country or geographic region. Exercise: Visit the IANA Web site now to view the many country codes.
- Netcraft – Webserver Search (*http://news.netcraft.com*): Netcraft is a company located in Bath, England. The company specializes in

EXHIBIT 9.1   *How to Interpret a Whois Record*

Domain Name: *www.msu.edu*

Tool used: Sam Spade – Do Stuff

www.msu.edu = [35.8.10.26] ◄— Domain name/URL = IP address

Domain Name: MSU.EDU

Registrant: ◄——— Name and contact information for the
   Michigan State University   person or organization who owns the
   220 Computer Center   domain name and Web site
   East Lansing, MI 48824
   UNITED STATES

Contacts: ◄——— Name and contact information for the
   Administrative Contact: person or organization responsible for
   DNS Administrator   maintaining the Web site, renewing the
   Michigan State University   domain name, and updating registrant
   220 Computer Center   and technical contact information.
   East Lansing, MI 48824
   UNITED STATES
   (517) 355-3600
   dnsadmin@msu.edu

Technical Contact: ◄——— Name and contact information of the
   DNS Technical Support   organization owning blocks of IP
   Michigan State University   addresses, such as an ISP, who distributes
   220 Computer Center   space on their servers to customers for
   East Lansing, MI 48824   Web site hosting, Internet access, and
   UNITED STATES   e-mail.
   (517) 353-2980
   dnstech@msu.edu

Name Servers: ◄——— Name Servers are also called hosts. These
   SERV1.CL.MSU.EDU   servers resolve (match) domain names to
   SERV2.CL.MSU.EDU   the correct numerical IP addresses. The
                                     servers direct e-mail to the proper e-mail
                                     accounts, allow access to Web sites, and
                                     provide Internet access.

Domain record activated: 06-May-1987 ◄— Date the domain name was registered
Domain record last updated: 21-Jun-2002 ◄— Date the domain name record
                                          was changed or updated

network security and Internet research and data analysis. Use this
site to locate operating systems, servers, and Web sites hosted on
those servers.

Exercise: In the textbox in the upper left corner of the Netcraft
Web site, type: *msu.edu*. Click on the *Search* button to view the
details returned.

- Link Popularity (*http://www.linkpopularity.com*): This tool locates
other Web sites that are linked to a particular Web site. It is useful
for finding "like" Web sites linked to pornographic, terrorist, and
any other identity theft-related sites.

  Exercise: Go to Link Popularity. In the textbox labeled *Enter Web
  Site URL*, type: *msu.edu*. Click on the *Tell me my popularity!*
  button.

- Internet Archive – Wayback Machine (*http://www.archive.org*):
The Wayback Machine is a tool for locating and viewing Web sites
that have been removed from the World Wide Web or older versions
of active sites. (The Wayback Machine is also useful for retrieving
Web sites involved in phishing scams.)

  Exercise: Let us go to the Wayback Machine. In the textbox, type the
  URL: *www.msu.edu*. Click on *Take Me Back* button. Here, you will
  find archived Web pages dating back to 1997.

Investigators at one time or another and in most every investigation will
visit the above Web sites when tracking the perpetrators. This chapter also
provided definitions and descriptions investigators may need on the witness stand. The chapter demonstrated how to locate IP and URL addresses, and illustrated how to interpret WHOIS records to locate servers
that may host suspect Web sites. Chapter 9 did not, however, cover e-mail
tracing, which is the topic of Chapter 10. E-mail messages analyzed from
a seized computer can contain information on the activities and whereabouts of a suspect at certain points in time.

CHAPTER 10

TRACING E-MAIL ADDRESSES

Tracing e-mail messages is a routine task for most identity theft investigations because ID theft criminals communicate with one another through personal e-mail addresses and use e-mail addresses to commit identity frauds, including online auction frauds, credit card frauds, e-shopping, drug and cigarette smuggling, bullying and harassing, and, of course, the online buying and selling of identities. The contents of an e-mail message can place the whereabouts of the computer user (the potential suspect) at a certain time and also reveal other important details from discussions with accomplices or victims. Following a brief overview of how e-mail works this chapter will show how to trace an e-mail message.

HOW E-MAIL WORKS

Software used to send e-mail messages are called "clients." Examples are Microsoft Outlook, Netscape, and Eudora. All clients receive "header" information, such as the time, date, and place the message was sent through the Internet, the name of the sender, the subject of the e-mail, and other information.

E-mail clients can be configured to show more information than is usually seen on an e-mail message, such as the routing of the e-mail through various servers on the Internet. All clients need a server, and messages sent through a client's server may travel through many other servers before reaching the destination—the designated recipient of the e-mail.

Further, each server has two subservers: the "Simple Mail Transfer Protocol" (SMTP) server handles outgoing mail, and the POP3 server handles incoming mail. Connecting servers can be traced. E-mail clients can be configured to show "full" headers instead of the "summary" headers—time, date, name address, and subject—shown on most e-mail messages. Let us configure your computer to show the full header. See Exercise 10.1.

EXERCISE 10.1 *Instructions for Viewing and Printing Full Headers*

Each e-mail client has its own methods for viewing and printing full headers and the steps change with new editions. The following instructions are for common e-mail clients used today. Configure your computer to show full e-mail headers.

Microsoft Outlook Express 6.0:
- From the File menu, select Properties.
- Click on the Details tab.
- Click on the Message Source button.
- Copy and paste into the notepad or a Word document.

Yahoo!:
- Open the e-mail message. In the right corner, click on: Full Headers.
- Click on Printable View to view and print the message with the full header.

AOL:
- At the top of the e-mail in the gray area, look for: *Sent from the Internet (Details).*
- Click on *Details* to view and/or print the complete header.

(continued)

EXERCISE 10.1 *(continued)*

MSN Hotmail:
- Select Options in upper right corner.
- On the left side of the page, click on Mail.
- Click on Mail Display Settings.
- *Under* the heading Message Headers, select the circle preceding Advanced.
- Click on Print View to print the message.

Netscape:
- Click on the yellow arrow (triangle) located in the bottom right corner of the condensed header to expand to full header.
- Under File, select Print.

Eudora 6.1.2 for Windows:
- On the toolbar, click on [[???]] to view full headers of all messages.
- Click on printer icon on toolbar to print.

Pine:
- From the Message Index or Message Text windows the "h" key will toggle full headers on and off.

Webmail:
- Click the Message Source link just below the name of the mailbox.

Mulberry:
- If using the 3 pane view, click the "Show/Hide Headers" icon on the Preview Pane toolbar.
- If the e-mail is open,or click Message -> Show Headers or hit Alt+Ctrl+H.

Now that your computer is configured to view and print the full e-mail header, which you will use in some phase of most identity theft investigations, let us move on to e-mail tracing.

TRACING AN E-MAIL MESSAGE: EXAMPLE #1

Exhibit 10.1 shows an actual e-mail message sent to *katzu@pilot.msu.edu* from "Richard K. Lee." Even though there was no syntax in the "Subject" field to indicate the contents of the e-mail, Katzu, thinking that "Richard Lee," the sender of the message, was someone she should know, opened the e-mail and found the following message:

> *"Stable & rock hard erections*
>
> *Increased stamina & endurance*
>
> *No. 1 recreative drug*
>
> *No prescription asked"*

Let us trace this e-mail. To start with, break the header down into three parts starting with the line that begins with "From:"

- Part 1. From: through the line that begins with X-Virus:
- Part 2. Received: through the line that begins with Message Id:
- Part 3. Return Path: through the line that begins with Envelope to:

In this simple e-mail there is only one "Received:" section in the header, however, when e-mails are sent through multiple servers, there will be two or more "Received:" sections. For example, computers in a large organization may send messages to the departmental server, which in turn may send the messages to a main server, which in turn sends the e-mail to the server for another company, and so on. In this case, the header would have three Received: sections, because at each location that a Mail Transfer Agent (a server) forwards the message, a new Received: line is inserted above the last.

The Received: lines are the most important in tracing e-mails, and, within the Received: lines, the most important part is the IP address— the address of the computer used to connect to the mail server that generated the Received header. The originating IP address should appear in [brackets]: a "red flag" should be raised if the IP address has no brackets or appears in (parentheses).

EXHIBIT 10.1 *E-mail Header*

Return-Path:	<Carrie@3-cities.com>
Envelope-To:	katzu@pilot.msu.edu
Delivery-Date:	Thu, 18 Nov 2004 13:14:28 -0500
Received:	From [216.85.17.12] (helo=216.85.17.12) by Sys33.mail.pilot.msu.edu with smtp (Exim 4.32 #22) id 1Cuqnb-00011U-SK for katzu@pilot.msu.edu; Thu, 18 Nov 2004 13:14:28 -0500
Message-Id:	517301c4cd96$2a10993a$d571199b@3-cities.com
From:	"Richard K. Lee" carrie@3-cities.com
To:	katzu@pilot.msu.edu
Subject:	=?iso-8859-1?B? Vm1hZ3JhIC0gTk8gcHJ1bWF0dXJ1IGVqYYWN1bGF0aW9uIQ==?=
Date:	Thu, 18 Nov 2004 17:47:32 +0000
Mime-Version	1.0
Content-Type:	multipart/related; type="multipart/alternativge"; boundary="----=_NextPart_000_0000_A53FEOF3.2B3OFA63"
X-Priority:	3
X-Msmail-Priority:	Normal
X-Mailer:	Microsoft Outlook Express 6.00.2600.0000
X-Mimeole:	Produced by Microsoft MimeOLE V6.00.2600.0000
X-Virus:	None found by Clam AV
	Stable & rock hard erections
	Increased stamina & endurance
	No. 1 recreative drug
	No prescription asked

The *originating IP address* is found in the bottom Received: lines, reading up, and in the first set of brackets. The *terminal* e-mail *server*—the one you access to read your e-mails—is found in the most recent, or top part, of the Received: lines. For the relatively simple e-mail in Exhibit 10.1, there is only one Received: part. (A following exercise will analyze a somewhat more complicated e-mail message containing two received headers.)

Analyze Part 1.

First become familiar with the following terms of header lines and the information they contain:

- *From: "Richard K. Lee" carrie@3-cities.com.* Programs can be written to instruct a computer e-mail client (e.g., Outlook, Netscape, Eudora) to use any e-mail address. In most fraud e-mails, the From: address is faked.
- *To: katzu@pilot.msu.edu.* The recipient's e-mail address.
- *Subject*: =?iso-8859-1?B? Vm . . . The sender did not indicate the subject and the various letters/numbers/symbols were added somewhere during the transmittal of this message. Interestingly, the number "ISO-8859-1" refers to a character set often used by international e-mail programs, and this type of character set is usually found in the Content Type: part of the header.
- *Date*: Thu, 18 Nov 2004 17:47:32 +0000 . . . The date and time of an e-mail, even if faked, can be important for an investigation. For this e-mail, "Richard K. Lee" sent the message on Thursday, November 18, 2004. On the 24-hour time clock, the message was sent at 17 hours, 47 minutes, and 32 seconds (which translates to 5:47 PM [and 32 seconds]). The plus digit and last four numbers (+0000) refer to the Greenwich Mean Time (GMT), or London, U.K. time. Plus means east of GMT and minus means west of GMT.

  The GMT and the importance of the date and time will be discussed in more detail when we come to the Received: part of the header. For now, however, note that an e-mail sent from someone in the GMT zone (Iceland, Ireland, United Kingdom) will usually have the time zone listed as "+0000" in the header of the e-mail.
- *MIME Version:* MIME (usually capitalized) is the acronym for Multipurpose Internet Mail Extensions, which are specifications that define how Internet messages are encoded. MIME version 1.0 is the standard format for Internet messages. The lines following the MIME version, if any, are auxiliary and usually extraneous for purposes of tracing e-mails.

- *Content Type:* "Multipart" indicates there will be several documents; "alternative" usually refers to where another variant of this document might be found, and the "boundary" term indicates encoding that separates each document. This information is meaningless for our purposes.
- *X-Priority:* Lines beginning with X- are added by the e-mailing system and are of little or no value for e-mail tracing. There also are no formal definitions for these X-terms. For example, an X-Priority script with the number three could mean that messages with values greater than three should be moved to a "work on later" folder, or it could refer to the priority delivery of an e-mail. X-Msmail Priority is another (nonstandard) priority script; X-Mailer is the mailer software used by the sender, which, in this case, is Microsoft Outlook, which, in turn, is produced by X-Microsoft Mimeole Version 6.0. Finally, X-terms can be forged.

Analysis Part 2: Received Lines

The "Received:" lines are of greatest interest for e-mail tracing. The IP address of the computer used to send the message is 216.85.17.12. The Received: line usually also includes the name of the mail server used to send the message, but in this e-mail, that information is missing. What is most important, however, is the IP address, which can be traced through the American Registry for Internet Numbers (ARIN), a nonprofit organization responsible for registering and administrating IP numbers for North America.

Go to *http://www.arin.net/index.shtml*. In the field located on the right side of the ARIN homepage, enter the IP address [216.85.17.12] and click on "Search WHOIS." The search returns the following information:

e.spire Communications, Inc. ESPIRE-8BL

(NET-216-84-0-0-1) 216.84.0.0 - 216.85.255.255

North Hills Auto NORTHHILLSAUTO

(NET-216-85-17-8-1) 216.85.17.8 - 216.85.17.15

North Hills Auto has been assigned IP numbers ranging from 216.85.17.8 to 216.85.17.15 (eight possibilities) by Espire Communications, Inc., a Domain Name Service. The IP address in the e-mail header falls within the assigned range. We have tracked the e-mail to its source—the IP address of the computer used to connect to the mail server that generated the "Received" header lines. (Espire Communications, Inc., by the way, is where this spam should be reported.)

The WHOIS information above is legitimate and can be trusted; however, the fact that the IP address reverts to North Hills Auto, Inc. does not point to the *person* who sent the e-mail. North Hills Auto could be a reputable business. The culprit spammer could be anyone who accessed a computer assigned to North Hills Auto, Inc. For an identity theft investigation, however, it is important to collect the information on the source of the e-mail.

The next step, therefore, is to locate North Hills Auto. In the field at the top of the page (*http://ws.arin.net/cgi-bin/whois.pl*), enter the term "North Hills Auto" and click on "Submit Query." The following information is returned:

CustName: North Hills Auto

Address: 8017 GRAPEVINE HWY

City: NORTH RICHLAND HILLS

StateProv: TX

PostalCode: 76180

Country: US

RegDate: 2003-08-12

Updated: 2003-08-12

NetRange: 216.85.17.8 –216.85.17.15

CIDR: 216.85.17.8/29

NetName: NORTHHILLSAUTO

NetHandle: NET-216-85-17-8-1

Parent: NET-216-84-0-0-1

NetType: Reassigned

Comment:

RegDate: 2003-08-12

updated: 2003-08-12

NOCHandle: ZI80-ARIN

NOCName: XSpedius IP Administrator

NOCPhone: +1-800-673-1900

NOC Email: ipadmin@xspedius.com

TechHandle: ZI80-ARIN

TechName: XSpedius IP Administrator

TechPhone: +1-800-673-1900

TechE-mail: ipadmin@xspedius.com

OrgAbuseHandle: ABUSE31-ARIN

OrgAbuseName: Abuse Department

OrgAbusePhone: +1-800-831-0309

OrgAbuseE-mail: NetAbuse@xspedius.com

OrgTechHandle: ZI80-ARIN

OrgTechName: XSpedius IP Administrator

OrgTechPhone: +1-800-673-1900

OrgTechE-mail: ipadmin@xspedius.com

OrgTechHandle: ZX7-ARIN

OrgTechName: XSpedius IP Administrator

OrgTechPhone: +1-877-962-1900

OrgTechE-mail: ipadmin@xspedius.net

 # ARIN WHOIS database, last updated 2005-08-13 19:10

Enter ? for additional hints on searching ARIN's WHOIS database.

From this search it can be concluded that:

- North Hills Auto is located at 8017 Grapevine Highway in North Richland Hills, Texas.
- The IP address was assigned to North Hills Auto on August 12, 2003.
- The IP address is still good, because it is still listed on ARIN.
- ARIN was last updated on August 13, 2005.

Note also the other information contained on ARIN, including the toll-free telephone number and e-mail address for reporting e-mail ABUSE, such as spam, e-mail viruses, harassments, or threats.

In this case, the culprit is unknown, and the only known factor is the IP address of the computer traced to North Hills Auto, Inc., who may be completely innocent of any spamming involvement. It is not yet time to start knocking on any doors, such as at North Hills Auto, Inc., though. If this were an identity theft case, it would most likely involve more than one perpetrator and any indication of suspicion would quickly reverberate throughout the crime network. However, for the future potential purpose of obtaining a search warrant, it is necessary to document the information on the Internet service provider (ISP). The ISP also is where you would report the spam abuse.

Therefore, search ARIN for the e.spire Communications, Inc. IP address. 216-84-0-0-1 returns the following address, allocated range of IP addresses, and dates when registration was last updated:

OrgName: e.spire Communications, Inc.

OrgID: ACSI

Address: 5555 Winghaven Blvd

Address: Suite 300

City: O'Fallon

StateProv: MO

PostalCode: 63366

Country: US

NetRange: 216.84.0.0 – 216.85.255.255

CIDR: 216.84.0.0/15

NetName: ESPIRE-8BL

NetHandle: NET-216-84-0-0-1

Parent: NET-216-0-0-0-0

NetType: Direct Allocation

NameServer: DNS1.XSPEDIUS.NET

NameServer: DNS2.XSPEDIUS.NET

NameServer: DNS3.XSPEDIUS.NET

Comment:

RegDate: 1998-09-24

Updated: 2003-10-03

The IP address in most headers is preceded by the name of the Domain Name Server (DNS) that sends the e-mail. In the present e-mail, the Return path: line indicates the e-mail message was sent from "*carrie@3-cities.com.*" We can check ARIN for the (unlikely) possibility that the IP address [216.85.17.12] would revert to *www.3-cities. com.* The ARIN search produced the following results:

No match found for 3-cities.com.

Most likely, there also is no such e-mail address as *Carrie@3-cities.com,* as shown in the Return Path.

In addition to the IP addresses, another potentially useful piece of information in the "Received:" part of the header is the time stamp—the date and time the message was received in the mailbox. In the present e-mail, the time stamp was:

Thursday, November 18, 2004 at 13:14:28 –0500

The –0500 is the time difference in hours from Greenwich Mean Time (GMT) in the U.S. Eastern Standard Time Zone. Thus, the complete time is:

1:14 PM (and 28 seconds) EST

Exhibit 10.2 lists the GMT zones for the United States. (Note that the GMT for Eastern *Daylight* Time is –0400.) The present e-mail was sent from the U.K. time zone (the GMT zone) at 5:47 PM and received in Katzu's mailbox at 1:14 PM. However, using the time zone converter at *http://www.greenwichmeantime.com/gmt-converter.htm*, an e-mail message sent from the GMT zone at 5:47 PM would have been received at –0500 time zone at 12:47 AM the same day.

EXHIBIT 10.2 *Greenwich Mean Time Table for Tracing E-mails*

State	Standard Time	Daylight Savings Time
Alabama	GMT-6	GMT-5
Alaska	GMT-9	GMT-8
Alaska Aleutian	GMT-10	NA
Arizona	GMT-7	NA
Arizona (Navajo)	GMT-7	GMT-6
Arkansas	GMT-6	GMT-5
California	GMT-8	GMT-7
Colorado	GMT-7	GMT-6
Connecticut	GMT-5	GMT-4
Delaware	GMT-5	GMT-4
Florida	GMT-5	GMT-4
Florida (W)	GMT-6	GMT-5
Georgia	GMT-5	GMT-4
Hawaii	GMT-10	NA
Idaho (N)	GMT-8	GMT-7
Idaho (S)	GMT-7	GMT-6

(continued)

EXHIBIT 10.2 *(continued)*

State	Standard Time	Daylight Savings Time
Illinois	GMT-6	GMT-5
Indiana	GMT-5	GMT-4
Indiana (E)	GMT-5	NA
Indiana (SW/NW)	GMT-6	GMT-5
Iowa	GMT-6	GMT-5
Kansas	GMT-6	GMT-5
Kansas (W)	GMT-7	GMT-6
Kentucky (E)	GMT-5	GMT-4
Kentucky (W)	GMT-6	GMT-5
Louisiana	GMT-6	GMT-5
Maine	GMT-5	GMT-4
Maryland	GMT-5	GMT-4
Massachusetts	GMT-5	GMT-4
Michigan	GMT-5	GMT-4
Michigan (W)	GMT-6	GMT-5
Minnesota	GMT-6	GMT-5
Mississippi	GMT-6	GMT-5
Missouri	GMT-6	GMT-5
Montana	GMT-7	GMT-6
Nebraska	GMT-6	GMT-5
Nebraska (W)	GMT-7	GMT-6
Nevada	GMT-8	GMT-7
New Hampshire	GMT-5	GMT-4
New Jersey	GMT-5	GMT-4
New Mexico	GMT-7	GMT-6
New York	GMT-5	GMT-4
North Carolina	GMT-5	GMT-4
North Dakota	GMT-6	GMT-5
North Dakota (W)	GMT-7	GMT-6
Ohio	GMT-5	GMT-4
Oklahoma	GMT-6	GMT-5

EXHIBIT 10.2 *(continued)*

State	Standard Time	Daylight Savings Time
Oregon	GMT-8	GMT-7
Oregon (E)	GMT-7	GMT-6
Pennsylvania	GMT-5	GMT-4
Rhode Island	GMT-5	GMT-4
South Carolina	GMT-5	GMT-4
South Dakota (E)	GMT-6	GMT-5
South Dakota (W)	GMT-7	GMT-6
Tennessee (E)	GMT-5	GMT-4
Tennessee (W)	GMT-6	GMT-5
Texas	GMT-6	GMT-5
Texas (W)	GMT-7	GMT-6
Utah	GMT-7	GMT-6
Vermont	GMT-5	GMT-4
Virginia	GMT-5	GMT-4
Washington	GMT-8	GMT-7
West Virginia	GMT-5	GMT-4
Wisconsin	GMT-6	GMT-5
Wyoming	GMT-7	GMT-6

Whatever the reason for the inconsistency, discrepancies in e-mail time stamps, such as when time sent/received entries are several hours apart, have the wrong time zone, or have nonsequential dates/times, can help determine if an e-mail is forged, as the present case indicates. Also, under most Internet traffic conditions, it takes only a couple of seconds to transmit a message from one server to another, even if an e-mail travels a great physical distance.

Of course, some time discrepancies may be due to the accuracy of time on a computer. To verify the accuracy of the time on your computer, go to: *http://wwp.greenwichmeantime.com*; the time shown at the top right side of the page is the current time for your computer.

In summary, this example showing the tracing of a simple e-mail suggests the following:

- Someone with access to computers at North Hills Auto, Inc. is sending spam.
- The spammer has altered (forged) portions of the e-mail header, including perhaps the time stamp showing the date on which the message was sent.
- And the alterations are particularly in the From: address (in part one) and the e-mail address in the Return Path: (in part three).

Next, let us analyze a somewhat more complicated e-mail message, one that has two Received: lines in the header.

TRACING E-MAIL: EXAMPLE #2

The easiest way to trace an e-mail is to remove from the header any information that is extraneous, such as, for example, the lines that begin with an "X." The X lines are added by the e-mailing system and can be faked. For brevity, the example below shows only the Received: lines of an e-mail message.

- **Received:** from *c-24-99-100-182.hsdl.ga.Comcast.net* ([24.99.100. 182]) by *sys10.mail.msu.edu* with smtp (Exim 4.44 #1) id 1E481x-0002CGZ; Sat, 13 Aug 2005 23:02:55–0400
- **Received:** from *ny-tupperlake0b-356.albyny.adelphia.net* (*pD636 D2D1.dip dialin.net* [179.218.136.248]) by *southeast.beonex.com* with ESMTP id 288B9C0219B for *htqxo@fastmail.ca.*; Sun, 14 Aug 2005 17:04:18 -0100

To *trace* an e-mail message from its origin to the final destination, read from the bottom up. However, to *analyze* an e-mail message with more than one "Received:" part in the header, it is easiest to read from the top down until you come to inconsistencies that would raise "red flags," such as in this e-mail.

The first "Received:" lines say that the *msu.edu* mail server (*sys10.mail.msu.edu*) received the message at 23:02:55 (GMT –0400) (translated, 11:02 PM (and 55 seconds), Eastern Daylight Time from a mail server at Comcast.net with the IP address 24.99.100.182.

The first step is to analyze the IP address shown in brackets as 24.99.100.182, for its authenticity: Does it revert to Comcast.net? Rather than using ARIN as above, another useful search system is *www.samspade.org*: Type the IP address in the first field and click on the "Do Stuff" button. The search returns the following information:

Server Used: [whois.arin.net]

24.99.100.182 = [c-24-99-100-182.hsd1.ga.comcast.net]

OrgName: Comcast Cable Communications Holdings Inc.

OrgID: CCCH-3

Address: 1800 Bishops Gate Blvd

City: Mt Laurel

StateProv: NJ

PostalCode: 08054

Country: US

NetRange: 24.98.0.0 –24.99.255.255

CIDR: 24.98.0.0/15

NetName: CCCH3-2

NetHandle: NET-24-98-0-0-1

Parent: NET-24-0-0-0-0

NetType: Direct Allocation

NameServer: DNS.INFLOW.PA.BO.COMCAST.NET

NameServer: DNS.CMC.CO.DENVER.COMCAST.NET

The IP address is consistent with Comcast.net—the last Message Transfer Agent (MTA) the message went through before reaching my ISP (msu.edu). This line can be considered authentic.

Still analyzing from the top down, the second Received: lines say that the adelphia.net mail server with IP address 179.218.136.248 received a message from a mail server at *beonex.com* sent by *htqxo@fastmail.ca* on Sunday, August 14, 2005 at 17:04:18, GMT –0100, (translated 5:04 PM and 18 seconds, WAT (West Africa Time Zone; see *http://wwp .greenwichmeantime.com/info/timezone.htm* for countrywide GMT zones).

Analyzing the IP address, 179.218.136.248, using *www.samspade.org,* returns the following information:

> *Server Used: [none]*
>
> *ERROR: IP Range Reserved by IANA.org*

IANA is short for *Internet Assigned Numbers Authority,* the organization responsible for assigning new Internet-wide IP addresses. According to *samspade.org,* the IP address has been reserved by IANA, that is, the IP address 179.218.136.248 has not been assigned. The message is spoofed and is not to be trusted. Let us go further nonetheless: In an identity theft case, further analysis of the "Received:" lines could prove informative.

The e-mail message originated at "*ny-tupperlake0b-356.albyny.adelphia.net.*" Using samspade's "Do Stuff" search reveals the following:

> *Server Used: [whois.networksolutions.com]*
>
> *ny-tupperlake0b-356.albyny.adelphia.net = [ ]*
>
> *Registrant:*
>
> *Adelphia Communications Corp.*
>
> *Main at Water*
>
> *Coudersport PA 16915*
>
> *US*
>
> *Domain Name: ADELPHIA.NET*
>
> *Administrative Contact:*
>
> *Admin domainadmin@adelphia.com*
>
> *Adelphia Communications Corp.*
>
> *1 N. Main St.*

Coudersport PA 16915

US

888-512-5111 fax: 814-274-1508

Technical Contact:

Adelphia Communications hostmaster@ADELPHIA.NET

Adelphia Communications Corp.

Main at Water Street

Coudersport PA 16915

US

888-512-5111 fax: 814-274-0780

Record expires on 24-Apr-2009.

Record created on 23-Apr-1996.

Database last updated on 17-Aug-2005 12: 15: 45 EDT.

Domain servers in listed order:

NS1.ADELPHIA.NET   24.50.78.2

NS2.ADELPHIA.NET   68.168.224.177

NS3.ADELPHIA.NET   68.168.192.17

Adelphia Communications exists. Note, however, the IP addresses for Adelphia's three domain servers: none include the IP address 179.218.136.248 (since, of course, IANA had not yet assigned them). The Received: lines in this header are inconsistent: the Adelphia mail server, suspiciously, failed to authenticate the IP address 179.218.136.248. The forgery should be reported to Adelphia.

The message was sent by *htqxo@fastmail.ca* through a server at *southeast.beonex.com*. We can use samspade to find information on *southeast.beonex.com*:

Server Used: [whois.corenic.net]

southeast.beonex.com = [ ]

Whois Server Version 3.12

Domain ID: D3434619-CNO

Domain Name: beonex.com

Domain Name IDN: beonex.com

Creation Date: 2000-11-03 09: 45: 53 UTC

Expiration Date: 2006-11-03 08: 45: 48 UTC

Last Modification Date: 2002-12-05 16: 02: 30 UTC

Sponsoring Registrar: CORE-39

Created by: CORE-39

Updated by: CORE-39

Last Updated By Registrar: CORE-39

Maintainer: 39

Registrant ID: COCO-14923

Registrant Name: Ben Bucksch

Registrant Address: Humboldtstr. 29

Registrant City: Wiesbaden

Registrant State/Province: Hessen

Registrant Postal Code: 65189

Registrant Country: DE

Registrant Phone Number: 49.611377777

Registrant Email: domains@bucksch.com

Admin ID: COCO-14923

Admin Name: Ben Bucksch

Admin Address: Humboldtstr. 29

Admin City: Wiesbaden

Admin State/Province: Hessen

Admin Postal Code: 65189

Admin Country: DE

Admin Phone Number: 49.611377777

Admin Email: domains@bucksch.com

Tech ID: COCO-14923

Tech Name: Ben Bucksch

Tech Address: Humboldtstr. 29

Tech City: Wiesbaden

Tech State/Province: Hessen

Tech Postal Code: 65189

Tech Country: DE

Tech Phone Number: 49.611377777

Tech Email: domains@bucksch.com

Zone ID: COCO-14923

Zone Name: Ben Bucksch

Zone Address: Humboldtstr. 29

Zone City: Wiesbaden

Zone State/Province: Hessen

Zone Postal Code: 65189

Zone Country: DE

Zone Phone Number: 49.611377777

Zone Email: domains@bucksch.com

Name Server: firespit.beonex.com

Name Server: ns3.knipp.de

Database last updated on 2005-08-17 16: 40: 36 UTC

CORE - [Internet Council of Registrars]

Notice the "Registrant Country": DE. Referring to RIPE NCC, the delegated registry for IP numbers in Europe, *http://www.ripe.net/info/resource-admin/rir-areas.html*, the country code DE refers to Germany. Interestingly, the message sent from Germany was stamped with a West Africa time zone (GMT −1) instead of GMT +2, which is what it should be.

To summarize the above exercise, the link in this e-mail was first broken with the inconsistency between *adelphia.net* and the IP address, which had not been assigned to anyone. With practice, investigators can quickly identify fake e-mail messages and know the Web sites to visit for authenticating information that can be used for writing affidavits for search warrants or subpoenas, for verification in courtroom testimonies, or for other related purposes. As these exercises have shown, it is not only the content of an e-mail message that can provide valuable leads, but it is the e-mail address itself that is essential to most investigations.

CHAPTER 11

SEARCHING AND SEIZING: THE INVESTIGATOR'S ROLE

SEARCHING AND SEIZING

The evidence obtained primarily from the Internet and also sometimes from surveillance, together with leads provided by a bank fraud investigator or police officer, often provides the basis for issuing a warrant. Investigators who are not authorized police officers may, or may not, be involved in the search and seizure of property related to the warrant. On occasions, investigators at the MSU Crime and Research Lab have participated in a search, after the police officers have secured the premises. Of paramount importance is the safety of the officers and any others who may be assisting the search.

In cases in which an investigator had assisted in the search, mostly involving credit card or bank fraud, the applications for search warrant and supporting affidavit included the name of the investigator. The investigator's assigned tasks were to search for documents, papers, and notes that contained Social Security numbers or credit card numbers of individuals not living at the premises. For example, the search of one premise for evidence of credit card fraud uncovered copies of hospital forms of various patients; the mother of the offender—the individual suspected of online fraud—was a nurse at a local hospital. The mother later confessed to being an accomplice. In another search of a premises, the Lab investigator found photocopies of Social Security cards and, in another case, crumpled notes in a wastebasket near a computer contained victims' names, addresses, and Social Security numbers.

Thus, warrants and affidavits for searches and seizure of properties involving crimes that are committed using stolen identities must include language that allow the investigator/officer to search for and seize "information," specifically, personal identifying information of individuals who may be victims of identity theft. In the previous chapters, the focus was on using the computer to investigate identity theft, whether or not the crime was committed online. Increasingly, however, the computer has become an *instrument* of the many crimes that use stolen identities to commit the frauds online.

THE INCREASING ROLE OF THE COMPUTER IN IDENTITY FRAUDS

The computer that is hacked into is the target of a crime, or a computer may be incidental to a crime when, for instance, it is used to traffic drugs or launder money.[1] In the case of the stolen identity that is used to commit credit card frauds, bank frauds, telecommunications frauds, or retail account frauds, the computer is the instrumentality of the crime,[2] but, in these cases, so also is the stolen identity. Therefore, applications for warrants and affidavits must include any and all language that, in addition to "information," pertains to the use of a computer and its peripherals, including, among others, fixed disks, external hard disks, floppy disk drives and diskettes, tape drives and tapes, optical storage devices, or other memory storage devices as well as keyboards, printers, monitors, modems, and any manuals that contain information and instructions on the operating system and software.

The Department of Justice's "Searching and Seizing Computers and Obtaining Electronic Evidence in Criminal Investigations" is the authority document for drafting warrants and affidavits and for searching and seizing computers as evidence. The document's author is Orin Kerr of the Computer Crime and Intellectual Property Section, Criminal Division, and the document itself can be fully downloaded from *www.cybercrime.gov/s&smanual2002.htm.*

The laws protecting information and digital privacy are strict; if violated, the evidence would be inadmissible. Therefore, to understand how to assist the police officer in an identity fraud case, the investigator, even though he or she may not be a member of the search team, should read this legal document.

The successful identity theft investigator, out of necessity, has already become knowledgeable about the inner sanctum of cyberspace. Now, for the search and seizure phase of the investigation, the investigator must also know of the technicalities involved in the confiscation of computers and equipment and in preserving the evidence they may contain. Often, the search team will include a specialist who knows how to secure a computer that is turned on and who also knows not to turn one on that is off, and who, further, knows whether or not to pull the power plug from the back of the computer or from the outlet in the wall. Two especially relevant information resources that address these and other issues are *The Cyber Crime Investigator's Field Guide* by Bruce Middleton and *Digital Evidence and Computer Crime* by Eoghan Casey. Investigators who may be assisting with a search should equip themselves with the technical expertise and tools required, which these texts describe.

Middleton's somewhat more technical volume, for the more advanced investigator, describes how to recover passwords and conduct forensic analysis on the computer's hard drives; and, in *Digital Evidence*, Casey describes the best practices for preserving, collecting, and documenting evidence, such as:

- Photographing evidence (serial numbers, wiring, computer screen).
- Taking notes, and making diagrams, to reconstruct the scene.
- Labeling, dating, and initialing all evidence.
- Protecting the drives by putting an unused floppy in each.

- Using evidence tape to seal the computer case and drives.
- Printing out, signing, and dating copies of documents.

Regarding the last point, one question raised recently by an investigator was, "Are computer printouts admissible evidence?" The same question also could be asked of the chain of evidence documents, those discovered through the Internet search that provided the basis for the warrant and affidavit applications. To answer this question, according to the Department of Justice Federal Rules of Evidence[3]:

> The best evidence rule states that to prove the content of a writing, recording, or photograph, the "original" writing, recording, or photograph is ordinarily required. See Fed. R. Evid. 1002. Agents and prosecutors occasionally express concern that a mere printout of a computer-stored electronic file may not be an "original" for the purpose of the best evidence rule. After all, the original file is merely a collection of 0's and 1's. In contrast, the printout is the result of manipulating the file through a complicated series of electronic and mechanical processes.
>
> Fortunately, the Federal Rules of Evidence have expressly addressed this concern. The Federal Rules state that [i]f data are stored in a computer or similar device, any printout or other output readable by sight, shown to reflect the data accurately, is an "original".
>
> Fed. R. Evid. 1001(3). Thus, an accurate printout of computer data always satisfies the best evidence rule. *See Doe v. United States*, 805 F. Supp. 1513, 1517 (D. Hawaii. 1992). According to the Advisory Committee Notes that accompanied this rule when it was first proposed, this standard was adopted for reasons of practicality. While strictly speaking the original of a photograph might be thought to be only the negative, practicality, and common usage requires that any print from the negative be regarded as an original. Similarly, practicality, and usage confer the status of original upon any computer printout. Advisory Committee Notes, Proposed Federal Rule of Evidence 1001(3) (1972).

The above Rules of Evidence provide valuable legal and technical information and advice; in addition, however, because of the dramatic increase in the use of computers to commit identity frauds, many if not most warrants should include contact addresses for Internet Service

Providers (ISPs). The Web site at *http://www.forensicsweb.com* contains a list of ISPs that can be downloaded at no charge. The list, which claims to be updated monthly, contains the names, mailing and street addresses, and fax and telephone numbers of contacts at the legal departments of a variety of ISPs and other information services.

THE FUTURE: IDENTITY THEFT AND INVESTIGATIONS

Identity theft can be expected to increase exponentially in the coming years, for many reasons. First, the names, addresses, Social Security numbers, and other identifying information of U.S. citizens are maintained in potentially hundreds of local, state, and federal government databases, including the Social Security Administration and all of its subdivisions (e.g., Medicare and Medicaid), driver's license bureaus, the Selective Service (all U.S. males), the Internal Revenue Service, including the database provided for under the Health Insurance Portability and Accountability Act (HIPAA)[4] of 1996 that contains complete and comprehensive data on anyone who has health insurance or has received health care, as well as all the data brokers, even those whose databases continue to be compromised, and, of course, the four credit reporting agencies: Experian, Equifax, Innovis, and Trans Union. Not yet mentioned are the databases maintained by the hundreds of banks, credit card companies, and other financial institutions and organizations—universities and other academic institutions, health clubs, and others—that maintain complete files on millions of Americans.

Opting out, the option of having a name removed from the database, works only temporarily. Eventually, a financial institution or one of the credit reporting agencies will again sell the opted-out identity to, for example, a business for marketing or product development or other planning purposes, and the name, address, and Social Security number are again in circulation and in the buy/sell market as a valued commodity. Thus, identities continue to be available for opportunistic criminals.

A second reason for the predicted increase in identity thefts is the lack of security for those hundreds, perhaps thousands, of databases. Several federal statutes, including the Identity Theft and Assumption Deterrence Act of 1998, the Identity Theft Penalty and Enhancement Act of 2003, HIPAA, the Gramm-Leach-Bliley Act, the Fair Credit Reporting Act, the Federal Trade Commission's Financial Privacy Rule as well as numerous federal bank regulatory agencies, such as the U.S. Treasury's Office of the Comptroller of the Currency, Treasury (OCC), the Federal Reserve System's Board of Governors, Federal Deposit Insurance Corporation (FDIC), and the Office of Thrift Supervision, Treasury (OTS), and many more, require that businesses secure the personal identifying information of their customers. Without exception, these Acts all emphasize Information Technology (IT) security, that is, computer and computer system security.

However, IT security alone cannot prevent identity theft. Since the Identity Theft Assumption and Deterrence Act was first passed in 1998, competitive computer companies in the business of securing hardware and developing software have flourished, flooding the market with varieties of tools and mechanisms aimed at information security. But IT security does not solve the problem because technology drives crime—criminals always find their ways around the latest security innovation, which is why computer users are constantly bombarded with e-mail messages providing links for patches to update compromised software or systems. Granted, IT security is essential, but it is not the answer to identity thefts.

The real answer lies in the securing of the workplace from culprit employees or other insiders, such as vendors, suppliers, and others, who have or can gain access to pass codes, key codes, or other means of entry to offices, departments, or computer systems. The so-called outside hackers most often have inside collaborators. Some, but not all, of the above-named laws do mention "employee training"; unfortunately, however, no law describes what the training should comprise, who should conduct it, and how the results are to be measured. And, surprisingly, only one law to-date, the Identity Theft Penalty and Enhancement Act, signed into law by President Bush in 2004, provides for increased fines and penalties for insider employees who have access to identities and who abuse their responsibilities for protecting them.

Thus, IT security alone is not the answer, because it is not failure-proof and also because computers do not steal identities, whereas people do. The solution to the problem of identity theft is to incorporate security into each and every facet of the personnel function, beginning with recruitment and including the selection of personnel, the socializing of these individuals into an honest company culture, and rewarding them for implementing and maintaining a workplace secure from the threats of identity theft. Personnel security must become an ongoing, continuous practice. Ironically, this country has *quality* standards for everything imaginable, from the manufacturing of millions of different kinds of products to the providing of all kinds of services, but there are no required *security* standards for the people who perform those jobs.

In addition to the database problems and the lack of workplace security, the practice of outsourcing also explains why identity thefts will continue to increase. Thousands of companies now outsource white-collar jobs to countries worldwide, including Russia, India, the Philippines, and Communist China—who claims that it would soon become the major outsource country, over India, for U.S. jobs.

The outsourcing of white-collar jobs, we are told, is good for the progress of our country, and I believe it is. Consider, however, the *types* of jobs that are outsourced: data management, accounting, legal work, and customer call centers; these and other white-collar jobs would not exist but for their job tasks that require the processing of identities. That is, to perform all of these and the many other outsourced white-collar jobs requires knowledge of names, addresses, Social Security, credit card, bank, and other forms of personal identifying information.

Outsourcing need not be a problem, provided the outsourcer requires as part of any contractual responsibilities the securing of personnel and personnel practices (see the uniform standards for security in *Preventing Identity Theft in Your Business: How to Protect Your Business, Customers, and Employees*[5]).

There are, however, yet additional reasons for the increase in identity thefts, and that is because identity theft is related to most or all crimes. One would be hard pressed to name a crime that does not use stolen identities as an instrument for its commission; consider, for example, the many frauds that this book focuses on (credit card, bank, retail account, telecommunications) as well as others not mentioned, such as arrests for driving violations (criminals certainly do not use their own names when arrested), wire fraud, chop shops (the stealing and tearing down of cars for their parts that are sold on the black market), prescription fraud, welfare fraud, vehicular crimes (hit and run), insurance fraud, cigarette smuggling (a big crime business), and, among many others, the manufacture and sale of methamphetamine, a major problem in the United States today.

The great implication is that the combination of the many crimes that are facilitated using stolen identities together with limited resources provided to local law enforcement to fight these crimes makes it highly likely they will go unresolved, and thus, identity theft and identity frauds continue. And this is why the role of the investigator of identity frauds has never been more important. By assisting police officers, identity theft investigators—whether they are victims or company or private fraud investigators—can provide a valuable service.

These investigators, with knowledge of the crime, the criminal, and the methods of identity theft investigations, can collect the probable evidence that police officers need to bring a case to trial and send a suspect to jail.

Many books have been written on how to investigate crimes, but this is the first, to my knowledge, to address the ONLINE investigation of identity theft crimes specifically. This book is not intended to be an exciting-to-read novel on the circumstances surrounding identity thefts; rather, the intention is to provide investigators with information learned since 1999 through experiences in solving identity theft cases. The book does not intend to be all-inclusive: this author is neither a police officer nor a lawyer. The book, however, is based on first-hand knowledge that, hopefully, will be useful for investigators who wish to become part of the identity theft solution.

LIST OF WEB SITES FOR IDENTITY THEFT SEARCHES

The majority of the Web sites on this list are registered in the names of major corporations or government agencies. The hyperlinks for these types of sites remain relatively consistent over time. At the time of this manuscript, all of the links below were accessible. However, it is important for investigators new to the Internet to know that most Web sites are routinely updated or taken down temporarily for maintenance. In both the cases, for updating or maintaining, a message will appear stating, "The page cannot be displayed." Investigators should try again later, because these sites will likely soon be up again, with additional, modified, or otherwise more current information.

Sometimes also, the Web *pages* within a Web *site* change locations. In these cases, the URL address for the Web site also will change. If a page cannot be displayed, key into the browser bar the first part of the URL address, eliminating the parts after the slash mark.

Example: for *http://www.landaccess.com/sites/oh/disclaimer.php? county=ohbrown*, use only *http://www.landaccess.com*, then, when at this homepage, search the site for the specific information of interest. In this example, the site contains land details for states and for the counties within states. The long URL above is for the State of Ohio, County of Brown.

The list of Web sites provided in the following sections are only a relatively few of the potentially millions of Internet sites that could contain valuable information for a criminal investigator. As they become proficient investigating crimes online, investigators will routinely encounter many Web sites that can be added to the list.

AUTOMATIC TELLER MACHINE (ATM)

MasterCard ATM Locator
   http://www.mastercard.com/atmlocator/index.jsp
Visa ATM Locator Quick Search
   http://visa.via.infonow.net/locator/global/jsp/SearchPage.jsp

BANKRUPTCY

Alaska Recorder's Office Search by Date
   http://www.dnr.state.ak.us/recorders/sag/DateSearchMenu.cfm
Alaska Recorder's Office Search by Document Type
   http://www.dnr.state.ak.us/recorders/sag/IndexSearchMenu.cfm
Alaska Recorder's Office Search by Name
   http://www.dnr.state.ak.us/recorders/sag/NameSearchMenu.cfm
Alaska Recorder's Office Search by Name of Subdivision
   http://www.dnr.state.ak.us/recorders/sag/SubDivisionSearchMenu.cfm
Alaska Recorder's Office Uniform Commercial Code Search by Date
   http://www.dnr.state.ak.us/recorders/sag/UCCDateSearchMenu.cfm
Alaska Recorder's Office Uniform Commercial Code Search by
   Document Type
   http://www.dnr.state.ak.us/recorders/sag/UCCIndexSearchMenu.cfm
Alaska Recorder's Office Uniform Commercial Code Search by Name
   http://www.dnr.state.ak.us/recorders/sag/UCCNameSearchMenu.cfm
Amador County, California Recorded Document Search
   http://www.criis.com/amador/srecord_current.shtml

Apache County, Arizona Recorder's Office Document Search
http://www.thecountyrecorder.com/(kktxyi55jpiie5jfcsnckfjc)/
Search.aspx?CountyKey=5

Arapahoe County, Colorado Public Records Index Search
http://www.co.arapahoe.co.us/Apps/LegalDocuments/default.aspx

Boulder County, Colorado Recorded Document Search
http://icris.co.boulder.co.us/icris/Login.jsp

Brevard County, Florida Clerk of Courts Land Records Index Search
by Name for 1981–1995
http://cfweb2.clerk.co.brevard.fl.us/

Brevard County, Florida Clerk of Courts Official Records Search
1995 to Present
http://cfweb2.clerk.co.brevard.fl.us/ORM/f_orm.cfm

Broward County, Florida Online Document Search
http://205.166.161.12/oncorev2/Search/AdvancedSearch.aspx?
Submit1=I+accept+the+conditions+above

Clark County, Washington Auditor Documents Search
http://auditor.co.clark.wa.us/auditor_new/index.cfm?fuseaction
=displaysearch

Cobb County, Georgia Clerk of Superior Court Real Property Records
Search by Grantor or Grantee Name
http://www.cobbgasupctclk.com/searchname.asp

Cobb County, Georgia Clerk of Superior Court Real Property Records
Search by Instrument Type
http://www.cobbgasupctclk.com/searchinstr.asp

Escambia County, Florida Court Records Search
http://205.152.130.14/cv_web_1a.asp

Escambia County, Florida Official Records Search by Name
http://205.152.130.14/or_1a.asp

Florida Statewide Official Records Search
http://www.myfloridacounty.com/services/officialrecords_intro.shtml

Fort Bend County, Texas Court Clerk Official Public Records Search
http://ccweb.co.fort–bend.tx.us/search.asp?cabinet=opr

Gadsden County, Florida Official Records Index
http://www.clerk.co.gadsden.fl.us/OfficialRecords/
Georgia Superior Court Clerk's Real Estate Index Search by Name
http://www.gsccca.org/search/RealEstate/namesearch.asp
Greene County, Ohio Recorder Document Search by Name
http://www.co.greene.oh.us/recorder/documentSearch.asp
Highlands County Florida Clerk of Circuit Court
Official Records Search
http://www.clerk.co.highlands.fl.us/official/search.html
Hillsborough County, Florida Clerk of Circuit Court Office Records
Index Search by Party or Business Name
http://207.156.115.73/or_wb1/or_sch_1.asp
Jefferson County, Colorado Clerk and Recorder Document Search
http://ww14.co.jefferson.co.us/crint/cri.jsp
Lake County, Florida Online Court Records Search
http://www.lakecountyclerk.org/online_court_records.asp
Larimer County, Colorado Index of Recorded Documents 1990 to
2-14-03
http://www.co.larimer.co.us/clerk/query/search.htm
Larimer County, Colorado Index of Recorded Documents 2-18-03 to
Current
http://www.co.larimer.co.us/clerk/query/search2.htm
Larimer County, Colorado Index of Recorded Documents Inquiry
Archive Data 1971 to 1989
http://www.co.larimer.co.us/clerk/query/arch_search.htm
Lee County, Florida Clerk of Courts Official Records Public Search
http://www.leeclerk.org/wb_or1/or_sch_1.asp
Manatee County, Florida Official Records Search by Subdivision
Name
http://www.manateeclerk.com/scripts/vfpwebn.exe
Maricopa County, Arizona Recorded Document Search
http://recorder.maricopa.gov/recdocdata/GetRecDataSelect.asp?
mcrs=1

Martin County, Florida Clerk of Courts Official Public Records Search
http://clerk–web.martin.fl.us/wb_or1/or_sch_1.asp

Miami–Dade County, Florida Recorder's Records Search
http://www.miami–dadeclerk.com/public–records/pubsearch.asp

Montgomery County, Ohio Recorder Document Search
http://www.mcrecorder.org/search_selection.cfm?letter=n

Nassau County, Florida Clerk of Court Official Public Records Search
http://www.nassauclerk.com/OfficialRecords/or_sch_1.asp

Ocean County, New Jersey Images of Public Records Search
http://webdev.co.ocean.nj.us/wb_or1/or_sch_1.asp

Pitkin County, Colorado Recorded Documents Search
http://webdev.co.ocean.nj.us/wb_or1/or_sch_1.asp

Routt County, Colorado Clerk and Recorder Reception Search Grantor/Grantee Name Search 1990 to Current
http://pioneer.co.routt.co.us/asp/clerk/search.asp?

Saguache County, Colorado Recorded Documents Search
http://www.thecountyrecorder.com/(f1m3h1eaevmv2rufzqn5cmfa)/Search.aspx?CountyKey=6

San Bernardino County, California Grantor/Grantee Records Search by Document Date
http://acrparis.sbcounty.gov/cgi–bin/osearchd.mbr/input

San Bernardino County, California Grantor/Grantee Records Search by Document Title
http://acrparis.sbcounty.gov/cgi–bin/Osearchc.mbr/input

San Bernardino County, California Grantor/Grantee Records Search by Name
http://acrparis.sbcounty.gov/cgi–bin/osearchg.mbr/input

St. Lucie County, Florida Clerk of Circuit Court Public Records Search
http://public.slcclerkofcourt.com/

Teller County, Colorado Recorded Documents Search
http://data.co.teller.co.us/AsrData/wc.dll?Doc~GrantSearch

U.S. Bankruptcy Court – District of Minnesota
http://www.mnb.uscourts.gov/ers–bin/mnb–651–main.pl

U.S. Bankruptcy Court, District of Minnesota Judges Calendars
http://www.mnb.uscourts.gov/Calendar/CalSelect2.html

U.S. Bankruptcy Court, District of Minnesota New Chapter 11 Cases
http://www.mnb.uscourts.gov/WebDir/Html/Chap11.html

U.S. Courts–District of Idaho Archived Bankruptcy Case Search
http://www.id.uscourts.gov/cfCourt/CourtArchives/
Archive_SearchForm.cfm

U.S. Courts–District of Idaho: Judicial Opinions/Court Documents:
Bankruptcy Case Opinions
http://www.id.uscourts.gov/wconnect2/wc.dll?
opinions~bk_opinions

Union County, Ohio Official Records Search
http://www3.co.union.oh.us/officialrecord/Search.asp

United States Bankruptcy Court for the Northern District of Illinois
Case Image Viewing–Western Division
http://www.ilnb.uscourts.gov/

United States Bankruptcy Court for the Northern District of Illinois
General Search
http://www.ilnb.uscourts.gov/search.html

United States Bankruptcy Court for the Northern District of Illinois
Judges Court Calendars
http://www.ilnb.uscourts.gov/Judgess.htm

United States Bankruptcy Court for the Northern District of Illinois
Mega Case Information
http://www.ilnb.uscourts.gov/chapter11/megacase.htm

United States Bankruptcy Court for the Western District of Pennsylvania
Calendars
http://www.pawb.uscourts.gov/calendar.htm

United States Bankruptcy Court–Eastern District of Washington
http://www.waeb.uscourts.gov/

Volusia County, Florida Clerk of Circuit Court–Public Records
http://www.clerk.org/index.html

Weld County, Colorado Recorded Document Search
http://icris.co.weld.co.us/icris/documentSearch.jsp

BANKS

Comptroller of the Currency Enforcement Actions Search
  http://www.occ.treas.gov/enforce/enf_search.htm
FDIC Institution Directory–Find a Bank Holding Company
  http://www3.fdic.gov/idasp/disabled.asp
FDIC Institution Directory–Find an Institution
  http://www3.fdic.gov/idasp/disabled.asp
FDIC Institution Directory–Find an Office
  http://www3.fdic.gov/idasp/disabled.asp
Federal Reserve Financial Services–Download E–Payments Directories
  https://www.fededirectory.frb.org/download.cfm
Federal Reserve Financial Services–Federal Reserve Routing
  Information
  https://www.fededirectory.frb.org/reserve.cfm
Federal Reserve Financial Services–Search for FedACHSM Participant
  RDFIs
  http://www.fededirectory.frb.org/search_ACH.cfm
Federal Reserve Financial Services–Search for Fedwire Participants
  http://www.fededirectory.frb.org/search.cfm
Federal Reserve Financial Services–Treasury Routing Information
  https://www.fededirectory.frb.org/treasury.cfm
National Information Center/Federal Reserve System–Bank Acquisi-
  tion History Search
  http://132.200.33.161/nicSearch/servlet/NICServlet?
  REQ=MERGEDOUT&MODE=SEARCH
National Information Center/Federal Reserve System–Foreign Banks
  with Branches in US Search
  http://132.200.33.161/nicSearch/servlet/NICServlet?
  REQ=AGY&MODE=SEARC
National Information Center/Federal Reserve System–Foreign
  Branches of US Banks Search
  http://132.200.33.161/nicSearch/servlet/NICServlet?
  REQ=FBR&MODE=SEARC

BULLETIN BOARDS, DISCUSSION FORUMS, AND CHAT ROOMS

AOL Chat Rooms
http://site.aol.com/community/chat/allchats.html
AOL Groups
http://groups.aol.com/
CafeArabia–The Arab–American Online Community Center
http://www.cafearabica.com/nuke/
Chechnya–sl Yahoo Group
http://groups.yahoo.com/group/chechnya–sl/
Class A Drivers Message Board
http://www.classadrivers.com/phpBB2/index.php
Confuddled.com
http://www.confuddled.com/
DC Message Board and Chat Room
http://www.darkconspiracy.com/
Delphi Forums
http://www.delphiforums.com/
Google Groups Usenet Discussion Forums Search
http://groups.google.com/
Hear Palestine
http://groups.yahoo.com/group/HearPalestine/messages/1
ICQ
http://www.icq.com
Islamic Awakening
http://www.as–sahwah.com/
Islamic Forums–IslamiWay.spyw.com
http://islamiway.proboards12.com/
Islamic News and Information
http://groups.yahoo.com/group/inin/messages/1
Islamic Web Conferences
http://www.myiwc.com/

It'sHappening
  http://www.itshappening.com/index.php
Life in Korea Discussion Forums
  http://www.itshappening.com/index.php
Linkspider UK Discussion Boards
  http://forums.linkspider.co.uk/
ListServ
  http://www.man.torun.pl/cgi–bin/wa
Madinat Al–Muslimeen ARCHIVE
  http://www.jannah.org/cgi–bin/yabb/YaBB.pl
Madinat Al–Muslimeen NEW
  http://www.jannah.org/madina/
mIRC
  http://www.mirc.com/
MSN Chat Rooms
  http://chat.msn.com/
MSN Groups
  http://groups.msn.com/home
Muslim Access
  http://www.muslimaccess.com/
Muslim Message Discussion Forum
  http://www.muslimmessage.net/discussion/
Offshore Financial Freedom Information
  http://www.offshoreinfo.com/
Sobs
  http://www.sobs.org/
Stay Informed–Be Heard
  http://www.geocities.com/casey_britton/
Yahoo!Chat
  http://chat.yahoo.com/
Yahoo!Groups
  http://groups.yahoo.com/

CDL AND SPECIAL LICENSES

American Truck Driving School Directory
http://www.infoporium.com/truckschools/
Best Trucking Schools
http://www.besttruckingschools.com/usmap.asp
Class A Driver Listing of All Trucking Companies with Profiles
http://www.classadrivers.com/index.php?
method=CompanyListing&ListAll=1
Class A Driver Online Trucking Job Search
http://www.classadrivers.com/index.php?method=JobSearch
Class A Driver Trucking Company Categories
http://www.classadrivers.com/index.php?method=CompanyListing
Class A Drivers Message Board
http://www.classadrivers.com/phpBB2/index.php
Class A Drivers Trucking Industry Related Links
http://classadrivers.com/links/links.php
FMCSA Safer Search
http://www.safersys.org/about.shtml
Michigan Waste Data System Search
http://www.deq.state.mi.us/wdspi/
Newbie Driver Online Receiver Database
http://www.deq.state.mi.us/wdspi/
Newbie Driver Online Shipper Database
http://www.newbiedriver.com/OnTheDock/Shippers/
All_Shippers.asp
Transport Canada: TDG Cylinder Requalifiers Database Search
http://www.tc.gc.ca/tdg/containers/cylinder/requalifier.asp
Transport Canada: Transportation of Dangerous Goods Training
Organizations Search
http://www.tc.gc.ca/tdg/training/trainorg.htm
Transport Canada: Transportation of Dangerous Goods Permit Search
http://www.tc.gc.ca/tdg/permits/permits.htm
United Motorcoach Association Member Directory Search
http://www.uma.org/directory/

CHARITIES AND NONGOVERNMENTAL ORGANIZATIONS (NGO)

Afghan Network–NGOs Operating in Afghanistan
http://www.afghan–network.net/Culture/aid–agencies.html
Afghanaid
http://www.afghan–network.net/Culture/aid–agencies.html
Afghanistan Relief International
http://www.afghan–ri.org/
Arizona Secretary of State Charitable Organizations System
http://www.azsos.gov/scripts/Charity_Search.dll
Arkansas Secretary of State Incorporations, Cooperatives, Banks, and
Insurance Companies Search
http://www.sosweb.state.ar.us/corps/search_all.php
CAIR Chapters
http://www.cair–net.org/default.asp?Page=chapters
CAIR–Council on American–Islamic Relations
http://www.cair–net.org/
California Department of Justice Charitable Trust Search
http://justice.hdcdojnet.state.ca.us/charitysr/default.asp
Colorado Secretary of State Charitable Organization Inquiry
http://www.sos.state.co.us
Colorado Secretary of State Current Solicitation Campaigns Inquiry
http://www.sos.state.co.us
Colorado Secretary of State Paid Solicitor Inquiry
http://www.sos.state.co.us
Colorado Secretary of State Professional Fundraising Consultants Inquiry
http://www.sos.state.co.us
Georgia Secretary of State Registered Charitable Organization Database Search by Name
http://www.sos.state.ga.us/securities/charitysearch.htm
Help the Afghan Children
http://www.helptheafghanchildren.org/
India Committee of the Netherlands
http://www.indianet.nl/english.html

Maine Secretary of State Corporate Name Search
  *http://www.informe.org/icrs/ICRS;jsessionid=aaa6rn7
  Dqputbsz3OWcu?MainPage=x*
Missouri Secretary of State Business Entity Database Search
  http://www.sos.state.mo.us/BusinessEntity/
Nonprofit Organization Search
  http://www.guidestar.org/
Oregon Department of Justice Charities Database Search
  http://www.state.or.us/cgi–bin/OrgQuery.pl
Pennsylvania Department of State Corporations Database: Orphan
  Name Search
  *https://www.dos.beta.state.pa.us/corpsapp/corpsweb/
  Search/wfFreeOrphanSearch.aspx?Public=1*
South Carolina Public Charities 2002 Scrooges List
  http://www.scsos.com/2002_scrooges.htm
South Carolina Public Charities Database Search by Keyword
  http://www.scsos.com/char_online.htm
South Carolina Secretary of State Public Charities Angels List
  http://www.scsos.com/2002_angels.htm
South Dakota Secretary of State Corporation Search
  http://www.state.sd.us/applications/st02corplook/corpfile.asp
Swedish Committee for Afghanistan
  http://www.dominoplaza.com/afghanK/afghankeng.nsf
TDH Afghanistan
  http://www.tdhafghanistan.org/home.htm
Washington Secretary of State Charitable Organizations and Commercial Fundraisers Registration Database Search
  http://www.secstate.wa.gov/charities/search.aspx
West Virginia Secretary of State Charitable Organizations and Professional Fundraiser Search
  http://www.wvsos.com/CharitySearch/main.asp

COUNTY LOCATERS

National Association of Counties–Search for County
*http://www.naco.org/Template.cfm?Section=Data_and_
Demographics&Template=/cffiles/counties/city_srch.cfm*
State and County QuickFacts
http://quickfacts.census.gov/qfd/
U.S. County Resources at RootsWeb
http://resources.rootsweb.com/USA/

COURT RECORDS (NATIONWIDE)

FindLaw.com
http://www.findlaw.com/
Legal Dockets Online
http://www.legaldockets.com/
PACER
http://pacer.psc.uscourts.gov/register.html

DIRECTORIES—BUSINESSES

411 Locate – Near Search
http://www.411locate.com/
411 Locate Yellow Pages
http://www.city–yellowpages.com/
American Universities
http://www.clas.ufl.edu/au/
ApartmentGuide.com–Apartments by State
http://www.clas.ufl.edu/au/
ArabDataNet
http://www.arabdatanet.com/
AT&T AnyWho Reverse Lookup
http://www.anywho.com/rl.html

AT&T AnyWho Yellow Pages
  http://www.anywho.com/yp.html
AT&T Toll–Free Number Lookup
  http://www.anywho.com/tf.html
ATF Federal Firearms License Check
  https://www.atfonline.gov/FFLeZCheck
Bell South Yellow Pages
  http://yp.bellsouth.com/
Better Business Bureau–Company/Keyword Search
  http://www.bbbonline.org/consumer/
Bio.com Company Profiles of Product Companies
  *http://www.bio.com/industryanalysis/industryanalysis_
  product.jhtml?action=cat*
Bio.com Company Profiles–Browse by Products
  *http://www.bio.com/industryanalysis/industryanalysis_
  product.jhtml*
Bio.com Company Profiles–Locate by Company Name
  http://www.bio.com/industryanalysis/industryanalysis_name.jhtml
Bio.com Company Profiles–Service Companies
  http://www.bio.com/industryanalysis/industryanalysis_service.jhtml
CBS Switchboard.com White Pages and Yellow Pages Search
  http://www.switchboard.com/
City of Davis, California Business Directory Search
  http://www.city.davis.ca.us/ed/business/
Contract Award Search–The World Bank Project Data
  *http://web.worldbank.org/WBSITE/EXTERNAL/PROJECTS/0,,
  menuPK:51565~pagePK:95864~piPK:95915~theSitePK:40941,00.
  html*
Corporate Information
  http://www.corporateinformation.com/
ELPS–Specially Designated Nationals and Blocked Persons
  http://www.epls.gov/

EPLS–Excluded Parties Listing System–Search Archives by Multiple
Names
http://www.epls.gov/epls/servlet/EPLSArchMain/2
EPLS–Excluded Parties Listing System–Search Archives by Name
http://www.epls.gov/epls/servlet/EPLSArchMain/1
EPLS–Excluded Parties Listing System–Search by Action Date
http://www.epls.gov/epls/servlet/EPLSSearchMain/6
EPLS–Excluded Parties Listing System–Search by Agency
http://www.epls.gov/epls/servlet/EPLSSearchMain/4
EPLS–Excluded Parties Listing System–Search by Dun & Bradstreet
Number
http://www.epls.gov/epls/servlet/EPLSSearchMain/3
EPLS–Excluded Parties Listing System–Search by Exact SSN/TIN and
Name
http://www.epls.gov/epls/servlet/EPLSSearchMain/8
EPLS–Excluded Parties Listing System–Search by Multiple Names
http://www.epls.gov/epls/servlet/EPLSSearchMain/2
EPLS–Excluded Parties Listing System–Search by Name
http://www.epls.gov/epls/servlet/EPLSSearchMain/1
EPLS–Excluded Parties Listing System–Search by State or Country
http://www.epls.gov/epls/servlet/EPLSSearchMain/5
EPLS–Excluded Parties Listing System–Search by Termination Date of
Action
http://www.epls.gov/epls/servlet/EPLSSearchMain/7
Euro Pages–European Business Directory
http://www.europages.net/
EuroPages
http://www.europages.com/
FCC Telephone Company Locator
http://gullfoss2.fcc.gov/cib/form499/499a.cfm
FDA Children and Tobacco Compliance Checker–Download Data
http://www.accessdata.fda.gov/scripts/oc/cftobacco/download.cfm

FDA Children and Tobacco Compliance Checker–Search by
Establishment
http://www.accessdata.fda.gov/scripts/oc/cftobacco/SearchEstablishment.cfm
FDA Children and Tobacco Compliance Checker–Search by Location
http://www.accessdata.fda.gov/scripts/oc/cftobacco/search.cfm
FFL Guide
http://www.shotgunnews.com/
Fone Finder
http://www.fonefinder.net/
Hoovers Online
http://www.fonefinder.net/
Infobel.com–International Telephone Directory
http://www.infobel.com/world/default.asp
InfoSpace Companies Online
*http://www.infospace.com/_1_4MJ9T9E04F6MWL2__
info/bizweb.htm*
InfoSpace Yellow Pages and White Pages
http://www.infospace.com/
International White and Yellow Pages
http://www.wayp.com/
Internet Address Finder
http://www.iaf.net/
Internet Toll–Free National Directory
http://www.internettollfree.com/
Internet Toll–Free National Directory Super Search
http://internettollfree.com/
Islamic Finder
http://www.islamicfinder.org/
MobilephoneNo.com Business Search
http://www.mobilephoneno.com/
MSN Yellow Pages
http://yellowpages.msn.com/

Muslim Yellow Pages
   http://www.muslimyellowpages.com/myphome.php3
National Association of Counties–Search for County
   *http://www.naco.org/Template.cfm?Section=Data_and_*
   Demographics&Template=/cffiles/counties/city_srch.cfm
Neighborhood Postal Centers Cross Reference City, Zip Code, and
   Area Code
   http://www.neighborhoodpostal.com/ZipCode.asp
Osha Data Online Search Utility
   http://www.oshadata.com/osu.html
Pay Phone Directory
   http://www.payphone–directory.org/
Pay Phone Project
   http://www.payphone–project.com/numbers/search.html
Phone Numbers
   http://www.infobel.com/teldir/
Search Bug
   http://www.searchbug.com/
SEC–EDGAR CIK Lookup
   http://www.sec.gov/edgar/searchedgar/cik.htm
SEC–EDGAR Company Search
   http://www.sec.gov/edgar/searchedgar/companysearch.html
SEC–EDGAR Current Events
   http://www.sec.gov/edgar/searchedgar/currentevents.htm
SEC–EDGAR Historical Archives Search
   http://www.sec.gov/cgi–bin/srch–edgar
SEC–EDGAR Latest Filings Received and Processed at the SEC
   http://www.sec.gov/cgi–bin/browse–edgar?action=getcurrent
SEC–EDGAR Search: Mutual Fund Prospectuses
   http://www.sec.gov/edgar/searchedgar/prospectus.htm
Smart Pages–Find a Business
   http://www.smartpages.com
Smart Pages–Reverse Area Code Look–up
   http://smartpages.infospace.com/yp.smart/npa/npa.html

Superior Business Network Toll Free Numbers Search
http://www.sbn.com/states/800/default.asp?ac=800&cobrandid=1
Superior Business Network Yellow Pages
http://www.sbn.com/
Telecodes – Dial–a–code.com
http://dial–a–code.com/
Telsakma International Telephone Directories
http://www.callbackservice.com/phonedir/
The Gulf Directory
http://www.gulfdirectory.com.bh/
The Ultimate Yellow Pages
http://www.theultimates.com/yellow/
Thomas Registry of American and Canadian Manufacturers
http://www.thomasnet.com/index.html
Toll Free Phone Business Directory
http://www.tollfreephone.com/
United States Patent and Trademark Office–Find Patent Attorneys and
Agents Registered to Practice before the USPTO
http://www.uspto.gov/web/offices/dcom/olia/oed/roster/index.html
United States Patent and Trademark Office–Search Patents
http://www.uspto.gov/patft/index.html
United States Patent and Trademark Office–Search Trademarks
http://www.uspto.gov/main/trademarks.htm
U.S. Copyright Registration and Document Search
http://www.copyright.gov/records/
U.S. County Resources at RootsWeb
http://resources.rootsweb.com/USA/
U.S. PIC Codes (Find a telephone carrier by searching the database
with telephone company name, country, city, state, and/or zip code)
http://davis–company.com/pic/dbsearch.html
Verizon Super Pages–Yellow Pages
http://yellowpages.superpages.com
White Pages International Telephone Directories
http://www.whitepages.com/intl_sites.pl

White Pages.com–Find a Business
http://www.whitepages.com/business
World Email Directory
http://www.worldemail.com/index.htm
World Legal Information Institute–Court Case Database
http://www.worldlii.org/cgi–bin/browse.pl
Yahoo! Consumer Yellow Pages
http://yp.yahoo.com/
Yellow Book USA
http://yp.yahoo.com/
Yellow Pages–USA and International Directories
http://www.yellowpages.com/Index.aspx

DIRECTORIES—INDIVIDUALS

411 Locate World Directories
http://www.411locate.com/
411 Locate–Email Lookup
http://www.411locate.com/index1.htm
411 Locate–White Pages
http://www.411locate.com/
American Universities
http://www.clas.ufl.edu/au/
AOL E-mail Finder
http://site.aol.com/netfind/emailfinder.adp
AOL Member Pages Search
http://hometown.aol.com/
Apartment Ratings
http://www.apartmentratings.com/
AT&T AnyWho Reverse Lookup
http://www.anywho.com/rl.html
AT&T AnyWho White Pages
http://www.anywho.com/wp.html

ATF Federal Firearms License Check
https://www.atfonline.gov/FFLeZCheck
Bell South Real Pages – Find a Person
http://yp.bellsouth.com/
CBS Switchboard.com White Pages and Yellow Pages Search
http://www.switchboard.com/
CBS Switchboard.com–Email Search
http://www.switchboard.com/bin/cgiemail.dll?LNK=3:71&MEM=1
Cellphone Directory Reverse Search by Cell Phone Number
http://www.cellphonedirectory.com/Search/html/reverse_lookup.cfm
Cellphone Directory Search by Email Address
https://www.cellphonedirectory.com/Search/html/home_e-mail.cfm?
Cellphone Directory Search by Home Telephone Number
https://www.cellphonedirectory.com/Search/html/home_phone.cfm?
Cellphone Directory Search by Last Name
https://www.cellphonedirectory.com/Search/html/lastname.cfm?
Ebay Search for Seller or Bidder by Email Address or User ID
http://search.ebay.com/ws/search/AdvSearch?sofindtype=1
ELPS–Specially Designated Nationals and Blocked Persons
http://www.epls.gov/
EPLS–Excluded Parties Listing System–Search Archives by Multiple
Names
http://www.epls.gov/epls/servlet/EPLSArchMain/2
EPLS–Excluded Parties Listing System–Search Archives by Name
http://www.epls.gov/epls/servlet/EPLSArchMain/1
EPLS–Excluded Parties Listing System–Search by Action Date
http://www.epls.gov/epls/servlet/EPLSSearchMain/6
EPLS–Excluded Parties Listing System–Search by Agency
http://www.epls.gov/epls/servlet/EPLSSearchMain/4
EPLS–Excluded Parties Listing System–Search by Dun & Bradstreet
Number
http://www.epls.gov/epls/servlet/EPLSSearchMain/3

EPLS–Excluded Parties Listing System–Search by Exact SSN/TIN and Name
http://www.epls.gov/epls/servlet/EPLSSearchMain/8
EPLS–Excluded Parties Listing System–Search by Multiple Names
http://www.epls.gov/epls/servlet/EPLSSearchMain/2
EPLS–Excluded Parties Listing System–Search by Name
http://www.epls.gov/epls/servlet/EPLSSearchMain/1
EPLS–Excluded Parties Listing System–Search by State or Country
http://www.epls.gov/epls/servlet/EPLSSearchMain/5
EPLS–Excluded Parties Listing System–Search by Termination Date of Action
http://www.epls.gov/epls/servlet/EPLSSearchMain/7
FCC Telephone Company Locator
http://gullfoss2.fcc.gov/cib/form499/499a.cfm
Fone Finder
http://www.fonefinder.net/
Freeality International Phonebooks
http://www.freeality.com/findi.htm
Hands Across the World
http://hatw.net/
ICQ Meet People Phone Number Search
http://www.icq.com/whitepages/phonesearch.php
ICQ Meet People–Advanced People Search
http://www.icq.com/whitepages/
Infobel.com–International Telephone Directory
http://www.infobel.com/world/default.asp
InfoSpace White Pages Reverse Lookup by Address
http://www.infospace.com/home/wp/reverse.htm
InfoSpace World Directories White Pages
http://www.infospace.com/_1_2VSZUP10GE7HMS__info/wp/intl/index.htm
InfoSpace Worldwide Email Address Search
http://www.infospace.com/_1_C4UVF04416HHM__home/wp/email/index.htm

InfoSpace Yellow Pages and White Pages
http://www.infospace.com/
International White and Yellow Pages
http://www.wayp.com/
Internet Address Finder
http://www.iaf.net/
Internet Address Finder–Area Code/Phone/City to Demographic
Information
http://search.peoplefind.com/phone2word/areacode.aspx
Internet Address Finder–Email Search
http://64.70.24.34/searchemail.asp
Internet Address Finder–Validate an Email Address
http://64.70.24.34/phone2word/validemail.aspx
MESA, Your Meta Email Search Agent
http://mesa.rrzn.uni–hannover.de/
MissingMoney.com
http://www.missingmoney.com/Main/Index.cfm
MobilePhoneNo.com
http://www.mobilephoneno.com/
MSN Member Directory
http://members.msn.com/
National Association of Counties–Search for County
*http://www.naco.org/Template.cfm?Section=Data_and_*
Demographics&Template=/cffiles/counties/city_srch.cfm
Neighborhood Postal Centers Cross Reference City, Zip Code, and
Area Code
http://www.neighborhoodpostal.com/ZipCode.asp
Network Abuse Clearinghouse Address Lookup
http://www.abuse.net/lookup.phtml
Pay Phone Directory
http://www.payphone–directory.org/
Pay Phone Project
http://www.payphone–project.com/

PBN Reunion Bureau Missing Person Post
  http://www.pbnreunion.com/missingpersonpostings.htm
Phone Numbers
  http://www.phonenumbers.net/
Phonebook Gateway to Colleges and Universities–University of Illinois
  http://webtools.uiuc.edu/ricker/PH?domainUrl=
  http://www2.uiuc.edu/cgi–bin/ph/lookup?Query=.
Return Path E-mail Finder and New E-mail Registration
  http://www.returnpath.net/
Search Bug
  http://www.searchbug.com/
Selective Service System Online Verification
  https://www4.sss.gov/regver/verification1.asp
Smart Pages–Reverse Area Code Look–up
  http://smartpages.infospace.com/yp.smart/npa/npa.html
Smart Pages–White Pages
  http://www.whitepages.com/
Superior Business Network White Pages
  http://sbn.whitepages.com/person
Telecodes – Dial–a–code.com
  http://dial–a–code.com/
Telsakma International Telephone Directories
  http://www.callbackservice.com/phonedir/
The Ultimate Email Directory
  http://www.theultimates.com/email/
The Ultimate White Pages
  http://www.theultimates.com/white/
U.S. Government Whois Lookup
  http://www.dotgov.gov/agree.aspx
U.S. Bureau of Industry and Security–Denied Persons List
  http://www.bxa.doc.gov/DPL/default.shtm
U.S. County Resources at RootsWeb
  http://resources.rootsweb.com/USA/

U.S. PIC
  http://davis–company.com/pic/dbsearch.html
UXN Spam Combat
  http://combat.uxn.com/
White Pages International Telephone Directories
  http://www.whitepages.com/intl_sites.pl
White Pages.com–Find a Person
  http://www.whitepages.com/person
World Email Directory
  http://www.worldemail.com/index.htm
World Legal Information Institute–Court Case Database
  http://www.worldlii.org/cgi–bin/browse.pl
Yahoo! Member Directory Search
  http://members.yahoo.com/
Yahoo! People Search
  http://people.yahoo.com/
ZabaSearch
  http://www.zabasearch.com/

DOMAIN NAME SEARCH

Access Whois Domain Name Search
  http://www.accesswhois.com/search/
AiS Alive Proxy Smart Traceroute
  http://atomintersoft.com/products/alive–proxy/smart–traceroute/
AiS Alive Proxy Smart Whois
  http://atomintersoft.com/products/alive–proxy/smart–whois/
American Registry for Internet Numbers
  http://www.arin.net/whois/index.html
Asian Pacific Network Information Centre
  http://www.apnic.net/
BetterWhois Domain Registrars Search
  http://www.betterwhois.com/index.htm

Department of Defense Network Information Center
http://www.nic.mil/dodnic/
Internet Archive
http://www.archive.org/
Internet Assigned Numbers Authority Root–Zone Whois Information
by Country
http://www.iana.org/cctld/cctld–whois.htm
Internet Assigned Numbers Authority Whois Service
http://whois.iana.org/
Latin–American and Caribean IP Address Registry
http://lacnic.net/en/index.html
Link Popularity
http://www.linkpopularity.com/
Netcraft
http://news.netcraft.com/
Network Abuse Clearinghouse Convert a Number to Dotted IP
Address
http://www.abuse.net/cgi–bin/unpackit
Network Solutions Whois
http://www.networksolutions.com/whois/index.jhtml
Ripe NCC Public Services
http://www.ripe.net/ripencc/pub–services/
Sam Spade
http://www.samspade.org/
U.S. Government Whois Lookup
http://www.dotgov.gov/agree.aspx
UXN Spam Combat
http://combat.uxn.com/
VisualRoute
http://www.visualware.com/demo/index.html
World Legal Information Institute–Generic Top Level Domain Name
Decisions
http://www.worldlii.org/int/cases/GENDND/

DRIVER'S LICENSES, VEHICLE IDENTIFICATION NUMBERS, AND LICENSE PLATES

Auto Check
> *http://www.autocheck.com/consumers/*
> *gatewayAction.do?&_209=0&_414=706*

California Vehicle Smog Test Query
> *http://www.dmv.org/vehicle–history.php?design=5*

Carfax Vehicle History Reports
> *http://www.carfax.com/cfm/general_check.cfm?partner=go2_6*

Consumer Guide Vehicle History Report
> *http://auto.consumerguide.com/product/vhr/index.cfm/partner/cg*

fakeid.tv
> *http://www.fakeid.tv/*

Florida Department of Law Enforcement Stolen Boat Search
> *http://www3.fdle.state.fl.us/fdle/boats_search.asp*

Florida Department of Law Enforcement Stolen License Plate Search
> *http://www3.fdle.state.fl.us/fdle/lic_plate_search.asp*

Florida Department of Law Enforcement Stolen Vehicle and Boat License Decals Search
> *http://www3.fdle.state.fl.us/fdle/lic_decal_search.asp*

Florida Department of Law Enforcement Stolen Vehicle and Boat Parts Search
> *http://www3.fdle.state.fl.us/fdle/vbparts_search.asp*

Florida Department of Law Enforcement Stolen Vehicle Search
> *http://www3.fdle.state.fl.us/fdle/vehicle_search.asp*

Minnesota Driver's License Number Check
> *http://www3.fdle.state.fl.us/fdle/vehicle_search.asp*

Minnesota Motor Vehicle Address Change Lookup
> *https://dutchelm.dps.state.mn.us/dvsinfo/vh14/vh14.asp*

Minnesota Motor Vehicle Registration Tax Paid Lookup
> *https://dutchelm.dps.state.mn.us/dvsinfo/vh80/mvregtax.asp*

Minnesota Vehicle Title Lookup
> *http://dutchelm.dps.state.mn.us/dvsinfo/info/DLTitleStatus/*
> *TitleStat1.html*

Unique ID–Drivers License Analyzer: Florida
http://www.highprogrammer.com/cgi–bin/uniqueid/dl_flr
Unique ID–Drivers License Analyzer: Illinois
http://www.highprogrammer.com/cgi–bin/uniqueid/dl_ilr
Unique ID–Drivers License Analyzer: Wisconsin
http://www.highprogrammer.com/cgi–bin/uniqueid/dl_wir
Unique ID–Drivers License Calculator: Florida
http://www.highprogrammer.com/cgi–bin/uniqueid/dl_fl
Unique ID–Drivers License Calculator: Illinois
http://www.highprogrammer.com/cgi–bin/uniqueid/dl_il
Unique ID–Drivers License Calculator: Maryland
http://www.highprogrammer.com/cgi–bin/uniqueid/dl_md
Unique ID–Drivers License Calculator: Michigan
http://www.highprogrammer.com/cgi–bin/uniqueid/dl_mi
Unique ID–Drivers License Calculator: Minnesota
http://www.highprogrammer.com/cgi–bin/uniqueid/dl_mn
Unique ID–Drivers License Calculator: New Hampshire
http://www.highprogrammer.com/cgi–bin/uniqueid/dl_nh
Unique ID–Drivers License Calculator: Pre 1992 New York
http://www.highprogrammer.com/cgi–bin/uniqueid/dl_ny92
Unique ID–Drivers License Calculator: Washington
http://www.highprogrammer.com/cgi–bin/uniqueid/dl_wa
Unique ID–Drivers License Calculator: Wisconsin
http://www.highprogrammer.com/cgi–bin/uniqueid/dl_wi
U.S. Driver
http://www.highprogrammer.com/alan/numbers/
dl_us_shared_mmm.html

E-MAIL

411 Locate–Email Lookup
http://www.411locate.com/index1.htm
AOL Email Finder
http://site.aol.com/netfind/emailfinder.adp

CBS Switchboard.com–Email Search
  http://www.switchboard.com/bin/cgiemail.dll?LNK=3:71&MEM=1
Ebay Search for Seller or Bidder by Email Address or User ID
  http://search.ebay.com/ws/search/AdvSearch?sofindtype=1
InfoSpace Worldwide Email Address Search
  http://www.infospace.com/_1_C4UVF04416HHM__home/wp/
  email/index.htm
Internet Address Finder–Email Search
  http://64.70.24.34/searchemail.asp
Internet Address Finder–Validate an Email Address
  http://64.70.24.34/phone2word/validemail.aspx
MESA, Your Meta Email Search Agent
  http://mesa.rrzn.uni–hannover.de/
Network Abuse Clearinghouse Address Lookup
  http://www.abuse.net/lookup.phtml
Return Path E-mail Finder and New E-mail Registration
  http://www.returnpath.net/
U.S. Government Whois Lookup
  http://www.dotgov.gov/agree.aspx
UXN Spam Combat
  http://combat.uxn.com/
World Email Directory
  http://www.worldemail.com/index.htm

ENCRYPTION

PGP–Pretty Good Privacy
  http://www.pgp.com/
VeriSign Digital ID Personal E–Mail Security
  http://www.verisign.com/products/trustedMessaging/index.html

FIREARMS

ATF Federal Firearms License Check
https://www.atfonline.gov/FFLeZCheck
FFL Guide
http://www.shotgunnews.com/
Shotgun News Gun Show Search
http://www.shotgunnews.com/

IMMIGRATION AND NATURALIZATION

Albany County, New York Naturalization Records Search 1821-1991
http://www.albanycounty.com/departments/achor/
naturalizationIndexes.asp
Albany County, New York Naturalization Records Search by Name
and Nation or Origin
http://www.albanycounty.com/departments/achor/
naturalizationindexes.asp?id=856
Ellis Island Immigration Records Search by Name
http://www.ellisislandrecords.org/
Finor–The Offshore Professionals
http://www.finor.com/
Green Card Plus
http://www.greencardplus.com/
U.S. Green Card Lottery
http://www.green–card–lottery.org/
Usafis
http://www.usafis.org/
York County, Pennsylvania Naturalization Records
http://www.york–county.org/cgi–bin/natural.cgi

INMATE SEARCHES

Alabama Department of Corrections Currently Incarcerated Inmates
http://www.doc.state.al.us/inmsearch.asp

Arizona Department of Corrections Inmate Datasearch
http://www.adc.state.az.us/ISearch.htm

Arkansas Department of Corrections Inmate Search
http://www.accessarkansas.org/doc/inmate_info/

Benton County, Oregon Sheriff Release Report by Date
http://www.co.benton.or.us/sheriff/corrections/bccf/reports/ releasec/releasec.pdf

Benton County, Oregon Sheriff's Release Report by Name
http://www.co.benton.or.us/sheriff/corrections/bccf/reports/ releasea/releasea.pdf

Broward County, Florida Sheriff's Office Arrest Search
http://www.sheriff.org/apps/arrest/

City and County of Denver, Colorado Convictions of Prostitution–
related Crimes
http://www.denvergov.org/johnstv/

Denton County, Texas Parole Notices List
http://www.dentoncounty.com/court/parole/paroleall.asp

Denton County, Texas Parole Notices Search
http://www.dentoncounty.com/court/parole/

Denton County, Texas Sheriff Jail Record Search
http://justice.co.denton.tx.us/SherSearch/jailfrmd.htm

Federal Bureau of Prisons Inmate Locator
http://www.bop.gov/iloc2/LocateInmate.jsp

Florida Department of Corrections Inmate Population Information
Search
http://www.dc.state.fl.us/ActiveInmates/

Florida Department of Corrections Inmate Release Information Search
http://www.dc.state.fl.us/InmateReleases/

Florida Department of Corrections Supervised Population Inmate Search
http://www.dc.state.fl.us/ActiveOffenders/

Florida Department of Corrections: Search all Offender Databases
   http://www.dc.state.fl.us/AppCommon/
Fresno County, California Sheriff Department Inmate Information
   System
   http://www.fresnosheriff.org/InmateInfoCenter/main.asp
Georgia Department of Corrections Offender Query
   http://www.dcor.state.ga.us/GDC/OffenderQuery/jsp/
   OffQryForm.jsp
Grayson County, Texas Sheriff Jail Record Search
   http://www.co.grayson.tx.us:3004/SherSearch/jailfrmd.asp
Gregg County, Texas Sheriff Jail Record Search
   http://www.co.grayson.tx.us:3004/SherSearch/jailfrmd.asp
Hillsborough County, Florida Sheriff's Office Arrest Inquiry
   http://www.hcso.tampa.fl.us/pub/default.asp?
   Category=Online&Service=SNAME01
Hillsborough County, Florida Sheriff's Office–Who's In Jail? Inquiry
   http://www.hcso.tampa.fl.us/pub/default.asp?
   Category=Online&Service=WHOSINJAIL01
Idaho Department of Corrections Offender Search
   http://www.accessidaho.org/public/corr/offender/search.html
Illinois Department of Corrections Inmate Search
   http://www.idoc.state.il.us/subsections/search/default.shtml
Indiana Department of Corrections Offender Public Information
   Search
   http://www.in.gov/serv/indcorrection_ofs
Kentucky Corrections Death Row Inmates
   http://www.corrections.ky.gov/inmateinfo/deathrow.htm
Kentucky Offender Online Lookup System
   http://apps.corrections.ky.gov/KOOL/ioffsrch.asp
Lane County, Oregon Adult Corrections Inmate Search
   http://e–airs.org/inmateinformation/InmateInformation.asp?
   lastname=@&firstname=@
Michigan Department of Corrections – OTIS
   http://www.state.mi.us/mdoc/asp/otis2.html

Minnesota County Jails Offender Search by Name
http://www.vinelink.com/offender/searchNew.jsp?siteID=24002
Minnesota County Jails Offender Search by Social Security Number
http://www.vinelink.com/offender/searchNew.jsp?searchBy=SSN
Minnesota Department of Corrections Offender Locator
http://info.doc.state.mn.us/publicviewer/main.asp
Missouri Department of Corrections
http://www.doc.missouri.gov/offender_search.htm
Missouri Offender Status Search
http://www.vinelink.com/offender/searchNew.jsp?siteID=26000
Montana Department of Corrections Offender Network Search
http://app.mt.gov/conweb/
Nebraska Department of Correctional Services Inmate Search
http://www2.ims.state.ne.us/Corrections/COR_input.html
Nevada Department of Corrections Inmate Search by Name
http://www.doc.nv.gov/ncis/search.php
New York State Department of Correctional Services – Inmate
Population Information Search
http://nysdocslookup.docs.state.ny.us/kinqw00
Oakland County, Michigan Sheriff's Office Inmate Locator
http://www.co.oakland.mi.us/sheriff/jail/
Inmate%20Locator%20Page.html
Ohio Department of Rehabilitation and Correction–Offender Name
Search
http://www.drc.state.oh.us/cfdocs/inmate/search.htm
Oklahoma County, Oklahoma Sheriff's Office Inmate Records Search
http://www.oklahomacounty.org/cosheriff/
Oklahoma Department of Corrections Offender Inquiry
http://docapp8.doc.state.ok.us/servlet/
page?_pageid=395&_dad=portal30&_schema=PORTAL30
Pennsylvania Department of Corrections Inmate Locator
http://www.cor.state.pa.us/DOCApps/locator.asp
Pierce County, Washington Current Corrections Jail Roster
http://www.co.pierce.wa.us/cfapps/linx/calendar/GetJailRoster.cfm

Pierce County, Washington Superior Court Records Search & Corrections Jail Roster Search
http://www.co.pierce.wa.us/cfapps/linx/Search.cfm
Pitkin County, Colorado Sheriff's Office–Jail Inmate Report
http://www.aspenpitkin.com/depts/28/inmates.cfm
San Diego County, California Sheriff's Department – Inmate Log
http://www.sdsheriff.net/wij/wij.aspx
St. Francois County, Missouri Current Warrant Arrests
http://www.sfcsd.org/wa.htm
Tennessee Bureau of Investigation Out of State Probation and Parole Supervision Registry
http://www.ticic.state.tn.us/Database/ISC_search.htm
Tennessee Felony Offender Information Lookup
http://www.tennesseeanytime.org/foil/search.jsp
Tom Green County, Texas Sheriff Jail Search
http://justice.co.tom–green.tx.us/SherSearch/jailfrmd.htm

INVESTIGATOR SITES—FEE–BASED SEARCHES

Note: Investigators at the MSU Crime and Research Lab do not use fee–based searches; most information can be found on the Internet at no charge.

AutoTrackXP
http://www.flpro.com/
ChoicePoint Online
http://www.choicepointonline.com/
Discreet Research, Inc.
http://www.discreetresearch.com/
Docusearch.com
http://www.docusearch.com/
Entersect Police Online
http://www.entersect.net/

KnowX
http://www.knowx.com/
LexisNexis
http://www.lexisnexis.com/
Merlin Information Services
http://www.merlindata.com/
NameBase
http://www.namebase.org/
PACER
http://pacer.psc.uscourts.gov/register.html
Rapsheets.com
http://rapsheets.com
U.S. Search
http://www.ussearch.com/consumer/index.jsp

INVESTIGATOR SITES—FREE SEARCHES

Black Book Online
http://www.crimetime.com/online.htm
docusearch.com–Free Searches
http://www.docusearch.com/free.html
Due Diligence Database
http://world.std.com/~mmoore/index.html
eInvestigator.com
http://www.einvestigator.com/links/default.htm
Foreclosure Free Search
http://www.foreclosurefreesearch.com/
ForensicsWeb
http://www.forensicsweb.com/
Fosson.com: Online Public Records Research System
http://www.fosson.com/
Investigative Resource Center
http://www.factfind.com/database.htm

Law Research–Public Records All States
   http://www.lawresearch.com/investigate/inv–pr–state.htm
NameBase
   http://www.namebase.org/
NETR Online
   http://www.netronline.com/public_records.htm
Public Record Finder
   http://www.publicrecordfinder.com/
Public Safety Task Patrol
   http://www.pstp.org/reference/State–Links.
   htmSearch Systems–Pacific Information
Search Systems–Pacific Information Resources, Inc
   http://www.searchsystems.net/
State and Local Government on the Net–Piper Resources
   http://www.statelocalgov.net/index.cfm
Virtual Gumshoe
   http://www.virtualgumshoe.com/

MAIL SERVICES (PACKAGE TRACKING, DROP BOXES)

Access USA
   http://www.myus.com/additional_services/
Airborne Express Drop–off Locator
   http://sbw.dhl–usa.com/Locations/USLocnsStart.asp?nav=DropOff
Airborne Express Tracking System
   http://track.dhl–usa.com/TrackByNbr.asp
All Connect
   http://www.allconnect.com/ConsumerWeb/showServiceability.
   do?cobrand=26300
FedEx Drop–off Locator
   http://www.fedex.com/Dropoff/start?locale=en_US
FedEx Package Tracking
   http://www.fedex.com/Tracking?cntry_code=us

iShip Packaging Tracking
  http://www.iship.com/trackit/track.asp?acct=AFFMB1MG8P
Mail Boxes Etc. and UPS Global Store Locator
  http://www.mbe.com/index.html
Neighborhood Postal Centers Airborne Package Tracking
  http://www.neighborhoodpostal.com/TrackAB.htm
Neighborhood Postal Centers Cross Reference City, Zip Code, and
  Area Code
  http://www.neighborhoodpostal.com/ZipCode.asp
Neighborhood Postal Centers FedEx Package Tracking
  http://www.neighborhoodpostal.com/TrackFE.htm
Neighborhood Postal Centers Locator
  http://www.neighborhoodpostal.com/
Neighborhood Postal Centers UPS Package Tracking
  http://www.neighborhoodpostal.com/TrackUPS.htm
Pak Mail List of International Stores
  http://www.pakmail.com/store/internationalStores.asp
Pak Mail Store Locator by City, State, or Zip Code
  http://www.pakmail.com/scripts/mqinterconnect.exe?link=find
PostNet National and International Store Locator
  http://www.postnet.com/locator99.asp
UPS Air Cargo Tracking System
  http://www.aircargo.ups.com/aircargo/using/services/actracking/
  actracking.html
UPS Drop–off Locator
  http://www.ups.com/using/services/locate/locate.html
UPS Package Tracking
  http://www.ups.com/tracking/tracking.html
UPS Worldwide
  http://www.ups.com/content/corp/worldwide/index.html
USPS Change Your Address Online
  https://moversguide.usps.com/mgservice/Home

USPS Post Office Locator
http://www.switchboard.com/bin/cgidir.
dll?Mem=1355&PR=138&CSF=LocatorPostOffice
USPS RIBBS (Rapid Information Bulletin Board System
http://ribbs.usps.gov/index.html
USPS Track and Confirm Mail/Packages
http://www.usps.com/shipping/trackandconfirm.htm

MAPS

Adams County, Colorado Maps
http://www.co.adams.co.us/gis/staticmaps/index.asp
Atlapedia
http://www.atlapedia.com/
City and County of Denver, Colorado Neighborhood Map (PDF file)
http://www.denvergov.org/admin/template3/forms/
DENVERNEIGHBORHOODOct03.pdf
City of Rochester Hills, Michigan GIS Maps
http://www.rochesterhills.org/reference_desk/maps.asp
Country Reports
http://www.countryreports.org/
Expedia
http://www.expedia.com/pub/agent.dll?qscr=over&rfrr=–357
Library of Congress Map Collections
http://memory.loc.gov/ammem/gmdhtml/gmdhome.html
Map Quest World Maps
http://www.mapquest.com/maps/
MapsOnUs
http://mapsonus.switchboard.com/
National Geographic Xpeditions Atlas
http://www.nationalgeographic.com/xpeditions/atlas/
Perry–Castaneda Library Map Collection
http://www.lib.utexas.edu/maps/

Super Pages Map–Based Search
  http://yellowpages.superpages.com/supermaps/mapform.jsp
TerraServer
  http://terraserver.homeadvisor.msn.com/default.aspx
Tiger Map Server Browser
  http://tiger.census.gov/cgi–bin/mapbrowse–tbl
Yahoo! Maps
  http://maps.yahoo.com/

OCCUPATION DATABASES (NATIONAL)

American Board of Medical Specialties Search
  http://www.abms.org/login.asp
American Hospital Search
  http://www.ahd.com/freesearch.php3?PHPSESSID
American Institute of Certified Public Accountants–Disciplinary Actions
  http://www.aicpa.org/pubs/cpaltr/discipli.htm
American Medical Association Physician Search by Name
  http://webapps.ama–assn.org/doctorfinder/home.html
American Medical Association Physician Search by Specialty
  http://webapps.ama–assn.org/doctorfinder/home.html
HRSA Health Education Assistance Loan Program Defaulted Student
  Loan Borrowers by Amount
  http://defaulteddocs.dhhs.gov/amount.asp
HRSA Health Education Assistance Loan Program Defaulted Student
  Loan Borrowers by Discipline
  http://defaulteddocs.dhhs.gov/discipline.asp
HRSA Health Education Assistance Loan Program Defaulted Student
  Loan Borrowers by Last Name
  http://defaulteddocs.dhhs.gov/name.asp
HRSA Health Education Assistance Loan Program Defaulted Student
  Loan Borrowers by School
  http://defaulteddocs.dhhs.gov/school.asp

HRSA Health Education Assistance Loan Program Defaulted Student
Loan Borrowers by State
http://defaulteddocs.dhhs.gov/state.asp
HRSA Health Education Assistance Loan Program Full List of Defaulted Student Loan Borrowers
http://defaulteddocs.dhhs.gov/FullList.asp
Martindale.com Lawyer Locator: Search by Location and/or Practice Area
http://lawyers.martindale.com/xp/Martindale/Lawyer_Locator/
Search_Lawyer_Locator/loc_search.xml
Martindale.com Lawyer Locator: Search by Name
http://lawyers.martindale.com/xp/Martindale/home.xml
Martindale.com Lawyer Locator: Search for In–house Lawyers at Cor-
porate Law Departments
http://lawyers.martindale.com/xp/Martindale/Lawyer_Locator/
Search_Lawyer_Locator/corp_search.xml
Martindale.com Lawyer Locator: Search for Law Faculty at US Law
Schools
http://lawyers.martindale.com/xp/Martindale/Lawyer_Locator/
Search_Lawyer_Locator/faculty_search.xml
Martindale.com Lawyer Locator: Search for Law Firms by Name,
Location or Size
http://lawyers.martindale.com/xp/Martindale/Lawyer_Locator/
Search_Lawyer_Locator/firm_search.xml
Martindale.com Lawyer Locator: Search for Lawyers Affiliated with
Government Agencies in Washington, DC
http://lawyers.martindale.com/xp/Martindale/
Lawyer_Locator/Search_Lawyer_Locator/govt_search.xml
Questionable Doctors
http://www.questionabledoctors.org/

PROXY SERVERS

Ais Alive–Free Proxy Server Lists
http://atomintersoft.com/products/alive–proxy/proxy–list/

RESOURCES FOR CRIMINAL JUSTICE PROFESSIONALS

Advanced Computer Examination Support for Law Enforcement
   https://www.acesle.com/
Consumer Sentinel Application–FTC
   http://www.ftc.gov/sentinel/cs_signup.pdf
Direct Access to the Cybercrime.Gov Website for Police Officers or
   Law Enforcement Agents
   http://www.cybercrime.gov/agents.html
Federal Trade Commission (FTC) Statistics
   http://www.consumer.gov/idtheft/index.html
ForensicsWeb
   http://www.forensicsweb.com/
HIPAA–Administrative Simplification
   http://www.cms.hhs.gov/hipaa/hipaa2/default.asp
Identity Theft First Responder Manual for Criminal Justice
   Professionals: Police Officers, Attorneys & Judges
   http://www.looseleaflaw.com/catalog/list.html
Michigan State University Identity Theft Partnerships in Prevention
   http://www.cj.msu.edu/~outreach/identity/
NICB
   http://www.nicb.org/
Searching and Seizing Computers and Related Electronic Evidence
   Issues
   http://www.cybercrime.gov/searching.html#A
U.S. Department of Treasury Designation Lists and Financial
   Advisories
   http://www.treas.gov/offices/enforcement/lists/
USA Patriot Act H.R.3162
   http://thomas.loc.gov/cgi–bin/bdquery/z?d107:h.r.03162:
Virtual Gumshoe
   http://www.virtualgumshoe.com/

SEARCH ENGINES

!metaEureka!!
  http://www.metaeureka.com/
7MetaSearch.com
  http://www.7meta.com/
All The Web
  http://www.alltheweb.com/
AltaVista
  http://www.altavista.com/
AOL Search
  http://search.aol.com/aolcom/webhome
ASIACO
  http://www.asiabot.com/
Ask Jeeves
  http://www.ask.com/
Ayan
  http://www.ayna.com/index.en.html
Better Brain
  http://www.betterbrain.com/
ByteDog
  http://www.bytedog.com/
CNET Search
  http://www.search.com/
Cybercafe Search Engine
  http://www.cybercaptive.com/
Dogpile
  http://www.dogpile.com/info.dogpl/
Excite
  http://www.excite.com/
Find Everything Faster–PC World.
  http://www.pcworld.com/resource/article/0,aid,55383,00.asp
Galaxy
  http://galaxy.einet.net/

Gigablast
  http://www.gigablast.com/
Google
  http://www.google.com
Hamza Islamic Search Engine
  http://www.theemiratesnetwork.com/islam/
Highway 61
  http://www.highway61.com/?id=bjorgul.com
HotBot
  http://www.hotbot.com/
IcySpicy
  http://www.icyspicy.com/
InfoGrid
  http://www.infogrid.com/
Internet Archive
  http://www.archive.org/
Invisible Web Gets Deeper–Search Engine Watch
  http://www.searchenginewatch.com/sereport/00/08–deepweb.html
Islamic Search Engines
  http://islamic-world.net/searchother.htm
Ithaki
  http://www.ithaki.net/indexu.htm
ixquick
  http://ixquick.com/
Jayde
  http://www.jayde.com/
KartOO
  http://www.kartoo.com
LookSmart
  http://search.looksmart.com/
Lycos
  http://www.lycos.com/
mamma
  http://www.mamma.com/

MetaCrawler
http://www.metacrawler.com/index.html
Metahoo!
http://www.metahoo.com/
MSN Search
http://search.msn.com/
Muslims Internet Directory
http://www.2muslims.com/
Northern Light
http://www.northernlight.com/
Peoplegroups
http://www.peoplegroups.org/default.aspx
ProFusion
http://www.profusion.com/index.htm
Proteus Internet Search
http://www.thrall.org/proteus.html
Query Server
http://www.queryserver.com/web_text_search.htm
Scrub The Web
http://www.scrubtheweb.com/
Search Bug
http://www.searchbug.com/
Searchy.co.uk
http://www.searchy.co.uk/
SurfWax
http://www.surfwax.com/
Teoma Search Engine
http://www.teoma.com/
The Deep Web: Surfacing Hidden Value–Bright Planet
http://aip.completeplanet.com/
The Emirates Network Directory
http://www.theemiratesnetwork.com/dir/
Thunderstone
http://search.thunderstone.com/texis/websearch/

Turbo 10
  http://turbo10.com/
Vivisimo
  http://vivisimo.com/
WebCrawler
  http://www.webcrawler.com/info.wbcrwl/
Widow Metasearch
  http://www.widow.com/
WiseNut
  http://www.wisenut.com/
Yahoo!
  http://www.yahoo.com/
ZabaSearch
  http://www.zabasearch.com/

SEARCH WARRANT INFORMATION

ForensicsWeb
  http://www.forensicsweb.com/
Searching and Seizing Computers and Related Electronic Evidence
  Issues
  http://www.cybercrime.gov/searching.html#A

SECURITIES AND EXCHANGE COMMISSION

Edgar Online Pro People Search
  http://pro.edgar–online.com/people/peopleSearch.asp
SEC–EDGAR CIK Lookup
  http://www.sec.gov/edgar/searchedgar/cik.htm
SEC–EDGAR Company Search
  http://www.sec.gov/edgar/searchedgar/companysearch.html
SEC–EDGAR Current Events
  http://www.sec.gov/edgar/searchedgar/currentevents.htm

SEC–EDGAR Historical Archives Search
   http://www.sec.gov/cgi–bin/srch–edgar
SEC–EDGAR Latest Filings Received and Processed at the SEC
   http://www.sec.gov/cgi–bin/browse–edgar?action=getcurrent
SEC–EDGAR Search: Mutual Fund Prospectuses
   http://www.sec.gov/edgar/searchedgar/prospectus.htm
SEC–Investment Advisor Search
   http://www.adviserinfo.sec.gov/IAPD/Content/Search/
   iapd_OrgSearch.aspx
SECinfo
   http://www.secinfo.com/

SITES THE PERPETRATORS (MAY) USE

Anarchist Central
   http://www.geocities.com/M_STANLEY_00/
Astalavista Group
   http://www.astalavista.com/
Banned Bookstore
   http://www.ariza–research.com/
Be A Hacker
   http://www.beahacker.com/
Beat the Bouncer
   http://www.beatthebouncer.com/
Belvine, The ID Card Specialist
   http://www.belvine.co.uk/
Bogus PhD
   http://www.bogusphd.com/
Brainstorm I.D. Supply
   http://www.brainstormidsupply.com/Cart/
Card Printer Warehouse
   http://store.yahoo.com/cardprinterwarehouse/

CardCheck
  http://www.xequte.com/cardcheck/
Credit Card Validator for Filemaker
  http://www.briandunning.com/filemaker–pro/
Digital Information Society
  http://www.phreak.com/
DisCard–Verify or Generate Credit Card Numbers
  http://www.elfqrin.com/hacklab/pages/discard.php
Fake Degrees
  http://www.fakedegrees.com/
Fake ID Information Centre
  http://www.fake–id.info/
FakeDiplomas.com
  http://www.fakediplomas.com/
fakeid.tv
  http://www.fakeid.tv/
Fakeidman
  http://fakeidman.net/
Fantasycard
  http://www.fantasy–card.com/
Fluxcard
  http://www.fluxcard.com/
Free credit card processing software
  http://216.228.12.229.dsl.redshift.com/misc/cc.html
Free Fake ID Template
  http://www.free–fake–id–template.com/
FreeCCS
  http://216.228.12.229.dsl.redshift.com/ccs/orderform.html
Hack Canada
  http://www.hackcanada.com/
Hackers Catalog
  http://66.40.78.100/Services/Index/
I.D. Checking Guides
  http://www.driverslicenseguide.com/

IBS–Information Bureau Services
  http://ibs–net.info/files/index.php?id=18
Ideal Studios
  http://www.fakephotoid.com/
Identacard
  http://www.identacard.co.uk/newsite/cards.html
International–IDs
  http://www.international–ids.com/
John The Ripper Password Cracker
  http://www.openwall.com/john/
Make Your Own IDs
  http://www.myoids.com/
Morphiss Press Bookstore
  http://www.morphiss.com/
New ID
  http://newid.com/
Next Day iD
  http://www.nextdayid.co.uk/
Phatism ID
  http://www.phatism.com/
PHIDENTITY
  http://www.fakeiduk.com/
Phony Diplomas
  http://www.phonydiploma.com/
Photo–ID
  http://www.photo–id.co.uk/
SnadBoy Software
  http://www.snadboy.com/
TheIDcentre
  http://www.theidcentre.com/
True Active Software
  http://www.trueactive.com/
Undercover Press
  http://www.undercoverpress.com/

Underground Review
  http://www.underground–review.com/
Unique ID–Drivers License Analyzer: Florida
  http://www.highprogrammer.com/cgi–bin/uniqueid/dl_flr
Unique ID–Drivers License Analyzer: Illinois
  http://www.highprogrammer.com/cgi–bin/uniqueid/dl_ilr
Unique ID–Drivers License Analyzer: Wisconsin
  http://www.highprogrammer.com/cgi–bin/uniqueid/dl_wir
Unique ID–Drivers License Calculator: Florida
  http://www.highprogrammer.com/cgi–bin/uniqueid/dl_fl
Unique ID–Drivers License Calculator: Illinois
  http://www.highprogrammer.com/cgi–bin/uniqueid/dl_il
Unique ID–Drivers License Calculator: Maryland
  http://www.highprogrammer.com/cgi–bin/uniqueid/dl_md
Unique ID–Drivers License Calculator: Michigan
  http://www.highprogrammer.com/cgi–bin/uniqueid/dl_mi
Unique ID–Drivers License Calculator: Minnesota
  http://www.highprogrammer.com/cgi–bin/uniqueid/dl_mn
Unique ID–Drivers License Calculator: New Hampshire
  http://www.highprogrammer.com/cgi–bin/uniqueid/dl_nh
Unique ID–Drivers License Calculator: Pre 1992 New York
  http://www.highprogrammer.com/cgi–bin/uniqueid/dl_ny92
Unique ID–Drivers License Calculator: Washington
  http://www.highprogrammer.com/cgi–bin/uniqueid/dl_wa
Unique ID–Drivers License Calculator: Wisconsin
  http://www.highprogrammer.com/cgi–bin/uniqueid/dl_wi
UwantiD
  http://www.uwantid.co.uk/
Warez
  http://www.warez.com/
YourPhoto–ID.com
  http://www.yourphoto–id.com/

SOCIAL SECURITY NUMBERS

Selective Service System Online Verification
https://www4.sss.gov/regver/verification1.asp
Social Security Death Index– Ancestry.com
http://www.ancestry.com/search/db.aspx?dbid=3693
Social Security Number Verification U. S. Info Search
http://www.usinfosearch.com/Free_ssn_search.htm
SSNDTECT – Comserv, Inc.
http://www.comserv–inc.com/downloads.html

STUDENT LOAN BORROWERS

HRSA Health Education Assistance Loan Program Defaulted Student
Loan Borrowers by Amount
http://defaulteddocs.dhhs.gov/amount.asp
HRSA Health Education Assistance Loan Program Defaulted Student
Loan Borrowers by Discipline
http://defaulteddocs.dhhs.gov/discipline.asp
HRSA Health Education Assistance Loan Program Defaulted Student
Loan Borrowers by Last Name
http://defaulteddocs.dhhs.gov/name.asp
HRSA Health Education Assistance Loan Program Defaulted Student
Loan Borrowers by School
http://defaulteddocs.dhhs.gov/school.asp
HRSA Health Education Assistance Loan Program Defaulted Student
Loan Borrowers by State
http://defaulteddocs.dhhs.gov/state.asp
HRSA Health Education Assistance Loan Program Full List of De-
faulted Student Loan Borrowers
http://defaulteddocs.dhhs.gov/FullList.asp

TIME SERVICE

Time Service Department–U.S. Naval Observatory
  http://tycho.usno.navy.mil/time.html

TRANSLATION SERVICES

Ajeeb Dictionary
  http://dictionary.sakhr.com/
Al–Misbar Online Word Dictionary
  http://www.almisbar.com/dict_page.html
Alta Vista Translation Services
  http://babelfish.altavista.com/
Content Analysis Language Identifier–xrce
  http://www.xrce.xerox.com/competencies/content–analysis/tools/
  guesser
Free Translation
  http://www.freetranslation.com/
Glossary of Islamic Terms
  http://www.islam101.com/selections/glossaryA.html
Google Language Tools
  http://www.google.com/language_tools
IslamOnLine Date Coverter
  http://www.islamonline.net/calculator/english/
  hijrigregoriancalculator.asp
Logos Multilingual Portal
  http://www.logos.it/pls/dictionary/new_dictionary.
  dictio_professional_window?u_name=&u_password=
  &u_code=4395&code_language=
NewsTran
  http://www.humanitas–international.org/newstran/index.html
PROMT's Online Translator
  http://www.online–translator.com/srvurl.asp?lang=en

Systran Online Translator
  http://www.systransoft.com/index.html
World Language Online Translation
  http://www.worldlanguage.com/Translation.htm
World Lingo
  http://www.worldlingo.com/en/products_services/
  worldlingo_translator.html

U.S. CENSUS BUREAU

American Fact Finder
  http://factfinder.census.gov/home/saff/main.html?_lang=en
State and County QuickFacts
  http://quickfacts.census.gov/qfd/
U.S. Gazetter–Search for a Place in the United States
  http://www.census.gov/cgi–bin/gazetteer

LAND AND VITAL RECORDS (BIRTH, MARRIAGE, DIVORCE, OTHER)

Land Records by Various States and Counties
  http://www.landaccess.com
Adams County, Colorado Clerk & Recorder Public Records Search
  http://www.co.adams.co.us/publicinquiry/index.aspx
Alachua County, Florida Civil Department Records Search
  http://www.clerk–alachua–fl.org/pa/pa.urd/pamw6500.display
Alachua County, Florida Clerk of Court Marriage License Search
  through 1969
  http://www.clerk–alachua–fl.org/pa/pa.urd/pamw6500.display
Alachua County, Florida Clerk of Court Public Records Search
  http://isol.clerk–alachua–fl.org/search.asp?cabinet=opr
Alaska Trial Court Name Index Search
  http://orca.courts.state.ak.us/names/

Amador County, California Recorded Document Search
http://www.criis.com/amador/srecord_current.shtml
Apache County, Arizona Recorder's Office Document Search
http://www.thecountyrecorder.com/(qcatya55kttafpvfxifvjcuy)/
Search.aspx?CountyKey=5
Arapahoe County, Colorado Public Records Index Search
http://www.co.arapahoe.co.us/Apps/LegalDocuments/default.aspx
Baldwin County, Alabama Marriage License Search
http://www.deltacomputersystems.com/AL/AL05/
mllinkquerya.html
Baldwin County, Alabama Probate Court Record Search
http://www.deltacomputersystems.com/AL/AL05/probatea.html
Beaufort County, South Carolina Register of Deeds Search
http://rodweb.co.beaufort.sc.us/or_web1/or_sch_1.asp
Berks County, Pennsylvania Marriage Records 1950 through 1974
http://www.berksregofwills.com/berks_marriage_3_search.asp
Berks County, Pennsylvania Marriage Records 1975 through 1999
http://www.berksregofwills.com/berks_marriage_4_search.asp
Berks County, Pennsylvania Marriage Records 2000 through Present
http://www.berksregofwills.com/berks_marriage_5_search.asp
Bernalillo County, New Mexico County Clerk's Document Search
http://cyclops.bernco.gov/splash.jsp
Bexar County, Texas County Clerk Deed Recordings Search by
Grantor or Grantee Name
http://www.countyclerk.bexar.landata.com
Bexar County, Texas Marriage License Database Search by Name of
Bride and/or Groom
http://www.countyclerk.bexar.landata.com
Boone County, Missouri Marriage Records Search by Name
http://www.showmeboone.com/Login/
Login.asp?A=RC_SEARCH_MARRIAGE&URL=/
RECORDER/MarriageLicenseSearchByName.asp
Boston, Massachusetts Public Library Obituary Database
http://www.bpl.org/catalogs/frame_obits.htm

Boulder County, Colorado Recorded Document Search
http://icris.co.boulder.co.us/icris/Login.jsp
Brevard County, Florida Clerk of Courts Land Records Index Search
by Name for 1981-1995
http://cfweb2.clerk.co.brevard.fl.us/Indexing/
if_indexing_search.cfm?CFID=93323&CFTOKEN=66871942
Brevard County, Florida Clerk of Courts Marriage License Application Search 1938 to 1982
http://webinfo4.brevardclerk.us/MarrLicense/
ml_inquiry_historical.cfm
Brevard County, Florida Clerk of Courts Marriage License Application Search 1981 to 1995
http://webinfo4.brevardclerk.us/MarrLicense/
ml_inq_hist_81_95.cfm
Brevard County, Florida Clerk of Courts Marriage License Application Search 1995 to 1998
http://webinfo4.brevardclerk.us/MarrLicense/
ml_inq_hist_95_98.cfm
Brevard County, Florida Clerk of Courts Marriage License Applications Search 1999 to Present
http://webinfo4.brevardclerk.us/MarrLicense/ml_inquiry.cfm
Brevard County, Florida Clerk of Courts Official Records Search
1995 to Present
http://cfweb2.clerk.co.brevard.fl.us/ORM/f_orm.cfm
Brevard County, Florida Clerk of Courts Scheduled Traffic Hearings
Search by Defendant's Name
http://webinfo4.brevardclerk.us/traffichearings/
if_def_name_search.cfm
Brevard County, Florida Clerk of Courts Tax Deed Sale Lists 1998 to
Present
http://www.clerk.co.brevard.fl.us/taxdeed/taxdeed.HTM
Broward County, Florida 17th Judicial Circuit Court Records Search
http://www.clerk-17th-flcourts.org/bccoc2/pubsearch/
public_search.asp?

Broward County, Florida Online Document Search
  http://205.166.161.12/oncorev2/Search/Advanced
  Search.aspx?Submit1=I+accept+the+conditions+above
Brown County, Ohio Recorder Land Records Search by Name
  http://www.landaccess.com/sites/oh/
  disclaimer.php?county=ohbrown p
California Death Records
  http://vitals.rootsweb.com/ca/death/search.cgi
Charleston County, South Carolina Probate Court Marriage Records
  Search
  http://www3.charlestoncounty.org/connect/
  LU_GROUP_2?ref=Marriage
Charlotte County, Florida Official Records Search
  http://208.47.160.70/magic93scripts/
  mgrqispi93.dll?AppName=MPI_webCH&PrgName=VAC
Citrus County, Florida Clerk of Circuit Court Public Records Database Search
  http://24.129.131.20/search.asp?cabinet=opr
City of Albany, Georgia Clerk of Court Records Search
  www.albany.ga.us/doco/co_clerk.htm
Clark County, Nevada Marriage Record Search by Name of Bride or
  Groom
  http://www.co.clark.nv.us/recorder/Mar_srch.htm
Clark County, Nevada Official Records Transactions Search by Name
  http://recorder.co.clark.nv.us/extReal/
  Navigate.asp?SimpleSearch.x=70&SimpleSearch.y=11
Clark County, Ohio Recorder Land Records Search by Name
  http://landmarc.landaccess.com/sites/oh/clark/shared/
  tract/tract_name.php
Clark County, Washington Auditor Documents Search
  http://auditor.co.clark.wa.us/auditor_new/
  index.cfm?fuseaction=displaysearch
Clermont County, Ohio Recorder Land Records Search by Name
  http://www.clermontauditorrealestate.org

Cobb County, Georgia Clerk of Superior Court Civil Case Search by Pleading Type
http://www.cobbgasupctclk.com/scripts/CourtsCV.dll/Civil SearchByPleading

Cobb County, Georgia Clerk of Superior Court Civil Case Search by Type
http://www.cobbgasupctclk.com/scripts/CourtsCV.dll/Civil SearchByType

Cobb County, Georgia Clerk of Superior Court Real Property Records Search by Grantor or Grantee Name
http://www.cobbgasupctclk.com/searchname.asp

Cobb County, Georgia Clerk of Superior Court Real Property Records Search by Instrument Type
http://www.cobbgasupctclk.com/searchinstr.asp

Collier County, Florida Clerk of Circuit Court Public Records Search
http://www.clerk.collier.fl.us/clerkspublicac/session/index.html?

Colorado State Archives–Divorce Records
http://www.colorado.gov/dpa/doit/archives/divorce/

Colorado Tri–County Obituaries for Pueblo, Huerfano and Las Animas Counties
http://www.kmitch.com/Pueblo/obits/obitindex.html

Comal County, Texas Civil Case Search by Name of Plaintiff and/or Defendant
http://www.comalcounty.net/JudicialSearch/CivilSearch/ civfrmd.htm

Connecticut Judicial Branch–Party Name Search for Civil and Family Cases
http://www.jud2.state.ct.us/Civil_Inquiry/GetParty.asp

Dakota County, Minnesota Catholic Church Records Search
http://www.dakotahistory.org/research/ Catholic_Church_Search.asp

Dakota County, Minnesota Cemetery Records Search
http://www.dakotahistory.org/research/Cem_Search.asp

Dakota County, Minnesota Obituary Search
http://www.dakotahistory.org/research/Obit_Search.asp

Delaware County, Ohio Recorder UCC and Land Records Search by
Name
http://oh–delaware–auditor.governmax.org/propertymax/rover30.asp

Denton County, Texas Civil Case Records Search
http://justice.co.denton.tx.us/CivilSearch/civfrmd.htm

Detroit Free Press Death Notices
http://www.detroitnewspapers.com/deathnotices/index.cfm?freep

Duval County, Florida Official Records Index Search by Document
Type
http://www.duvalclerk.com/OnCoreWeb/

Duval County, Florida Official Records Index Search by
Grantor/Grantee Name
http://www.duvalclerk.com/OnCoreWeb/

Eaton County, Michigan Divorce Decrees
http://www.eatoncounty.org/County_Services/Divorce/Divorce.htm

Eaton County, Michigan New Marriages
http://www.eatoncounty.org/County_Services/marriage/Marriage.htm

El Dorado County, California Recorder's Index Query By Name
http://main.co.el–dorado.ca.us/CGI/WWB012/WWM501/R

El Dorado County, California Vital Statistics Query By Name
http://main.co.el–dorado.ca.us/CGI/WWB012/WWM500/C

Escambia County, Florida Court Records Search
http://205.152.130.14/cv_web_1a.asp

Escambia County, Florida Marriage Search 1996 to Present
http://205.152.130.14/marriage_1a.asp

Escambia County, Florida Official Records Search by Name
http://205.152.130.14/or_1a.asp

Fairfield County, Ohio Clerk of Court Records Search by Attorney
Name
http://www.fairfieldcountyclerk.com/Search/byAttorney.asp

Fairfield County, Ohio Clerk of Court Records Search by Date Range
http://www.fairfieldcountyclerk.com/Search/byDay.asp

Fairfield County, Ohio Clerk of Court Records Search by Judge
http://www.fairfieldcountyclerk.com/Search/byJudge.asp

Fairfield County, Ohio Clerk of Court Records Search by Name of Individual or Company
http://www.fairfieldcountyclerk.com/Search/byName.asp

Florida Statewide Official Records Search
http://www.myfloridacounty.com/services/officialrecords_intro.shtml

Fort Bend County, Texas County Clerk's Birth Certificate Search
http://ccweb.co.fort–bend.tx.us/search.asp?cabinet=birth

Fort Bend County, Texas County Clerk's Death Certificate Search
http://ccweb.co.fort–bend.tx.us/search.asp?cabinet=death

Fort Bend County, Texas County Clerk's Marriage Records Search
http://ccweb.co.fort–bend.tx.us/search.asp?cabinet=marriage

Fort Bend County, Texas County Clerk's Probate Court Records Search
http://ccweb.co.fort–bend.tx.us/search.asp?cabinet=probate

Fort Bend County, Texas Court Clerk Official Public Records Search
http://ccweb.co.fort–bend.tx.us/search.asp?cabinet=opr

Fort Logan National Cemetery Records, Denver County, Colorado
http://www.interment.net/data/us/co/denver/logan/index.htm

Fulton County, Ohio Recorder UCC and Land Records Search by Name
http://landmarc.landaccess.com/sites/oh/disclaimer.php?county=fulton

Gadsden County, Florida Official Records Index
http://www.clerk.co.gadsden.fl.us/OfficialRecords/

Grand County, Colorado Clerk and Recorder Data Search by Date Recorded
http://co.grand.co.us/Clerk/lookup/date.php

Grand County, Colorado Clerk and Recorder Data Search by Grantee's Name
http://co.grand.co.us/Clerk/lookup/grantees.php

Grand County, Colorado Clerk and Recorder Data Search by Grantor's Name
http://co.grand.co.us/Clerk/lookup/grantors.php

Grand Traverse County, Michigan Death Records Search
http://www.tcnet.org/cgi–bin/deathseek.pl
Grand Traverse County, Michigan Marriage Records Search
http://www.tcnet.org/cgi–bin/marriseek.pl
Grayson County, Texas Civil/Probate Case Search
http://www.co.grayson.tx.us:3004/CivilSearch/civfrmd.asp
Greene County, Missouri Recorded Document Search
http://www.greenecountymo.org/web/About/publicinfo.php
Greene County, Ohio Court Records Search
http://198.30.12.230/pa/pa.urd/pamw6500*display
Harris County, Texas County Clerk Informal Marriage License Inquiry System
*http://www.cclerk.hctx.net/coolice/default.
asp?Category=InforMarriage&Service=im_inquiry*
Harris County, Texas County Clerk Marriage License Inquiry System
*http://www.cclerk.hctx.net/coolice/default.
asp?Category=MarriageLic&Service=ma_inquiry*
Harris County, Texas County Clerk Vital Statistics Inquiry System
*http://www.cclerk.hctx.net/coolice/default.
asp?Category=VitalStats&Service=vs_inquiry*
Hawaii State Judiciary Court Records Search
*http://www.courts.state.hi.us/page_server/LegalReferences/
Records/6FEC5FEBB44D2621EC4446A8DE.html*
Hernando County Florida Clerk of Circuit Court Civil/Probate/Marriage License Search
http://www.clerk.co.hernando.fl.us/searchCivilCases.asp
Hernando County Florida Clerk of Circuit Court Marriage License Search Through 9-30-02
http://www.clerk.co.hernando.fl.us/searchMarriageLicenses.asp
Hernando County Florida Clerk of Circuit Court Official Records Search by Document Type 1983 through Present
*http://www.clerk.co.hernando.fl.us/SearchOR.
asp?System=DR&SearchType=DocTypeDate*

Hernando County Florida Clerk of Circuit Court Official Records
Search by Grantor/Grantee
http://www.clerk.co.hernando.fl.us/SearchOR.
asp?System=DR&SearchType=GrantoreeName
Highlands County Florida Clerk of Circuit Court Civil Case Search
http://www.clerk.co.highlands.fl.us/civil/search.masn
Highlands County Florida Clerk of Circuit Court Official Records
Search
http://www.clerk.co.highlands.fl.us/official/search.html
Hillsborough County, Florida Clerk of Circuit Court Office Records
Index Search by Party or Business Name
http://207.156.115.73/or_wb1/or_sch_1.asp
Ingham County, Michigan Death Records Search
http://www2.ingham.org/icors/clerks/deaths.asp
Ingham County, Michigan Marriage Application Search
http://www2.ingham.org/icors/clerks/marriages.asp
Jackson County, Missouri 16th Judicial Circuit Court Probate Record
Inquiry
http://www.16thcircuit.org/ProbateApps/probateonlinenameinq.asp
Jackson County, Missouri Marriage Records Search
http://records.co.jackson.mo.us/search.asp?cabinet=marriage
Jefferson County, Colorado Clerk and Recorder Document Search
http://ww14.co.jefferson.co.us/crint/cri.jsp
Kentucky Vital Records Index University of Kentucky
http://ukcc.uky.edu/~vitalrec/
Kern County, California Birth Certificates Search
http://recorderonline.co.kern.ca.us/cgi–bin/bsearchnofunction.mbr/
input
Kern County, California Death Certificates Search
http://recorderonline.co.kern.ca.us/cgi–bin/dsearchnofunction.mbr/
input
Kern County, California Marriage Certificates Search
http://recorderonline.co.kern.ca.us/cgi–bin/msearch.mbr/input

Kern County, California Recorded Document Search by Document
Class
http://recorderonline.co.kern.ca.us/cgi–bin/Osearchc.mbr/input

Kern County, California Recorded Document Search by Document
Date
http://recorderonline.co.kern.ca.us/cgi–bin/osearchd.mbr/input

Kern County, California Recorded Document Search by Document
Number
http://recorderonline.co.kern.ca.us/cgi–bin/osearchn.mbr/input

Kindred Pursuits Adoption Registry Search
http://www.kindredpursuits.org/search.htm

King County, Washington Recorder's Office Records Search
http://146.129.54.93:8193/legalacceptance.asp?

Lake County, Florida Clerk of Circuit Court Public Record Search by
Party Name
http://www.lakecountyclerk.org/wb_or1/or_sch_1.asp

Lake County, Florida Online Court Records Search
http://www.lakecountyclerk.org/online_court_records.asp

Lamar County, Texas Cemetery Records
http://userdb.rootsweb.com/cemeteries/TX/Lamar/

Larimer County, Colorado Index of Recorded Documents 1990 to
2-14-03
http://www.co.larimer.co.us/clerk/query/search.htm

Larimer County, Colorado Index of Recorded Documents 2-18-03 to
Current
http://www.co.larimer.co.us/clerk/query/search2.htm

Larimer County, Colorado Index of Recorded Documents Inquiry
Archive Data 1971 to 1989
http://www.co.larimer.co.us/clerk/query/arch_search.htm

Lee County, Florida Clerk of Courts Official Records Public Search
http://www.leeclerk.org/

Legacy.com: Find a Legacy Life Story, Notice or Guest Book in the
UnitedStates or Canada
http://www.legacy.com/Obituaries.asp?

Legacy.com: Search Canadian Newspapers for Obituaries
http://www.legacy.com/Obituaries.asp?

Legacy.com: Search U.S. Newspapers for Obituaries
http://www.legacy.com/Obituaries.asp?Page=SelectNewspapers

Leon County, Florida Clerk of Courts Databases Search
http://cvweb.clerk.leon.fl.us/index.asp

Leon County, Florida Clerk of Courts Marriage Records Search by Name
http://cvweb.clerk.leon.fl.us/index_marriage.html

Leon County, Florida Clerk of Courts Official Records Search by Party Name
http://image.clerk.leon.fl.us/official_records/

Lucas County, Ohio Online Court Records Search
http://co.lucas.oh.us/ClerkDockets/Dockets.asp

Lucas County, Ohio Recorder
http://co.lucas.oh.us/Recordings/logon.asp

Macomb County, Michigan Death Records Search
http://macomb.mcntv.com/deathrecords/

Madison County, Ohio Recorder UCC and Land Records Search by Name
http://landmarc.landaccess.com/sites/oh/disclaimer.
php?county=madison

Maine State Archives Death History Search Form
http://portalx.bisoex.state.me.us/pls/archives_mhsf/archdev.
death_archive.search_form

Maine State Archives Marriage History Search Form
http://portalx.bisoex.state.me.us/pls/archives_mhsf/archdev.
marriage_archive.search_form

Manatee County, Florida Clerk of Circuit Court Information Processing System
http://www.manateeclerk.com/mpa/cvweb.asp

Manatee County, Florida Official Records Search by Subdivision Name
http://www.manateeclerk.com/scripts/vfpwebn.exe

Maricopa County, Arizona Recorded Document Search
   http://recorder.maricopa.gov/recdocdata/
   GetRecDataSelect.asp?mcrs=1
Marin County, California Vital Records Search
   http://www.co.marin.ca.us/depts/AR/VitalStatistics/index.asp
Marion County, Florida Clerk of Circuit Court Case Search by Name
   http://www.marioncountyclerk.org/index.
   cfm?FuseAction=CaseSearch.Search
Marion County, Florida Clerk of Circuit Court Search by Party Name
   http://www.marioncountyclerk.org/index.
   cfm?FuseAction=RecordsSearch.Home
Martin County, Florida Clerk of Courts Official Public Records
   Search
   http://clerk-web.martin.fl.us/wb_or1/or_sch_1.asp
Miami Herald Obituaries
   http://www.miami.com/mld/miamiherald/news/obituaries/
Miami–Dade County, Florida Clerk of Courts Civil, Family, Probate
   Justice System Record Search
   http://www.miami-dadeclerk.com/civil/pubsearch.asp
Miami–Dade County, Florida Recorder's Records Search
   http://www.miami-dadeclerk.com/public-records/pubsearch.asp
Minnesota Death Certificate Search
   http://people.mnhs.org/dci/
Mobile County, Alabama Probate Court Records Search
   http://www.mobilecounty.org/probatecourt/recordssearch.htm
Monroe County, Florida Clerk of Circuit Court Civil Cases Search
   http://www.clerk-of-the-court.com/searchCivilCases.asp
Monroe County, Florida Clerk of Circuit Court Official Records
   Search
   http://www.clerk-of-the-court.com/searchOfficialRecords.asp
Montgomery County, Ohio Recorder Document Search
   http://www.mcrecorder.org/search_selection.cfm?letter=n
Naples Daily News Death Notices
   http://marketplace.naplesnews.com/mach2/nap/home/Home.action

Nassau County, Florida Clerk of Court Official Public Records Search
http://www.nassauclerk.com/OfficialRecords/or_sch_1.asp
New Castle County, Delaware Recorded Documents Advanced Search
http://www.ncc–deeds.com/recclkshr/Navigate.
asp?AdvancedSearch.x=109&AdvancedSearch.y=16
New Castle County, Delaware Recorded Documents Simple Search
http://www.ncc–deeds.com/recclkshr/Navigate.
asp?SimpleSearch.x=84&SimpleSearch.y=19
Olmsted County, Minnesota Guardianship Records Search
http://www.selco.lib.mn.us/apps/ochs/guard.cfm
Olmsted County, Minnesota Obituary Search 1993-1997
http://www.selco.lib.mn.us/apps/ochs/rpbobits.cfm
Peoria Journal Star–Matters of Record
http://www.pjstar.com/news/index.shtml
Pierce County, Washington Marriage Records Search
http://hartweb.piercecountywa.org/search.asp?cabinet=oprmarriage
Pierce County, Washington Official Public Records Search
http://hartweb.piercecountywa.org/search.asp?cabinet=opr
Pitkin County, Colorado Recorded Documents Search
http://www.pitkinassessor.org/Clerk/search.asp
Routt County, Colorado Clerk and Recorder Reception Search
Grantor/Grantee Name Search 1990 to Current
http://pioneer.co.routt.co.us/asp/clerk/search.asp?
Saginaw County, Michigan Death Certificate Search
http://www.saginawcounty.com/clerk/search/death.html
Saginaw County, Michigan Marriage Certificate Search
http://www.saginawcounty.com/clerk/search/marriage.html
Saguache County, Colorado Recorded Documents Search
http://www.thecountyrecorder.com/(1f13tjex0yfoi0y3cuahelzh)/
Search.aspx?CountyKey=6
San Bernardino County, California Grantor/Grantee Records Search
by Document Date
http://acrparis.sbcounty.gov/cgi–bin/osearchd.mbr/input

San Bernardino County, California Grantor/Grantee Records Search
by Document Title
http://acrparis.sbcounty.gov/cgi–bin/Osearchc.mbr/input
San Bernardino County, California Grantor/Grantee Records Search
by Name
http://acrparis.sbcounty.gov/cgi–bin/osearchg.mbr/input
Santa Cruz County, California Official Records Database Inquiry
http://sccounty01.co.santa–cruz.ca.us/clerkrecorder/Asp/ORInquiry.asp
Sarasota County, Florida Clerk of Courts Marriage License Database
Search
http://www.clerk.co.sarasota.fl.us/marrapp/marrinq.asp
Sarasota County, Florida Clerk of Courts Official Records Search
http://www.clerk.co.sarasota.fl.us/oprapp/oprinq.asp
Selective Service System Online Verification
https://www4.sss.gov/regver/verification1.asp
Snohomish County, Washington Marriage Records Search
http://198.238.192.100/search.asp?cabinet=oprmarriage
Snohomish County, Washington Official Public Record Search
http://198.238.192.100/search.asp?cabinet=opr
Somerset County, New Jersey Official Public Record Search
http://209.92.88.21/search.asp?cabinet=opr
Southern Colorado Obituaries
http://www.pueblolibrary.org/web2/tramp2.
exe/log_in?SETTING_KEY=English&servers=
obituary&guest=guest&screen=obitadvancedsearch.html
St. Cloud Times Obituaries Search
http://miva.sctimes.com/miva/cgi–bin/miva?Web/page.mv+2+Obits
St. Louis County, Minnesota Death Records Index RootsWeb
http://www.rootsweb.com/~mnstloui/slcmndin.htm
St. Louis, Missouri Death Notices and Obituaries 1880 to present
http://www.slpl.lib.mo.us/libsrc/obit.htm
St. Lucie County, Florida Clerk of Circuit Court Public Records
Search
http://public.slcclerkofcourt.com/

Teller County, Colorado Recorded Documents Search
http://data.co.teller.co.us/AsrData/wc.dll?Doc~GrantSearch

Texas Death Records–RootsWeb
http://userdb.rootsweb.com/tx/death/search.cgi

Texas Department of Health Divorce Indexes 1968-2001
http://www.dshs.state.tx.us/vs/default.shtm

Texas Department of Health Marriage Indexes 1996-2001
http://www.dshs.state.tx.us/vs/default.shtm

Texas Divorce Records Search–CourthouseDirect
http://www.courthousedirect.com/TexasDivorceSearch.asp

Texas Marriage Records Search–Courthouse Direct
http://www.courthousedirect.com/TexasMarriageSearch.asp

The Philadelphia Inquirer and Philadelphia Daily News Death Notices
http://www.legacy.com/philly/LegacyHome.asp

Union County, Ohio Clerk of Courts Documents Search
http://www3.co.union.oh.us/clerkofcourts/main.htm

Union County, Ohio Clerk of Courts Public Records Search
http://court.co.union.oh.us/cgi–bin/db2www.pgm/cpq.mbr/
main?nuser=07:12:59

Union County, Ohio Official Records Search
http://www3.co.union.oh.us/officialrecord/Search.asp

Van Wert County, Ohio Recorder Land Records Search by Name
http://landmarc.landaccess.com/sites/oh/vanwert/shared/tract/
tract_name.php

Vine Funeral Home of Rochester, Minnesota Records Search
http://www.selco.lib.mn.us/apps/ochs/vine.cfm

Volusia County, Florida Clerk of Circuit Court – Public Records
http://www.clerk.org/index.html

Wabasha County, Minnesota Cemetery Records
http://www.selco.lib.mn.us/apps/ochs/cemwab.cfm

Weber County, Utah Marriage License Search
http://www.co.weber.ut.us/marriage/

Weld County, Colorado Recorded Document Search
http://icris.co.weld.co.us/icris/documentSearch.jsp

Wisconsin Circuit Court Access – Advanced Case Search
   http://wcca.wicourts.gov/caseSearchSelect
Wisconsin Circuit Court Access – Simple Case Search
   http://wcca.wicourts.gov/simpleCaseSearch

ZIP CODES

City/State/Zip Code Associations
   http://zip4.usps.com/zip4/citytown_zip.jsp
Zip+4 Codes for United States Vessels
   http://216.228.12.229.dsl.redshift.com/cgi/navy.html
Zip+4 Look–up
   http://zip4.usps.com/zip4/welcome.jsp
ZipInfo–Zip Code Lookup
   http://www.zipinfo.com/search/zipcode.htm

NOTES

Chapter 2

1. U.S. Department of Justice, Al Qaeda Training Manual, retrieved February 23, 2004, from *www.usdoj.gov/ag/trainingmanual.htm*.
2. Woolsey, James, as reported by Daniel McGrory, Saturday, September 22, 2001, retrieved Friday, May 27, 2005, at *www.papillonsartpalace.com*.
3. Ibid, Woolsey.
4. Lormel, Dennis M., Testimony before the Senate Judiciary Committee Subcommittee on Technology, Terrorism, and Government Information, July 9, 2002, Hearing on S. 2541, "The Identity Theft Penalty Enhancement Act," retrieved Friday, May 27, 2005, from *http://www.fbi.gov/congress/congress02/idtheft.htm*.
5. Ibid, U.S. Department of Justice, Al Qaeda Training Manual.
6. Ibid, U.S. Department of Justice, Al Qaeda Training Manual.
7. Ibid, U.S. Department of Justice, Al Qaeda Training Manual.
8. Ibid, U.S. Department of Justice, Al Qaeda Training Manual.

Chapter 5

1. *Preventing Identity Theft in Your Business: How to Protect Your Business, Customers, and Employees*, Judith M. Collins, published by John Wiley and Sons, Inc., Hoboken, NJ, *http://www.wiley.com/WileyCDA*. The book is available in hard cover or over the Internet as an e-book; at the top of the Wiley Web site, type into the textbox: Judith Collins.

Chapter 11

1. Carter, David L. (1995). "Computer Crime Categories, How Techno-Criminals Operate," *FBI Law Enforcement Bulletin*, July.
2. Ibid. Carter.
3. Kerr, Orin S. (2002). "Searching and Seizing Computers and Obtaining Electronic Evidence in Criminal Investigations." Computer Crime and Intellectual Property Section, Criminal Division, United States Department of Justice.
4. Health Insurance Portability and Accountability Act of 1996, Public Law 104-191, 104th Congress (Washington, DC: U.S. Government Printing Office August 21, 1996), *www.hhs.gov/ocr/hipaa/*.
5. *Preventing Identity Theft in Your Business: How to Protect Your Business, Customers, and Employees*, Judith M. Collins, published by John Wiley and Sons, Inc., Hoboken, NJ, *http://www .wiley.com/WileyCDA*. The book is available in hard cover or over the Internet as an e-book; at the top of the Wiley Web site, type into the textbox: Judith Collins.

INDEX